GROUP HARMONY

GROUP HARMONY

The Black Urban Roots of Rhythm & Blues

STUART L. GOOSMAN

University of Pennsylvania Press

Philadelphia

10   9   8   7   6   5   4   3   2   1

Published by
University of Pennsylvania Press
Philadelphia, Pennsylvania 19104-4011

Text design and composition by Ellen Beeler

Library of Congress Cataloging-in-Publication Data

Goosman, Stuart L., 1953–
Group harmony : the Black urban roots of rhythm & blues / Stuart L. Goosman
p.   cm.
Includes bibliographical references (p.) and index.
ISBN-13: 978-0-8122-3886-0 (acid free paper)
ISBN-10: 0-8122-3886-9 (acid-free paper)
1. Rhythm and blues music—Maryland—Baltimore—History and criticism.
2. Rhythm and blues music—Washington (D.C.)—History and criticism.
3. African Americans—Maryland—Baltimore—Social conditions—20th century.
4. African Americans—Washington (D.C.)—Social conditions—20th century.
5. Baltimore (Md.)—Race relations.
6. Washington (D.C.)—Race relations.
I. Title
ML3521.G66 2005
782.421643'089'9607307529—dc22   2005046521

FRONTISPIECE: Quality Music Co., 1836 Seventh Avenue,
Northwest, 1948. Courtesy of the Afro-American Newspapers.

Contents

Preface

Herman Denby and Ernest Warren, former singers in the Swallows and the Cardinals, sat next to each other one afternoon in Catonsville, Maryland, just outside Baltimore. They went back and forth about vocal groups and values, gangs and social clubs, and what they had learned from their youthful experiences on Pennsylvania Avenue, in Baltimore, during the 1940s. They spoke thoughtfully, openly and were generous, like the avenue itself. Their talk, more like a good lecture, began with the social clubs they ran with, like the Amboy Dukes and the Vulcans. Some knew them as gangs. Herman put it cryptically. "There were gangs, and then there was tradition."

They went on to the subject of parents, peer pressure, drugs, and finally to Herman's thoughts on what affected a young person back then. "When you come in to this world, you are what you are." He pointed to Ernest. "Look this man and I, we've been all up and down the avenue."

Ernest added, "Been exposed to everything."

They go back and forth when they talk.

"You know what I mean? And saw everything."

"Everything there is, we've been exposed to it."

They ran down the kinds of bad things they had run into as kids, on the avenue, and sounded absolutely convinced that they were born with their sound judgment and good sense.

Herman remarks, "It's in me when I came into the world."

They both looked squarely at the person on the other side of the table recording their conversation. Ernest finalizes matters. "I could sit here and look at you and tell the way you talk and the way you carry yourself. I can tell you what you are, what you going to be." And to that he adds, "But that's the truth there. That's the truth."[1]

The late Eazy E once said about rap and hip-hop artists, "We're telling the real story of what it's like living in Compton. We're giving the fans reality. We're like reporters. We give them the truth" (quoted in Cross 1993: 37).

The singers and other participants, like Denby and Warren, who helped in this study were and are very much like rap artists who give us the truth, though their truth is of a different time and place. Indeed, this book does not draw comparisons between the landscape of Compton in the 1990s and black neighborhoods of Baltimore from the 1940s. Nevertheless, we can seek in the music and the stories of group harmony vocalists, from their own time and place, that "real story."

This book is about how young black males came to sing rhythm & blues group harmony in the 1940s and 1950s. I focus on participants who were from Baltimore, Maryland, and Washington, D.C., but given the patterns in segregated cities at mid-century, it is reasonable to draw some broader conclusions based on what occurred in those two areas.

The book is also about the character of those places during that period, and the significant effect "place," as both urban geography and social sphere, had on music making. I write about people's lives, city neighborhoods and businesses, the black schools, local radio, and the vagaries and intricacies of both segregated urban districts and the areas common to both blacks and whites. These elements were fundamental to the emergence of this particular music and vital to the personal narratives of those with whom I spoke. Thus I examine music in several aspects: the emergence of black harmony groups out of black neighborhoods, the music industry during the time period of rhythm & blues, the entrepreneurial promise of popular music—rhythm & blues in particular—and the convergence of music, place, and business, including the business of radio, managers, producers, and song writers.

In addition, this book is about race. At face value, I write about how segregated cities such as Baltimore and Washington affected youngsters in the 1940s and 1950s and how that influenced their music making. However, beyond that, there are a multiplicity of racial consequences on group harmony, rhythm & blues, and ultimately on what we generally understand as "black" music and its reciprocity with other music. There is, then, the issue of perspectives about race, but race in its very broadest sense, including ideas that people carry around with them about what does or does not constitute "black." My goal from the beginning was to give voice to racial perspectives based in part on participants interviewed. Race was a powerful idea that singers confronted on a number of different levels, from walking the street to choice of material to performance style, the latter especially important when groups went to record and companies went to market, sell, and thus categorize the style.

Our understanding that "black sells"—the idea that a constructed blackness in a multitude of guises has been marketable and profitable—is a concept that I explore throughout the book. It is predicated on the established fixed images or ideas about what is or is not black, and adds yet another layer of complexity to the intersection of race and music. The isolation and reification of blackness was something that enabled white people to acquire, manipulate, package, and market it (something that you could say began with enslavement). Emerging from the nineteenth century there was in this a conflation of blackness as a social concept, a cultural icon and form, and ultimately a stereotype essentialized by whites and well understood by blacks—internalized by some, as Malcolm X asserted. In this book's narrative about group harmony at mid-twentieth century, these themes are present on two levels: on the street level, where living in a segregated city affects people in everyday ways, and on a broader level in how the music industry in particular treated group harmony and rhythm & blues as product and how black performers ineluctably were a part of that process and how some of them came to view and manage their role in that process.

Young black males in Baltimore and Washington of the 1940s and 1950s had to carefully negotiate segregated streets and neighborhoods and public behavior just as black vocal groups so carefully straddled notions of race in their renditions of Tin Pan Alley standards and blues-derived material—two music types fundamental to twentieth-century popular music. These strategies speak to the much larger conundrum of African American experiences and cultural forms over time—the "apart from" and "a part of" aspects of black culture in white society. At its broadest, the core issue really is one of perspective, what distinguishes "blackness," not as skin color or morphology, but as social affiliation and, in turn, a cultural or musical idea or ideal. All of this plays out in the drama to control, label, package, and market cultural forms such as music—not to mention the day-to-day struggle from a black perspective to control one's own image and integrate into a grossly segmented society.

Throughout the book, I consider all these issues through the interpretive lens of oral histories provided by individuals who performed or participated in post-World War II secular black group vocal harmony. They help us understand the nature of group harmony, the many spheres out of which it emerged and developed, who controlled it, and what it meant. Through examining Baltimore and Washington, we find that group harmony was as much a way of life as it was a purely musical activity. It was for a period a source of empowerment for young singers, for it provided them with a means of expression and some aspect of control over their lives where there were limited alternatives. It also became a significant resource for the popular music industry. Through group harmony, African American youngsters celebrated and musically confounded, when they could not overcome, complex issues of separatism and assimilation during the postwar period. This study is social and cultural music history grounded in the human experience of a particular time and place. It is also a deeper and more general reflection on relationships and representations in black music—beyond the time and place of postwar group harmony.

The book employs the term "group harmony" to delimit postwar secu-lar, black male, vocal quartets and quintets, performed either with small band accompaniment or a cappella. The musical sources for these groups came from Tin Pan Alley "standards" and sentimental pop of the period, as well as blues and jump material. The vocal performance style of black group harmony drew from both black and white styles such as earlier pop, gospel, and jubilee group singing. Although socially the style emanated from black neighborhoods, there clearly were racial complexities at work. The record industry marketed group harmony under the broad category "rhythm & blues," beginning in 1949. Trade publications of the period, such as *Billboard*, at first referred to male groups simply as "vocal units" (or quartets, quintets) and their standard material as "pop ballads" or "stan-dards." Today, many know and market those groups and their style simply as "doo-wop," a term that at one time denoted a specific type of back-ground vocal accompaniment, often in the bass voice. Marketing terms such as rhythm & blues, doo-wop, rock 'n' roll, and oldies-but-goodies, came from the dominant culture and singers eventually came to use them. But during their time, the singers themselves almost never had a name for what they did, they simply got together to sing.

In Baltimore and Washington, as well as in other cities, young males formed vocal groups at home, on blocks and streets, in neighborhoods, and around town. They gained impetus through urban institutions: talent shows, social clubs, public schools, and churches. During this period, the popularity of local amateur male vocal groups (they already had antecedents in African American sacred and secular music), grew in pro-portion to the number of professional, successful, and well-known ones. Groups like the Orioles, Swallows, and Cardinals from Baltimore and the Clovers from Washington rose to national prominence between 1948 and 1951. Indeed, among the most seminal, influential and popular groups of the period were the Orioles from Baltimore and the Clovers from Wash-ington, and the dynamics of that region were important in fostering the development of group harmony on a national level.

The origins of these and other groups were in black communities, where a tradition of hanging out and harmonizing had long been in place. First, art mirrored life, and then life mirrored art. The Orioles, for instance, came out of West Baltimore, sang locally, and eventually made records that sold nationally and changed considerably the charismatic drift of black popular music. It was a model that younger groups would surely follow, just as the Orioles used earlier vocal groups like the Ink Spots and Ravens as their models. After about 1950 especially, the popularity and success of harmony groups fueled enthusiasm and professional aspirations back in the neighborhood and on the block. Urban grassroots harmony, which is the focus of this book, proliferated throughout the 1950s under the guise of the industry category "rhythm & blues."

These kids of the 1940s and 1950s initially made vocal harmony music of their own determination, with help from managers, producers, parents, DJs, radio stations, recordings, songwriters, schoolteachers, and others. Record companies reconstructed this music to market as "rhythm & blues" and to a certain degree altered its sound and meaning as it went from a purely local sphere to a national one. Others later resurrected group harmony as "doo-wop," part of the post-1960s "oldies-but-goodies" nostalgia for the 1950s era. Record collectors and dealers now prize the more obscure recordings from the period. The style made money in the end for the record industry, but not so for the singers, save for a very few. Today group harmony provides remuneration for a new generation through record collectors, dealers, and record reissues.

Despite these issues of money, commercial categories, and their attendant meanings, the acceptability of song and harmony singing as a form of expression remains a vital African American form and, historically, communities have nurtured it as such. Youngsters who participated in group harmony celebrated a black oral tradition, but they did so within repressive social limits of severely segregated cities such as Baltimore and Washington. They sang because it was something they surely wanted to do, but they also sang because often there were few alternative activities. On the one hand, they harmonized to empower themselves against social limitations — and many tried to take advantage of the style's commercial viability. On the other hand, they sang for the fun of it, to celebrate, so to speak, and to celebrate in color, regardless of remuneration.

In spite of the time- and place-specific aspect to group harmony in this book, there are broad historical ties that bind. This book ultimately walks that fine line between celebrating diversity within black America and exploring the notion that black America perpetuates through specific times, specific places, and through complex relationships, essentially as a kind of oneness because of both shared continuities within the group and because it does so within the framework of white America. The complex interrelationships between black and white, as both intellectual abstracts and on-the-street realities constitute the protean subtleties and intricacies of music, blackness, and race, which is what group harmony — and this book — are about.

1

Antecedents

Flow

Where did group harmony come from? Well, partly, it was just as Howard says.

"We just went with what's easy, the flow, because we could do anything. If he wanted to do the tenor, no problem. Like I told you we go to the football games. When we sing the National Anthem—"

Howard Davis pauses to let Mel Lipscomb, who sits next to him, finish the thought. "It amazes us."

The two of them have been friends since meeting at Washington, D.C.,'s Dunbar High School in 1943. They remained best friends for years after their harmony group the Hi Fis performed together. The other two members are gone, but occasionally Howard and Melvin sing when they happen to be together. They continue to exude that matter-of-fact attitude of "we could do anything." Their reference is musical, but you get the feeling that there was more there, that "we could do anything" flowed from something deeply within. Bear witness to the optimistic and bright soul of black youth as it still radiates in these two men. You hear it today as you would have heard it in their music, in the 1950s. The flow that Howard said they went with is just as it has always been—one singer picks up a vocal part where the other leaves off. That was how they patterned their harmony, music, and sometimes even their lives. You notice that same principle at work in their social actions and in conversation, as Melvin completes Howard's thought.

Here, Howard describes how he and Melvin spontaneously exchange vocal parts (and attract some attention) when they sing the National Anthem at football games. This was just the way they performed in the 1950s, the way it has always been for them.

"And you see the people turn around. Because through the National Anthem, he'll drop off to the baritone line and I go from the baritone, go right

1

up to where he left off. You know. Or he might, say, in a song, 'Do that,' I mean, 'You take that up there.' And that's all it's ever been. And I don't know a note. Well I don't know the names for them, but I know what I feel."

When young black males during the period around World War II got together to sing, they put music into their lives. Conversely, they put their lives—collective and individual attitudes, styles, and strategies—into the music. The result was that group harmony was as much a way of life as it was a musical activity. This played out in a myriad ways, but one nice example was the way Howard and Melvin—and other singers who appear in these pages—call and respond with each other in song as well as conversation. One picks up where the other leaves off. One expresses the other, answers the other, and affirms the other. They go with the flow of the moment.

What singers put into their music they culled from the city street, public school, church, family, home, and a shared history. The flow to which Howard alludes occurs from one singer to another and one friend to another, but it just as well roots one sphere of life in another and each generation in the previous one. Howard's is a casual use of the word flow, as many of us would use it. Beneath the casual, there is something more meaningful, something deeply fundamental to black music culture and in the emergence of postwar group harmony.

The anthropologist Victor Turner wrote about the concept of "flow" in creative experience. Flow is a sensation present "when we act with total involvement." Flow can occur when we are "in control of our actions, and in which there is little distinction between self and environment—or between past present and future."[1] Young singers socialized this notion of flow as they established relationships with each other and their surroundings. Music making was a way in which youngsters put themselves in control of their actions. And the nature of urban life made them do so in close relation to—if not quite in harmony with—their immediate, sometimes unfriendly environment.

These are defining qualities specifically in postwar group harmony and in black music culture more generally. One of these characteristics is a use of music in the everyday, a flow between shared values, home, school, church, and music. There is also another component to this, the flow from one generation to the next—a total involvement of another kind, with history, from past to present to future as one generation builds on the last. In all of these senses, "flow" transverses musical and social processes.

Another element of flow that seems particularly fitting here is this: "To flow is to be as happy as a human can be" (quoted in Turner 1982: 58).

When these vocalists performed, even informally, out of difficult times, singing brought great joy. It is perhaps the one great, unvoiced truth here. Howard Davis alludes to it as he tries to connect music and urban, social circumstance for us:

"If I hear a funny chord, I get a chill. We used to sing, man, and you know what we used to do? The chords would be so good we'd almost have tears in our eyes. Say, what the hell are we doing? And where do we, where, you know, we come from different parts of the city, through kind of the same kind of stuff, you know?"

Behind what Howard tells us is a long road.

Antecedents

Black rhythm & blues vocal harmony had antecedents in older, historical traditions of vocal music, which in turn drew from a myriad of both African and European-derived vocal traditions that ranged broadly from church hymns to folk tunes. Harmony groups were an early part of modern gospel music, beginning in the 1920s, and had a place in both sacred and secular song performances much earlier. The Fisk University Jubilee Singers, for instance, was a group of about eight male and female voices. Their success from an 1871 concert tour to raise money for the school spawned a number of other black college groups in the 1870s, such as the Hampton Institute Singers. These groups focused on sacred music, and the result was a newer, formally arranged and harmonized version of older folk spirituals. Here was the beginning of "concert" harmony in black religious music that clearly drew as much from white traditions as black, but it later became an important element in the development of gospel quartets, after the late 1920s. It was also the beginning of spiritual performances intended for white audiences, which accounted in part for the formalized style. Concertized spirituals were also evidence of both generational and class differences emerging in black music, whereby young college students performed "cleaned up" spirituals, in a departure from the older folk style that some would have considered a vestige of enslavement.

Other types of black harmony singing most certainly occurred earlier, before the mid-nineteenth century. Although West Africans taken for the slave trade preferred multi-part singing, they did not use four-part, tonal harmony. As they encountered Europeans, though, they acquired it, used it, and adapted it for their own purposes as they learned Western music. As Lovell recounts (1986: 109), Frederick Law Olmstead wrote that he heard slaves harmonizing in the 1850s. Lynn Abbott's account of early harmony

groups and their social setting establishes a black origin of barbershop harmony, a particular style of male quartet harmony that had a defining influence on "America's cultural fabric" (Abbott 1992: 319) and on the black
pop quartets that predated rhythm & blues. (That particular style of four
or five part block harmony singing was a good example of how nineteenth-
century African Americans learned and adapted European styles.)

Within this rich authoring by black harmony groups, there was a particular affection for harmonizing among male singers in quartets and quintets. The black writer James Weldon Johnson cites numerous examples of
vocal quartets he heard in southern black communities during the late nineteenth century (Johnson and Johnson 1925: 35–36). Louis Armstrong,
during the first decade of this century in New Orleans, sang for pennies on
the sidewalks with a quartet of youngsters. Later Armstrong recounted listening, singing with, and presumably learning from male "barroom quartets" in New Orleans (Armstrong 1954: 86). Both sacred and secular male
quartets and quintets flourished in different forms throughout the twentieth century.

Any narrative about rhythm & blues group harmony is inseparable from
the desire to make recordings. The history of black vocal group performance
recordings begins as early as 1893, with the Unique Quartet performing
"Mama's Black Baby Boy."[2] In 1894, the Standard Quartette recorded both
sacred and secular songs in Washington for Columbia (Funk 1991).[3] Black
vocal harmony—as performance and as a recorded commodity—continued
to develop with early gospel groups such as the Dixie Hummingbirds,
formed in 1928, and later ones like the Golden Gate Jubilee Quartet, popular in the 1940s. There were hundreds of other black groups throughout
the 1930s, 1940s, and 1950s. Well-known secular groups included the Mills
Brothers (formed 1920s) and Ink Spots (1930s), while the Deep River
Boys (1936) and the Delta Rhythm Boys (1937) originated as college
groups and had mixed repertoires of both secular and sacred material
(Southern 1997: 513). Of all the groups that came of age before World War
II, the Ink Spots seem to have made the most lasting impression on younger
singers during the early and mid-1940s.[4]

The Ink Spots after 1939 became a uniquely popular and visible group.
They made records, received a lot of recognition, and became solid crossover artists well-liked by both black and white audiences—a fact not lost
on aspiring singers.

Before the R&B era, before the Ravens, Orioles, and Clovers, young
black males who wanted to sing wanted to be just like Bill Kenny and the
Ink Spots. The group had the sound and they had the look. During the

1950s, Harold Winley sang bass for the Clovers and remembered the impact of the Ink Spots.

"But, during that time," he said, "you know, the groups that you would hear around on the corner singing were mostly singing Ink Spots. You hear cats going down the street, you know guys that had tenor voices man, in the morning, at night, singing Bill Kenny and doing the hands, like he used to do. It was either Bill Kenny or Billy Eckstine.[5] Understand what I'm saying? Those were the voices you would hear."

The peak years of the Ink Spots were the 1940s. Beginning in 1939, after Bill Kenny joined the group as lead tenor, the group consisted of Orville "Hoppy" Jones, bass/baritone vocal, Ivory "Deek" Watson, and Charlie Fuqua on background harmony and guitar. The Ink Spots perfected their distinctive sound with sweet, sentimental, Tin Pan Alley ballads. Between Kenny, the high tenor lead, and the low range of Jones, the group further popularized a high voice/low voice combination (already present in period gospel quartets), as well as Jones's signature "talking choruses." The Ink Spots had vocal superiors, to be sure, in the dynamism of the sacred music singers like the Golden Gate Jubilee Quartet, or in the abilities of jump vocal groups like the Delta Rhythm Boys, who were contemporaries. The Ink Spots, however, were better known, and the reasons were probably difficult for singers to ignore.

The group's trademark sound was Bill Kenny's airy tenor voice. The overall aesthetic of the group sound was staid, but Kenny had a polished voice, gorgeous tone, effective range, and perfect diction with rolling r's equally reminiscent of Rudee Vallee and the Fisk Jubilee Singers. There remained, however, an unmistakable patina to the group's sound.[6] Behind Kenny were the quiet background harmonies, even-strumming guitar chords, and on some recordings a string bass and piano. It was a reassuring sound, perfect for the years of World War II. The group recorded for the Decca label and had fifty hits between 1939 and 1951 (Clarke 1989: 580).

The other thing about the Ink Spots, and Eckstine too, for that matter, was the look—white suits, flowers in the lapels; they were clean and pressed, but not over the top. Winley remembered that look. It transformed the group's stage appearance, the formal posturing, "doing the hands," the low-key gestures. There was no shuck, no jive, and no blackcrobatic dancing for white Hollywood. The Ink Spots were not stereotype. The only aspect of the group that by today's standards disturbs is the Hoppy Jones talking chorus. He always maintained a contemplative, sad aspect to his voice—not clearly a submissive dialect, but very close on some recordings (e.g., "We'll Meet Again") to the stereotype of a 1930s-era world-weary black male. Talking choruses were not new and were used by both black and white singers in a great variety of genres, but Jones's style was certainly copied and even parodied over the years. There is in this aspect of the group a kind of covert dynamism that straddled two worlds, one black, one white. The demeanor, sound, and success of the group empowered in that it looked to crossover, perhaps integrationist possibilities. The group certainly appealed in different ways to its constituents—to blacks, the group was successful and respected; to whites, talented and "respectful" enough to listen to.

But that talking chorus of Hoppy Jones, which appeared in many though not all songs, is something of a drag on contemporary ears. This was a juncture, because later black singers used talking choruses as well— or just talking through portions of a song—to great effect, but it was the younger, rhythm & blues-era singers that imbued a freshness and assertiveness into that older concept. Ultimately black performers, from the 1960s on, transformed it into a distinct, powerful communicative tool within the context of a song.

Nevertheless, the Ink Spots were still cool, reserved, and respected. It was before the R&B vocal groups incorporated dance steps and their own postwar type of stylized posturing. The Ink Spots communicated "appealing" (read respectable) values in the sense that the group crossed lines of both race and class. Young singers appreciated the strategic aspect of that, the business side of music. They knew that the result of those values could mean success. White expectations often played off shuck and jive, which is absent with this group, and yet their demeanor had enormous appeal for those same whites, and Hoppy Jones as a foil to Bill Kenny was part of the formula. This is the crossover conundrum of black performance vis-à-vis white expectations—be black, but not too black. For African Americans of the time, however, the Ink Spots must have struck a dignified, successful pose. They smiled, but they did not grin, and got over.

"But we knew they were a smooth operation on that stage," Winley said. "Yes. So you knew you had to dress well. You had to present yourself well, and you carried, you know, the demeanor."

The Ink Spots, along with similar groups like the Mills Brothers, Cats and the Fiddle, Four Vagabonds, and Delta Rhythm Boys, drew from Tin Pan Alley to develop their crossover sounds in the 1930s and early 1940s. "Crossover" meant both black and white audience appeal and in that, greater commercial success. Groups maintained a kind of musical and racial middle ground, sometimes (but by no means always) by taking a standard song and rearranging it in a jump or jive style (it never went the other way).[7]

When youngsters in the later 1940s copied crossover groups like the Ink Spots, who performed standard material almost exclusively, they furthered a particular kind of black style and tradition—one more inclusive, rather than exclusive. They performed material they liked, and material that they thought an audience would identify with. They did material that they also thought was "classy" and commercially viable. For the latter, inevitably, white audiences had to be part of the formula, whether performers articulated the point or not—and the point was not to sell out to whites, but to buy in to success. This drive created some terrific ironies for black groups.

To some derisive industry insiders, for instance, Bill Kenny and the Ink Spots (as well as the Mills Brothers and other similar groups) "sugared" their sound to appeal to white audiences (Shaw 1978: xvii). Perhaps they did, but so what? Did that make them somehow less black? Black musicians like the Ink Spots were shrewd enough to play with the notion of blackness. They did so with obvious irony, in light of their fly-in-the-milk kind of name choice that called attention to color (as did the Ravens, the Lewis Bronzeville Five, Brown Dots, Cap-Tans, and numerous others).[8] This was decades before scholars wrote about social constructions of race, but these artists had long known the score of that game. Indeed, playing with the notion of blackness (which was not a new thing in the 1930s and continues into our present era under updated guises) must be predicated on the idea that "blackness" as a concept endures (albeit in changing ways over time) in opposition to a mainstream that isolated it to begin with. That said, you cannot play with the idea of "white" in quite the same way, unless it is in opposition to black ("white on!" as a sarcastic pun only works in opposition to the black affirmation, "right on!"). The point here is that groups like the Ink Spots, and subsequent ones, were forced to engage with race and concepts of "blackness." The result was shifting perceptions of what "black" was or was supposed to be.

Clearly, the Ink Spots knew what they wanted to do musically and commercially (even if the entertainment world may have limited the choices to begin with). Clearly, the group appealed to young black males also, especially during the mid-1940s, and not just as a strategy for mainstream success. The group's crossover success was part of the inspiration, yet black youngsters at that time were intuitive enough not to essentialize music. They went with the popular flow, took what came their way in those years, and eventually made something uniquely their own.

In cities like Baltimore and Washington that constituted a sound considerably more "mainstream" than blues, for instance, for which the old line black residents in those cites most likely had only a limited appreciation, and the Ink Spots, though unapologetically black, were definitely not blue.[9]

Blues, just like Tin Pan Alley standards, was an undeniable influence on American popular music as a whole. Blues was to become a blessing for white musicians learning about rock 'n' roll in the 1950s and white teenagers who craved something on the other side of Perry Como and Vic Damone. There was also the historical connection between blues and black culture, and that inescapable influence of a black consciousness on this nation. By the mid-1940s, you could no more ignore blues than Tin Pan Alley as a musical structure, attitude, and as a cultural form. Inevitably, group harmony drew as much from one as it drew from the other. For performers to attain a certain level of professional success in popular music, at the time meant they had to be open to sing anything, to see what worked and what did not.

Groups like the Ink Spots were enormously successful with both black and white audiences, but then fell into the trap, to some, of not sounding (or acting) "black" enough, thus the idea that they "sugared" their sound. This is another familiar story—be black enough to make whites comfortable, but neither black enough to make them feel threatened nor white enough to imply parity (or parody). This is one of those historical ties: blacks, especially those who work in public, have to do so in the context of white expectations.

By 1947 changes in American popular music were underway. There occurred a shift away from large swing bands to the smaller jump bands after the early 1940s, the development and subsequent popularity of small format, modern jazz (the trade name became "bebop"), and urban blues as well. In addition, changes in popular dances helped incite a tighter rhythmic feel in fast tempo music, especially pronounced in the rhythm sections. One result was a more pronounced "backbeat," a distinct off beat accent in common time usually hammered out as rim shots by the drummer on 2 and 4. You can hear the backbeat antecedents at least as far back as New Orleans style rhythm sections from the 1920s, but it became so typical of rhythm & blues / rock 'n' roll during the late 1940s and 1950s that today it is a cliché (though still a useful one), a good example of an enduring black sound image.[10]

These and other changes in black popular music resulted in a more emotional climate that began to define the rhythm & blues vocal group era. As popular and influential as the Ink Spots were, even in the late 1940s, they still had established their sound before World War II and by the war's end tastes began to change.

Arguably, the one most influential vocal group of the postwar period was the Ravens, billed as "The Greatest Group of Them All." The Ravens, like the Ink Spots, performed mostly Tin Pan Alley standards, although they also recorded a few original blues compositions (e.g., "Write Me a Letter"), as well as some novelty numbers. The emotional qualities of the Ravens' blues recordings, while nowhere near the intensity of electric urban blues or gospel, were something of a departure from the more dispassionate demeanor of the Ink Spots and others. The emotion was enough to inspire younger groups who did not necessarily come out of the gospel or blues traditions, but who reflected the emergent tastes of the period—it was that yearning by the young for something different, something more exciting. The Ravens were less restrained than the Ink Spots, and, by recording some blues numbers, they further opened the door for that material as more mainstream and acceptable, beyond jazz and swing.[11]

Between 1947 and 1950 the original group recorded their best material for the National label. The Ravens were a sensational harmonizing group and they further popularized the strong bass lead and the equally strong falsetto lead—both became a staple of vocal groups in the 1950s and beyond. Jimmy Ricks (1924–1974) of the Ravens brought to popular music a strong but extremely supple bass lead, but he was just as good with the background figures and grounding harmonies. Ricks was originally from Jacksonville, Florida. He began his singing career in a choral group at Stanton High School. After he graduated, he spent two years in Greensboro, North Carolina, where he sang in a quartet. Ricks made his way to New York where, early in 1946, he formed the Ravens with the group's baritone, Warren Suttles, a church soloist from Alabama. Ricks found the group's second tenor, Leonard Puzey, at an Apollo Theater amateur show. The first tenor and falsetto voice, Maithe Marshall, joined the group after he performed on Broadway, in Billy Rose's *Carmen Jones*, the adaptation of Bizet's *Carmen*.

> The RAVENS easily rank as America's top harmony singing unit of the day. They also are unquestioned champs of the Juke boxes. They won the unchallenged claim on the music machine title with a smashing victory in the 1948 balloting by CASH BOX, the "bible" of the music box and recording industry. This famed group of distinctive song stylists have added further to their laurels in 1948 by winning the coveted first place spot in the annual poll of the Pittsburgh COURIER, largest circulated Negro weekly in the country. (*Baltimore Afro-American* June 21, 1948; emphases original)[12]

After 1946, the Ravens began to have a considerable influence on what would soon become rhythm & blues vocal harmony. This occurred primarily because of the group's solid harmonies, their sweet falsetto singer, the strong bass vocal (they often featured a dual lead), and their balance of up-tempo standards, sentimental ballads, blues, and novelty numbers. The group's arrangements, usually with piano, guitar, and bass, though formulaic, were simultaneously jazzy, catchy, low-key, and cool, but compared to the Ink Spots, stunning and alive.

The Ravens were a seminal rhythm & blues group, but most followers of this period cite the Orioles as the first true rhythm & blues group after they had their first hit in 1948, "It's Too Soon to Know." The Orioles and then the Clovers in 1951 were the two groups to come right after the Ravens and to help establish rhythm & blues vocal harmony as we know it today.

The Orioles came from Baltimore. They subtly, but completely, transformed the music into a noticeably more emotional sound and a more physical performance than the restrained style of the earlier established black "pop" vocal groups. The Orioles, like the R&B groups that followed them, continued to use standard material that either was, or resembled, Tin Pan Alley songs, well after the period of the Ink Spots and Mills Brothers.[13] Although the Orioles did not, other late 1940s and 1950s groups also copied (or tried to) the predominant bass voice (sometimes as lead), and falsetto lead (or floating tenor), of Jimmy Ricks and Maithe Marshall of the Ravens. Save for the enduring influences of the Ravens, after the Orioles hit groups never really looked back for much else. The Orioles articulated the movement and yearning of postwar youth in even the most standard of material. The lead singer, Sonny Til, wound up, pulled, and squeezed the words and melody of a song while the alternate lead, George Nelson, contrasted with a rhythmically irregular delivery. The result was a quiet, yet slightly taut sound. The group's early performances were far from the raucous stereotype of rhythm & blues, as they still used restrained bass and guitar backing. Nor did the Orioles have the wide-open emotionalism of gospel quartets. In the Orioles, those influences seem more felt than heard. The group held in their emotion, it was close-coiled, and yet there was something slightly dissolute about the vocal lead, in a charming sort of way. It was smooth. It was different. It was all style and performance. It was immensely appealing.

Meanwhile in Washington the Clovers built on what they heard the Orioles do. They first sang standards a cappella and then with guitar accompaniment, in the tradition of early pop groups. In 1951, with a contract and some significant re-shaping by Atlantic Records, the Clovers created a rock-steady harmony sound—also very appealing, well executed, blues-based, danceable, young, and fun. If the Orioles were seminal, then the Clovers were developmental. They helped define a decade with songs like "Don't You Know I Love You," "Fool, Fool, Fool," "One Mint Julep," "Your Cash Ain't Nothing But Trash," "Lovey Dovey," "Devil or Angel," and "Love Potion Number Nine."

Together the Orioles and Clovers provided grounding for many subsequent groups, not just vocal rhythm & blues in the 1950s, but vocal harmony for the future, the 1960s, 1970s, and beyond. During their time, the Orioles and Clovers created a good musical mix for young, emerging teenage minds that favored danceable rhythms and emotional performances that were different from 1940s swing. These two groups also became successful models for many amateur groups.

After the Orioles hit in 1948, other groups followed, and with the Clovers' success in 1951, group harmony developed throughout the 1950s until it became a dominant style for a period of time. As early as September 1951, *Billboard* reported that, "vocal groups have taken the play in the R&B field" (Gart 1986: 448). Young groups emerged on a national level, with names still familiar today: the Cadillacs, Cardinals, Five Keys, Flamingos, Moonglows, and Swallows—there were hundreds of other, lesser known groups. Localized traditions formed through amateur or semi-professional neighborhood groups, in churches, or in the public schools. Throughout the 1950s, these kinds of groups were especially popular in, but certainly not limited to, cities such as New York, Philadelphia, Chicago, Los Angeles, and of course Baltimore and Washington, D.C. The vocal groups harmonized a cappella or with piano, guitar, or a small band. The instrumental accompaniment ranged from slow, triplet-backed dance ballads to jump blues to piano boogies. The standout instrumental centerpiece for many of the faster arrangements continued, from the jump band tradition, to be tenor saxophone.[14] By the mid-1950s or so, the electric guitar began to predominate.

The postwar vocal groups, like their antecedents, maintained a varied repertory of sweet sentimental songs, pop standards, and blues, jump, and novelty numbers. They balanced formulaic renditions of Tin Pan Alley with other material in response to their interests, the recording industry, and popular tastes of the period. Group repertoires, it seemed, sometimes came down to either a ballad or a fast blues. Nevertheless, some originality and individuality could cut through the basic formulas, and that was what gave each group its identity and what distinguished the successful ones. If a group did not have its own signature sound at first, then they copied or adapted an already popular one (always a trusted strategy in music). Thus groups like the Orioles and Clovers, because of their national success, became models for many local groups, just as they themselves had modeled themselves on the Ink Spots and Ravens. In this way, groups maintained continuity with earlier black music styles. That said, they also changed and adapted to conform to newer musical sensibilities and tastes, especially as they came into contact with music producers, managers, and record companies. Part of this process had to do with learning what record companies wanted, and then giving it to them. Thus groups oftentimes worked to become active participants in the whole creative process, even if that meant they learned how to harmonize differently, on top of what they already knew, to provide what a producer or arranger wanted. This is not to suggest that record industrialists did not take advantage of musicians. At the very least, however, the singers became aware of the whole industry process and tried to become a part of it as best they could. The challenge was to create or maintain a sound and repertoire that would make the group commercially viable. This was the inevitable popular music imperative and one that young black males could and would embrace.

Blues Alley

To seek that imperative, young singers of the 1940s jumped off the dominant popular music of their period—swing, jump, urban blues, Tin Pan Alley standards, and gospel music. This was music they heard at home, over the radio or on records, learned in school, or performed at church. Blues in its older folk form, however, was probably the music least heard among young singers in the north, although blues forms and blues derivatives were commonly heard.

Many in this book say that what music they heard and liked, they got as much from radio as they did from home, school, or church. Radio, as we shall see, was a ubiquitous, pivotal presence in communities. That had its bad points, as well as its good ones. African Americans, for example, had to listen to broadcasts, including those aimed at black audiences, dictated by the white-dominated media for the most part, but because of that, they were familiar with a wide variety of music.

Blues and Tin Pan Alley were fundamental to group harmony in particular and American popular music in general. They constituted the dominant, entwined, yet contrasting sound images for much of the twentieth century after the 1920s, the importance of country music strands not influenced by those two styles notwithstanding. Blues and Tin Pan Alley broad-cast peculiar, particular, though sometimes ambiguous and racialized atti-tudes that affected not only the artists themselves, but audiences and the music industry as well. To some, for instance, Tin Pan Alley was simply "class," and blues simplistically "crass." But blues was neither simple, nor monochromatic. It appeared in a variety of shades and guises: as an emo-tion, a feeling, a musical form and structure, and on particular instruments. A good singer could make anything a blues with the right performance technique, the right vocal inflection, and the right emotion. It is next to impossible to say the same thing about a standard, that is, to make any kind of song sound like one. Standards were song architecture, structure, melody, and harmony; blues had structures, but were far more performative. Blues could be sublime (Billie Holiday), or strident (Robert Johnson). Blues could be rural or urban. There is no such thing as "down home" Tin Pan Alley, although jazz performers certainly turned many of those songs around. Good blues performers of any type must be convincing, if not "authentic," which is a problematic term. At one time, in the latter half of the nineteenth century, blues had to be a lived experience, and it was black experience, too, clearly marked by the lower classes. This is quite the oppo-site of Tin Pan Alley standards.

The rural folk blues remained somewhat obscure to many urban dwellers in the north, but certainly not those derivations found in female Classic singers, jazz, jump, swing, or urban blues. The popularity among African Americans of female blues singers after 1920—the first blacks to record in any great numbers—had perhaps more to do with race pride than with enjoyment of the style. African Americans who demurred when it came to blues, for reasons of religion or social standing, nevertheless took it for granted as a black cultural legacy, albeit with some reservations.

"But you also know the attitude people had toward that music," Harold Winley says of blues. "And Buddy, you sure couldn't sing that stuff in my mother's house. My oldest brother is about six feet tall. I'll never forget the day he walked into the house singing 'Jelly, Jelly, Jelly.' My mother was about four and a half feet; jumped in his chest."

Gradually, one aspect of blues became a produced, constructed form; a 12-bar structure detached from the original cultural and social underpin-nings, became a vital part of the American popular musical terrain, from jam sessions to jingles. Part of that process was that you did not always have to live the blues to sing the blues; you simply needed to master the style. Tin Pan Alley standards, while no less difficult to master in a musical sense, were never actually a lived cultural form. You would like to wish you could live your life as in the song, but first you have to suspend your belief in reality. Eventually, blues became as Tin Pan Alley had begun—a formal, musical construction of cultural life that required good musical and production tools to perform credibly. This was how the Clovers came to know the style, as we shall see, and this probably accounts for the popularity of both blues and Tin Pan Alley forms among a younger generation of vocalists familiar with big band jazz, which used both blues and Tin Pan Alley forms almost exclusively. The younger generation of singer simply recognized both as styles to learn, if not live, and you could acquire one just as easily as you could acquire the other.

For some whites, though, blues grew from crude obscurity to become an exotic, enticing sound image. Until about 1960, it often entered the white consciousness not directly through black artists, but through popular standards that referenced it, as in George Gershwin songs, and later through jazz and rock 'n' roll. Blues also influenced early country styles— from Jimmie Rodgers to bluegrass to Honky Tonk—just as influences flowed from country and folk styles into early blues. Tin Pan Alley songs (blues-tinged or not) became enormously popular with black swing and jazz musicians. Between the 1920s and the end of the 1940s, much black popular music derived from blues, gospel, or standards. As those interpretations became popular, they reinforced the general swirl of influence that popular white composers and musicians derived from black music and musicians—and so goes the cycle. These imprecise mixes and re-mixes acted on popular music and group harmony in the 1940s.

Most of the postwar rhythm & blues groups kept variations of both blues and Tin Pan Alley type songs in their repertoires, whether recording known material or creating original compositions. Indeed, the two music styles and structures, combined with the emotional power of black gospel (sometimes wound together in the same song) have helped define most of what we have been listening to as a nation for the past century. The Tin Pan Alley sentimental standards strain in rhythm & blues era group harmony was particularly strong, at least early on, simply because of the earlier group models and because it was the dominant music of the period. In addition, as singers testify here, they liked the music, the songs, melodies, and lyrics.

Some have also suggested that this kind of material in vocal harmony was part of a postwar optimism among African Americans. Diz Russell, a singer in the third version of the Orioles, phrased it as a "chicken in every pot" and "folks just wanted to fall in love" interpretation of postwar vocal harmony ballads (quoted in Maultsby 1986: 15). His point was that things were getting better for blacks after the war and they wanted to sing about it. Based on these assertions of an emergent, idyllic period in urban black history, Maultsby suggests that group harmony ballads and sentimental songs "captured the mood and feelings of the times" (15). In one sense, she is quite correct, but for different reasons. Indeed, standards captured the mood, feeling of the musical times, but not necessarily the positive sentimentality that Diz Russell implies. Socially, there had always been a disjuncture between Tin Pan Alley romance and the way people really lived their lives, especially for a great deal of black America. Indeed, there was as much to lament after the war as before, vis-à-vis the social circumstances of African Americans in cities like Baltimore and Washington and everywhere else in America. What changed?

This point tells us something about the vocalists, and others involved in music at the time, that had the presence of mind, in spite of social circumstance, to hear musical possibilities in what citizens had not yet realized socially or politically. It points to the musical interrelationships that define American popular music over the course of the twentieth century. As youngsters warmed to the popular music of their time, they began to change it. Singers of the period tell us that very often distinctions between "black" and "white" music meant little on the grassroots level. Indeed, the recirculation of music between blacks and whites is a refining and defining process for much of the twentieth century that points not to independence, but to interdependence. That relationship stands in stark contrast to social segregation. It is not a circumstance people have easily understood, but is at the heart of a very basic research question asked early on in this project. Why did vocal groups—and many other black musicians—interpret and embrace Tin Pan Alley standards to such a degree? As a predominant style at the time, there was no good reason not to embrace the music, and the music's qualities obviously resonated with blacks as well as whites.

There is another answer to the question, and it comes from James McPhail, a well-known singer in Washington since the 1950s. In the 1940s, he sang in a vocal group called the Armstrong Four, associated with the black high school of the same name. McPhail says that the popularity of Tin Pan Alley resulted from something musically valuable and appreciated by the singers.

"You knew where you were going in the standard songs, you know. You could just about hum it and you'd get through it. But we were doing those things, like I said Billy Eckstine, the Ink Spots, the Mills Brothers, the Cats and the Fiddle. But they were the ones that happened to be doing the music that we liked. And that's what we tried to [do]."

What McPhail tells us is that his generation liked standard material and its structural elegance and compositional simplicity. A good Tin Pan Alley song had a good melody and logical chord progression, so you could hum it and get through it. There was also a strong precedent in black performances of the style, and the kids emulated that. Harold Winley, the bass singer with the Clovers, said something very similar. He also clearly indicates that with this kind of song, a group could sing their way into places. That was what mattered. Money may not have mattered, initially, but still the singers were thinking in terms of getting over. To be popular was the first step toward professional status, and those songs meant status.

"If you wanted to do anything, I mean, any entertainer you know or had seen, what were they singing? They were singing standard songs. Classy acts. I mean you go see the Ink Spots, man, my god. Class. You know, Eckstine, Prysock, when he was young, in Buddy Johnson's band. The Delta Rhythm Boys. All class. These songs must be the way. And they're very appealing songs. You know you can sing these songs anywhere."

The term "standards" refers to Tin Pan Alley songs, such as those composed between the years beginning around World War I through roughly the end of World War II or early 1950s. What distinguished them? They had formal musical structures—as in verse/chorus, 32-bar AABA, ABAC, or similar variants of form (Hamm 1979: 361)—good, underlying harmony, great tunes, some with comfortable melodies, easy to discern or remember, and standard orchestral accompaniment. Tin Pan Alley lyrics evoked either an ethos of sentimentality, or one that was charming, but cynically urbane. If blues brought you face to face with a particular reality, then Tin Pan Alley tried to take you as far away as possible. The core audience for Tin Pan Alley was mostly, though not exclusively, mainstream—white, urban, upper-middle class, probably oriented more to the North than South. The appeal of the songs clearly crossed over to many African Americans (and other whites across a broad spectrum of classes) because the sentiments often voiced a modern romanticism open to anybody socialized to identify the signs. Tin Pan Alley also had strong ties to Broadway shows and Hollywood movies, and a particular stable of composers/lyricists. These would be the familiar names of white writers, almost exclusively male: Arlen, Berlin, Gershwin, Hammerstein, Kern, Porter, Rodgers, and many others. There was considerable involvement by black writers also, like Eubie Blake, Shelton Brooks, Andy Razaf, and Noble Sissle, among others. In addition, nearly a century's worth of black artists have been interpreting and recording Tin Pan Alley standards.

Tin Pan Alley was no simple phenomenon, by any means, because it had so many constituent parts. It was a place (in New York City, where the music publishing industry centered itself for so many years), a way to compose, to perform, and in some ways, it became a way to think. It was the music business par excellence, with strong ties to stage shows and film as well-known standards often originated there. It invoked a formal musical architecture, well-constructed tunes, particular sentiments and attitudes in the lyrics, and well-known professional writers who knew the craft. Tin Pan Alley also had a sublime, maybe subliminal association with white, urban attitudes.

Nevertheless, despite this mainstream sphere, Tin Pan Alley was neither separate from African American culture nor entirely a distinct intellectual movement. Indeed, "blackness" in some cases became a necessary defining element for Tin Pan Alley composers, at least in some of their songs—Irving Berlin, George Gershwin, and Johnny Mercer, to name just three. Black musicians obviously enjoyed performing and interpreting standards and they contributed significantly to their popularity, especially as the songs became a dominant movement throughout the 1930s and 1940s. As they performed material based on black "images"—think of Johnny Mercer's gospel sermon-inspired "Ac-Cent-Tchu-Ate the Positive" (1944)— black artists ended up reinterpreting white interpretations of their own culture, as in songs from George Gershwin's "Porgy and Bess" or Jerome Kern's "Showboat." If you wanted to make successful popular music in the 1940s, you had to engage with the right material. For whites, that material ironically was black music, at least a respectable taste of it, blues or jazz for instance (though often through the interpretive lens of whites); for African Americans, it was Tin Pan Alley. Young singers tried to engage with the right material.

Buddy Bailey was one of those young singers. He became the lead singer in the Clovers and spoke in the same way about his early influences as others did about theirs: the Ink Spots, Billy Eckstine, those singers that had the sound and the look. They were pop idols of the 1940s and performed standards. "Yeah. Oh yeah. King Cole Trio. And I liked Billy Eckstine. I admired Billy Eckstine's songs, "Cottage for Sale," stuff like that. I liked the, there was something about the lyrics, you know, the meaning. They were meaningful to me. They told a story. Great love songs."

Johnny Page, who lived in Baltimore and sang in the 1950s, brought up the issue of his public image as a singer and the notion of race. There is a particular sentiment that his comment evokes—that a certain sound, like that of the Ink Spots, and certain kinds of songs, such as standards, were for everyone. At the same time, he feels a particular rhythmic feel was "black." "Well, the rhythm and things that I felt was black, you know, but the projection I wanted to give to the public was pop style, anybody's style. See, because anybody could relate to it, because it was that type. Because the Ink Spots was like that, and numerous other groups. The Platters were like that, and they didn't have any racist thing, or 'I'm going to sing just to black people.' "

Andrew Magruder, who sang lead and recorded with a group called the Five Blue Notes, grew up in Washington during the 1940s. "O.K., before the Orioles came on the scene I was listening to the Andrews Sisters, Donna Costa, Nat King Cole, Ink Spots. Listen to what I'm saying now. Yes, the Mills Brothers—because my father liked them. And, going to the movies, Gene Autry, Roy Rogers, Sons of the Pioneers. "Cool Water." But I'm just saying, you know, I can't understand what the problem is, because music was music to me. I don't care what kind of music it was. I can take your music and turn it around and make it my music."

Magruder here casually drops what could very well be a proverb of African American performance values—"I can take your music and turn it around and make it my music."[15] This is one reason why vocal groups would learn and internalize mainstream Tin Pan Ally material, certainly enjoy it, and at the same time appeal to a wider audience. Part of this was a function of the time in which pop vocal groups emerged, when standard tunes dominated popular vocal music. Yet, another perspective on this suggests that these groups were like entrepreneurs. They emerged into a public sphere eager to engage with commodity and exchange. This is not quite the bourgeois public sphere of Habermas. It is, rather, a black public sphere that is "more expansive than the realm of public debate and deliberation" (Austin 1995: 248, n. 66) and one that inevitably, necessarily, engaged with whites. It is also a sphere that perhaps blurs the distinctions between "private" and "public," necessitated by the continual public imaging—white expectations—of black America and the consequent role private citizens had to play. The vocal groups, in their time and place, entered this sphere, engaged with it, and built on what had preceded them to make it their own, with an eye and ear on musical stock in trade. Thus, as we shall see, they were emerging entrepreneurs.

Musically then, to summarize, postwar rhythm & blues group harmony resonated between blues and Tin Pan Alley. The overall trajectory of group harmony touched on several historical points as it developed a nicely emotional core that emanated in part from gospel crossover and blues, and was fueled by young, postwar sensibilities in popular music. The professional posture of singers, too, was that blues, Tin Pan Alley standards, whatever, all fit into a strategy for musical success. Artists no longer had to live the blues to sing the blues; they only had to learn the blues. In addition, there were emotional qualities of another kind in harmony groups as described by participants. This had to do with the "flow" of singing and hanging out, a kind of psychological attitude and musical connection between singers. It allowed them, for instance, to trade voice parts almost intuitively. Beyond the immediacy of performing, young males singing in harmony groups connected with the world around them and did so through and with music. Unlike the professional disjuncture that might exist between the singer and a song, here vocalists integrated music into their everyday lives. It was more than becoming the song, or the song becoming them, because often it did not matter, on this level, what the song was. Vocalists integrated the act of singing into their lives. The process of singing became them, no matter what they sang. This concept has earlier and deeper roots.

The power of African American religious music and its influence over the years on secular music remains inarguable. Gospel music is powerful because it is a transformative music. If successful, it becomes a part of one's everyday as well as spiritual life. African American gospel quartet singers in Memphis, for example, "integrate their music into everyday life" and "try to live the life about which they sing" (Lornell 1990: 8). How could it be otherwise? It happens all of the time in ways measureless throughout the world.

African practice maintained a persistent, pervasive, and compelling integration of music, worship, and everyday life that carried over to the New World. The Memphis gospel quartets both sang and lived their spirituality—clearly an African and African American preference that occurs in other black styles, not just sacred music. This was precisely the kind of occurrence typical for secular group harmony. The participants both sang and lived their music.

On a general level, it is difficult to imagine someone who has not tried to turn the theory of a song into the practice of living and, in that way, integrate music into everyday life. It seems that one function of much successful music is precisely that, whether African-based or not. Popular music in particular gives us a melody and some lyrics—a story—and compels us to believe we can live that story or confirms that we already have. Tin Pan Alley standards certainly were prescriptive in that many of them constructed a world of fantasy and make-believe, a world as far from reality as could be. Yet, in listening to a convincing performance, we still believe that we can, that we should, fall into life under the blue moon and when it turns to gold, love happily ever after. Blues, on the other hand, before moving too far beyond its cultural underpinnings, was a descriptive music that confirmed much about the human condition to those that lived the life and knew the story. Rap and hip-hop, especially in the late 1980s through the mid-1990s, before it became too much like pop, would also purport to tell us the truth and also tell us what to do about it. In the world of popular music, many of us do not (and do not care to) distinguish between our lives and the poetry of the music. In any case, these genres have high entertainment value and provide a good return on our emotional investment. On one level, the stakes remain low, even if things don't quite work out as in the song. It is, however, on another level that precisely what is at stake distinguishes African American music making.

For blacks in America, the stakes in making music were much higher than for whites, and the integration of song and everyday life more persuasive. Song was both entertainment and a technology—a means to survive. In so many instances you had to live the song and sing your life in a seesaw motion, and this was what juba, work songs, spirituals, blues, gospel, jazz, and other related styles were all about. Blacks have had to consider controlling factors like enslavement, disenfranchisement, and segregation, as well as others that followed. Music constituted part of a survival methodology but that did not diminish its entertainment value, its professional possibilities, or the pure celebration of a song. Whites have so often failed to understand this, this political agency—the "had to"—that black performance inevitably has had to embrace, no matter the song, no matter the style, and no matter the historical period.

What should seem obvious by now, and what has become a postulate for intelligent music study, is that music does not occur in a social vacuum. There is connectivity between music and everyday life, a multitude of daily occurrences performed or celebrated through or with music. African Americans also have historically observed and lived life through music, diversity within black America notwithstanding. This is celebration in its broadest sense. This is the use of music for its intrinsic goodness, because we value it, and, as such, is an end in itself. It was something people did for each other, not solely in response to anything or anyone, least of all whites.

But there was another, deeper dimension to it.

Herman Denby was the lead vocalist for the Swallows in the early 1950s. He said about Baltimore of the 1930s and 1940s that there were lots of things black kids wanted to do, lots of places blacks wanted to go but couldn't because of segregation. At the same time, Herman tells us, "We wanted to sing. So that's what we did. We sang, day after day."

Others will say something quite similar in the coming pages. In the story of black group harmony from the 1940s, there are relationships between spatial limitations, spatial perspective, and social interaction. This had everything to do with being black and living in the city. The "mobility, travel patterns, individual's field of contact, activities: all affected by the characteristics of the urban system and the quality of physical channels of movement" (Herbert 1972: 238–39). To this, we can add "social" channels of movement—factors that helped map the lives of young singers in Washington, Baltimore, and no doubt, most other places with racial borders.

One question is whether singers opposed or resisted a lack of social mobility, in part, through the act of singing, through what they sang, and how they sang. The segregation and segmentation in Baltimore and Washington was stifling, and simply to negotiate the streets took some doing. The notion of "territory" or "place" framed everything that a black youngster might do in a segregated city, and black areas could be just as distinct from one another as from white areas. Denby, of the Swallows, and Ernest Warren, of the Cardinals, both grew up in Baltimore in the 1930s and 1940s. They both knew well the consequence of difference, that is, between the East Side and the West Side.

Herman Denby would say, "Well, you weren't allowed over here. I mean, that's the thing. That's the territory."

To which Ernest Warren replies, "You can live over there and don't come over here."

Herman completes the formula, "And I didn't belong over there, where he came from."

Limited mobility was a fact of African American life, always.[16] For group harmony, specifically the kind that took place on the local, grassroots level, singing was set against a wider and less forgiving urban sphere—a pervasive repression. As black voices sang, they did so in a white America. The story of group harmony illustrates the connection between human experience and music making and these two historical and extant human actions, which have largely shaped black music in the United States— celebration and resistance. Here we have not bipolar opposites, but rather a functional expanse of behaviors and flexible strategies that might range from celebration to acquiescence, accommodation, assimilation, opposition, or outright resistance. All these worked through simple, everyday, and creative gestures.

Resistance can take the form of momentous acts of organized, planned, and disciplined protests, or it may consist of small, everyday actions of seeming insignificance that can nevertheless validate the actor's sense of dignity and worth—such as refusing on the basis of inferiority to give up a seat on a bus or covering one's self in shame. It can rise out of the small-est conviction, such as knowing that an old woman can transmit an entire culture simply by touching a child. (Caldwell 1995: 276)

Oppositional behavior consists of individuals or group survival tactics that do not challenge the power in place, but make use of circumstances set up by that power for purposes the power may ignore or deny. (Chambers 1991: 1)

African Americans have used music performance to a considerable degree to enact celebration and resistance. These two forces have not been mutually exclusive of one another. Over the course of the past nearly 400 years, the flow of celebration and the force of resistance, played out in everyday life, grew to be interdependent in that one became the function of the other. The larger historical issue here simply is that African Americans lived and proliferated, celebrated, made music, but most often under con-ditions shaped by white society—large urban areas, for instance, where group harmony also proliferated in the 1940s and 1950s. The result is an overall music consciousness that embraces both celebration and resistance.

It is the singularity of African-derived culture, the singular institution of enslavement as practiced here in the United States, and the resultant racism and other persistent social practices that established and perpetu-ated patterns of interaction unique between African and non-African. Those patterns forever (at least for the meanwhile) shaped differently the social consciousness of both blacks and whites. One result was an African American use of music with which to both celebrate life and spirituality and resist repression. African Americans used those strategies in unique ways that had not, need not have been, used before.

There is a challenge to any overarching theory or explanation of social phenomenon, such as one that tries to see a black unity in music celebra-tion and social resistance. The challenge is to find clearly (as clear as some-thing like this can be) discernible oppositional voices and evidence of resistance that come directly from the phenomenon's actors. The narratives in this book strive to meet that challenge.

Clearly, something was at work here, when singers lamented, as a kind of riddle, that yes, they wanted to sing, but often had little else to do. This riddle resides inside the time, place, and social sphere of group harmony, to which we now turn our attention.

2

Time and Place

People adjust to their surroundings and extract structure and identity out of the material at hand.

—Lynch (1960: 46)

———

The black public sphere—as a critical social imaginary—does not centrally rely on the world of magazines and coffee shops, salons and highbrow tracts. It draws energy from the vernacular practices of street talk and new music, radio shows and church voices, entrepreneurship and circulation.

—Black Public Sphere Collective (1995: 3)

———

On the corner, on somebody's porch or something—you could hear groups, I mean, from all over when you come down the street, you know, especially in the summer months when you out of school. Everybody's tuning up. Then that made you popular, too—with the young ladies and all that. And everybody knew you. You know, that was part of growing up.

—Alphonso Feemster

Imageability

Some lines of musical inquiry point beyond the extant literature around a particular style and refer us back to the street. Rhythm & blues group harmony began on the street, and was of a particular time and place. It was a postwar style and a city style. What youngsters had in singing was powerful for them. Singing had, unlike the city that contained it, a limitless, unbounded quality. Yet, to a remarkable degree, the urban environment in which it took place shaped vocal harmony—not only the musical aspects, but the social. Perhaps the vertical briefing urban structures provide, the space and pace of the city, suggested to singers a certain musical attitude that complimented what they already had in their heads, heard on recordings, over the radio, or in church. At least that could have been part of the story. It is seductive to consider the relationships between spatial dimensions within a city and those of group harmony. The straight-up stacking of voices in postwar harmony singing, with the rhythmic attitude of young singers, certainly reminds one more of the city than the country. Certainly the physical and psychic aspects of a city and, in particular, the restrictions of urban segregation helped shape a consciousness, a constant awareness of physical place in the minds of black citizens. The limitlessness of singing, however, engages the imagination to surge beyond the limitations of place. This was especially true for young black males who, in the eyes of whites, would have been the most "suspect" if they drifted into white areas as they moved around segregated city streets. When singers from Baltimore and Washington were asked about their musical influences, they inevitably talked more about the streets, neighborhoods, and cities than they did the music. The importance that place had to them is reflected in this chapter.

Ernest Warren of the Cardinals commented on the thought of crossing over from his Baltimore neighborhood into a white neighborhood to the north, at Pennsylvania and North Avenues. "Pennsylvania Avenue across North Avenue? Sheeeeeeeeeeee…"

Baltimore and Washington, like other cities during the 1940s, provided a singular social sphere for African Americans. The city was, in one sense, the same place for blacks as it was for whites, but in another sense, it was distinct and different. Blacks and whites lived in the same general geographical location, passed each other on sidewalks, but lived different social lives and interpreted any shared, interrelated experiences differently. The streets were the same, but walking the sidewalks was different: same place, different space. The question, simply, is what consequence on music making did this have.

With this in mind, a number of vocalists from the 1940s and 1950s tell their stories, in this and subsequent chapters, of growing up in Baltimore and Washington. Ernest Warren and Herman Denby, along with Howard Davis and Mel Lipscomb, Alphonso Feemster, Andrew Magruder, George Tillman, James McPhail, Harold Winley, John Buddy Bailey, and Buddy Slaughter, were among first generation singers in the rhythm & blues era in and around Baltimore and Washington. Their groups include, respectively, the Cardinals, Swallows, Dunbar Four / Hi Fi's, Four Bars of Rhythm,

Five Blue Notes, Melodaires, Armstrong Four, Clovers (both Winley and Bailey), and the Buddies / Cap-Tans. This group of vocalists, generally, was born before 1935 and came of age as singers by about 1947. Below they discuss the neighborhoods where they grew up. We also meet a younger generation of singer, generally born after 1935. This group includes Lawrence Berry, Melvin Coles, George Jackson, and Carroll Williamson. All of the stories, not surprisingly, spin around lines of segregation, race, place, class, age, and by virtue of these principle characters being male, issues of gender.

Almost without exception, the singers who told their stories made striking references to sections of town, physical landmarks, streets, and blocks. Even after 40 to 50 years, the references to place and the effects of space remained very much a part of their thinking.

The Cardinals' lead singer Ernest Warren was born in Norfolk, Virginia, in 1929. When he was eleven, Ernest moved with his youngest sister and their mother up to Baltimore.

As a teen, Ernest joined with a group called the Charms. Later they became the Mellotones, and finally the Cardinals, just before they recorded for Atlantic Records beginning in 1951. Ernest had a solid, graceful tenor voice. Yet, he had a matter-of-fact delivery, almost detached, and he carried that practicality with him over the years he spent away from music.

Ernest said he and his family moved from one side of Baltimore to the other a number of times over the years. Families often moved frequently in response to economics and the shifting boundaries of a class segmented and racially segregated city. There was continual overlap between where and with whom youngsters lived—their social geographic place—and how and why they made music—their cultural space. There was also the historical dimension of African Americans living within a dominant society. These factors combined to more than limit mobility, for they had an impact on other aspects of life—like who you met walking out of your door. Jack Johnson was one of the singers with whom Ernest subsequently worked in the Cardinals. Johnson heard Ernest sing as a youngster in the projects where they both lived. Many of the projects of that era were low, rectangular brick buildings laid out in lines, rows, and diagonals, like the surrounding city streets.

"Jack Johnson and I lived in the same court. We lived in the projects in East Baltimore, and he had heard me sing and he asked me to go with him one evening. I went down on the Point, that's where the boys—Meredith Brothers and Leon [Hardy]—were living. After you cross Baltimore Street; there's something called The Point. South Baltimore. And I was living in North Baltimore. I was on this side of Baltimore Street and they was on that side. And I went down—mean down there, too—and I went down there and got along with everybody and we did a few songs."

Families, neighborhoods, networks of interpersonal relationships, local businesses, churches, and schools were institutions important to areas that were hard-hit and poor as well as those middle class or assimilated. These institutions created meaning, motion, and equilibrium within constraints imposed by the larger, dominant society. African Americans had to live and work through these constraints—segregation in particular—which were not only spatial, but social and emotional as well. In some ways, just to exist within such a society is temptation to acquiesce to it, to become what it insists you become. Yet in most ways, there were few choices save to endure, oppose, or resist whenever, however possible. The phenomenon of racialized place and space in particular, when recalled by those who lived it, is something historian and architect Dolores Hayden so accurately terms "territorial history." It emerges through narratives about "political territories—bounded spaces with some form of enforcement of the boundaries" (Hayden 1995: 22–23). With these kinds of histories, we can better understand the relationships between making music, "spatial dimensions," to borrow from Hayden (23), and people's lives. For black youngsters, the impact of space and place could mean something as basic as negotiating the streets and establishing an alternative territory for play or performance, as countless male groups established local, geographic affiliations—East Side, West Side, Northwest, Southeast. This was much like the generation or two that followed who, in the 1980s, territorialized and regionalized rap and hip-hop—Bronx, Brooklyn, East Coast, West Coast. These East Side and West Side affiliations were lived experiences, partially the result of established racial boundaries. But they were also categories constructed and understood from within, rather than specific categories that the dominant society imposed.

White folks made neighborhoods segregated, but they neither created the idea of East Side or West Side vocal groups nor the related emotions, experiences, and affiliations within those areas. For a young black male to have, say, an "East Side" affiliation was a category whose power came from the ground up. From a black perspective, then, these territorial affiliations had the potential to be as empowering as they were limiting.

It is perfectly reasonable to interpret this as a type of opposition because youngsters, whenever they could, found ways to get through certain places and situations by "transforming imposed structures...codes, rules, etc." (Chambers 1991: 6). Transforming is an old art. "Change the joke and slip the yoke," in the words of Ralph Ellison (1964: 45). If young-sters could not change the streets, they certainly could change the meaning of those streets and the music that they sang on them.

For blacks in segregated cities, mobility and access to specific places were clearly limited, and limiting. Movement within the city was just as affected by emotional structures or images of segregation, as it was by enforced physical or legal limits—the two could hardly be separate. With a lack of freedom of movement, so goes what a youngster thinks about— or does not think about. James McPhail from Washington phrased it this way:

"And like I say, we didn't know, I didn't know anything about white neighborhoods because we didn't venture out that much. We knew where everybody, all the black people went, and that's where we went, you know. Didn't even think about it. Didn't even think about. Didn't even, didn't even think about it."

Ernie Warren was supremely conscious of Pennsylvania and North and the consequences of stepping into the white district while Jimmy McPhail as a youngster remained hardly conscious of white areas. This gives us pause to consider what effect this had on young people as they grew up. Kevin Lynch uses the term "imageability" to refer to the "physical environment" and "structures" of cities. He defines imageability as, "that quality in a physical object [in a city] which gives it a high probability of evoking a strong image in any given observer" (Lynch 1960: 9). For Lynch, imageability is also legibility (9), and one presumes in that a clarity and comprehension on the part of a city's inhabitants to understand the physical structure of the city. His purpose is to probe the "mental images" citizens have of their cities in order, ultimately, to help urban planners consider the "visual quality" (2) of the American city. Lynch discovers that city dwellers each have their own, unique internal images of the city in which they reside. Urban patterns vary, depending on the place, person, or group.

Images of the city, however, can include the non-material—the emotional, social, cultural, political, or economic. In segregated cities, folks knew where they could or could not go, knew where they needed or wanted to go. Black citizens knew where they wanted or needed to stay, or how to negotiate paths beyond the black areas. Segregation, by law or custom, often dictated those paths. The social and emotional structures imposed by whites made a lasting imprint on the urban totality. A very young child, as its social consciousness forms, thinks it is where it should be. The notion of "place" took on new meaning for black youth in segregated cities as they grew up. The very young, as McPhail suggests, made little if any connection to the white areas, until they got older. Then they needed to come to terms with negotiating the streets, neighborhoods, and the concept of "whites only." For whites, the idea of being "out of your territory" was quite different, if not absurd when compared to blacks. In the 1940s a young white male who, for instance, wandered into a black neighborhood would at worst, face a confrontation with other youth. He always had the option of running to the police. A young black male, on the other hand, who wandered into a white section, would inevitably find the police confronting him.

Andrew Magruder sang in Washington during the 1950s with the Blue Jays, Blue Notes, and then later as a solo performer (as Andy Mack). He was born in Washington on October 16, 1936. The family lived in Georgetown. His father, an African American, was a meat cutter and worked for a white grocer up in Chevy Chase, just outside of Northwest Washington. Magruder's mother was white and was from Lynchburg, Virginia. She played guitar and taught Andy what he called "hillbilly" songs that his father also learned. The Magruders were Catholic; Andy did not sing in church.

He describes an incident that happened to him when he was about fourteen or fifteen years old: "Must have been around 1950. Yeah, about '50 or '51. Because I'll never forget that, because we did a show for the guys in the hospital at Walter Reed and they wanted us to sing spirituals so we was trying to put spirituals together. They had the Red Cross bus, the army bus, pick us up. I missed the bus and had to walk from Georgia Avenue and Butternut all the way over to 26th and P, and the police stopped me because I was black. They wanted to know what I was doing in that neighborhood. I said, 'Man, I missed my bus, but I walked.' They didn't lock me up or nothing. They let me keep going, because I had my white dinner jacket on, bow tie, and tucked pants and whatnot. But I was scared to death. I was scared to death, man."

Black citizens in cities like Baltimore and Washington in the 1940s needed to keenly employ a heightened sense of place in their local world. They devised strategies with which to position themselves, literally and in their own minds, in the segregated city. These were factors beyond the physical boundaries within a city, the emotional feel of racial limits that we cannot transcribe, yet are unmistakable. They are an outgrowth of the material boundaries established through segregation and whites-only policies. This is a social imageability, to borrow from Lynch, which constitutes a powerful marker and surely required of black citizens mapping of a very pedestrian, literally, and practical kind. The result was both the wicked dis-

comfort of segregation and a comfortable insularity for black neighborhoods, businesses, and entertainment districts.

Typically, an urban black neighborhood during this period centralized
"the perspectives of poor and working-class folks," to borrow a phrase from
bell hooks (1995: 151). The black districts, however, were not necessarily
the complete social pathology preached by the likes of E. Franklin Frazier
(1940), or Gunnar Myrdal (1944). As some might say of that time and
place, "We were poor, but not in poverty." There was severe economic pri-
vation in black neighborhoods, to be sure, but also economic gain for black
businesses, although many whites operated stores and businesses in those
areas as well (on this more below).

Black neighborhoods in cities like Baltimore and Washington were
complex and pluralistic. African Americans in those cities knew that they
self-segmented, by intra-racial divisions, along class, regional, urban, and
rural lines. This was an especially resonant image inside of Washington,
with historical antecedents. Older black families distinguished themselves
from the new in-migrants, for instance. The intersection of race and class
in the development of postwar group harmony is not a clear one, but like
segregation, a clearly felt one.

The notion still lingers that there were some positive aspects of segregation, from African American perspectives. This is precisely why some
older African Americans might refer nostalgically to the "we all had each
other" sensibility. This, interestingly, is the opposite nostalgia of the "things
were getting better" sentiment referenced above. Nelson George argues
that rhythm & blues, along with self-sufficiency and race pride, dissipated
with integration (George 1988). This "was integration what killed rhythm
& blues" argument is a familiar feeling felt by more than a few older vocalists from the era. It points to the relationship between integration, assimilation, and culture — what blacks have had to "give up" in the process to
gain — and is a part of the story of how segregation and the city found a
way into music production. The formula is that through assimilation (literally, absorption), one loses indigenous culture. This is ironic in light of, for
example, the Clovers, whom Atlantic Records felt compelled to make
sound more "black" in order to be successful as a "rhythm & blues" group.
The catch is, though, that inevitably rhythm & blues moved towards mainstream acceptability. Thus the Clovers, willing participants in pursuit of
success, had to obtain a "black" sound (what presumably they were supposed to lose, that is, not to sound too black) in the process of achieving
mainstream success as performers (which was the point to begin with).
This, along with creating the marketing category, is precisely how whites

created "rhythm & blues" as a concept. In fact, one could argue that African American music has curiously become more "black" through the twentieth century, precisely because of white structured and broadcast categories, not just musical ones, either, but social and cultural ones as well. Even more curious, but still plausible, is the conclusion that whites first created rhythm & blues as a category and then, partially because of integration and their involvement in the music, eventually killed it as a style.

Part of what blacks managed to create in spite of (or because of) segregation resided in the neighborhoods, schools, churches, and footpaths (footpaths both real and figurative). All in all, the imageability of black Baltimore and black Washington during the 1940s and 1950s invited feelings of both repression, in light of segregation, and celebration, for "what we did have in spite of it all." Indeed, it must have been an extraordinary, mysterious combination of contrary feelings.

Lawrence Berry was born in Washington, D.C., on January 25, 1942. He grew up on Belmont Street, off 14th and about four blocks from U Street, Northwest, part of black Washington's premier business district. His mother used to sing in the house; his father lived elsewhere. His interest in music began at a Boys Club summer camp in southern Maryland, where counselors would play the rhythm & blues records "over and over and over again and, after a while, you just couldn't get away from it." Berry managed some groups in the 1960s and remained active in Washington music throughout the 1970s and 1980s.

He said of the Washington that he knew in the 1950s, "Well, O.K., we had our theaters, we had our labels, we had everything, I guess, that whites had, and we were comfortable with what we had. That's why I'm telling you that integration was the worst thing that could happen, to a certain degree, because it split our culture in two, and we lost it.

"Most people had their own during those days. Like I said, blacks had their own, whether you lived in Washington, Baltimore, or wherever. You had your own section, your own. You didn't have to go, I mean, far as the movies are concerned, we had our own movies; we didn't have to go downtown to the white movies. We had our own. To be honest with you, I didn't even know that they [white movie houses] existed down there because we had no reason to go down there. Only time we went downtown would be on a field trip. They may take us down to the monument or the Capitol, or take us to see how that operated. But after that you came right back to your section and that was it."

James McPhail, a generation older than Berry, states something quite similar. "We couldn't go to the movies downtown. But, you know, in reality we really didn't miss it because we enjoyed being with each other, and it was no problem. I think, well I'm going to tell you the truth now. I think integration hurt us more than it helped us because we lost some of our values, the things that we used to have, that we used to cling to that made us survive and keep going, you know. Now it just doesn't seem to have the punch to it."

The "it" to which McPhail refers was something akin to values, to use his word, something from within, not imposed from without. It was not a direct result of segregation, but rather strength in the face of adversity. Segregation, though, clearly was the frame.

Alphonso Feemster was a lead singer in the vocal group Four Bars of Rhythm in the 1950s. A third generation Washingtonian on his mother's side, he was born in 1936 and lived in Southeast Washington.

"Well, mostly in the '50s, you know, there was still a lot of places we couldn't go. Parts of town, like downtown, the National Theater, you couldn't go there. And Ford's Theater and all the rest, like we can go now. So we had are own little"—he paused—"U Street, which we had our theaters on. All the businesses, eating places. You dress up to go to U Street, you know, that was ours. And of course T Street, where the Howard Theater was. So you had your own little area and it was pleasant, to me it was. We had everything there, we were comfortable, and doing all right. And this is the early '50s. We were in a confined area, I guess you would say. But we [blacks] all got along, you know. We're used to each other and everything else."

Here Alphonso suggests that "confinement," as he put it, had an effect on music making. "That's what fuel and kept, I think, the black music going because, hey, it was just certain areas that you could work in even. Like Forestville, Northeast Casino, Turner's Arena, and you couldn't go down to Constitution Hall and work. You know, so that's what made it so great, I think, because everything was flourishing right in one area."

As Alphonso mentions places you could not go in one breath, in another he talks about the places you could go, albeit in "one area," the black parts of town. In Washington and Baltimore (as many other places), there were one or two main black districts. There were also other, smaller neighborhoods, blocks, and streets where blacks lived. Youngsters mapped out their early years in ways that reflected their side of town or neighborhood, or places they could go—from institutions, establishments, businesses, to blocks and even streets. This was a linear, horizontal orientation, common to segmented cities like Baltimore and Washington.

Melvin Coles was typical of the second generation of R&B vocalists. They all listened to and emulated the Orioles, Cardinals, Clovers, Swallows, and others that had come of age in the late 1940s. Melvin was born in 1940, at 510 Saint Mathew Street in East Baltimore, what he called the "heart" of East Baltimore—and "rough." His parents had moved to Baltimore from Farmville, Virginia, outside of Richmond, with five of his brothers and sisters, before Melvin was born. Melvin says his brothers got him interested in music.

"Oh, my brothers, I think they were responsible for that. You see I had four older brothers. I had five older brothers, but I had one pretty close to my age. The other ones were, you know, say like ten or fifteen years older than we were. And they would all sit around the house on the weekends. They had a raggedy guitar and they would just bang on it. They would sing a lot of Ink Spots and Mills Brothers and stuff like that."

Melvin sang in neighborhood recreation centers and schools and went on to record in the duo Bobby & Melvin. In the 1980s he joined revival versions of the Cardinals and the Swallows and performed with both Ernest Warren and Herman Denby.

Herman Denby, the original lead singer for the Swallows, was also a Baltimore native, born on June 26, 1931. He stayed there with his family until he was about five years old before they left for Detroit. They returned to West Baltimore when Herman was twelve.

Herman's memories of Baltimore are less than sanguine and provide yet another perspective to growing up there. He notes, in particular, unfortunate social circumstance offset by the beauty of making music.

"I've had very, a lot of bad memories here, you know, I mean growing up. You see your father everyday. When you're very small you don't understand it, but you can feel it. You know, he have a job this month and next month there is no job. You know, being on welfare, that type of thing. It was horrible. So I think the only thing that we had was the music. That's about the most beautiful thing you had in your life was the music. And that was the only thing that, except your behavior, was restricted to the point that it must be right. You know, you don't sing off key. You play it right; you sing it right. I mean, that was very important, to do it right. Do it right to make it sound good."

Here, Denby's comments suggest that the pervasive social restrictions of black Baltimore in the 1940s were in some way related to the singers' need to get "right" what they did have control over—their voices. This is a good example of how the singers worked around one liability to profit in another manner. This is a sentiment intimated in other narratives, as when someone says that guys got together to sing, in part, because they had little else to do. Often they turned to the streets. Herman Denby and the Swallows as well as other groups used what of the streets they could to negotiate the city and to learn, rehearse, and perform. It would seem that young males roaming around a city in groups was an image of many places at different times, but hanging out to sing in harmony was a phenomenon particular to young black males in twentieth-century America, a function of a particular time and place.

"Oh, we used to sing on the street corners. We used to sing on the street corners all the time. And people would give us money and what have you. And the tenor, who started the group, had a brother-in-law that played bass. Earl Hurley started the group. He had a brother-in-law that was a bass player and I asked him and he allowed me to practice on his bass. That's how I learned to play upright bass. And we used to go out on the street and sing. What else, what else did we have? Nothing. I mean, there were places that we wanted to go, you couldn't even go. We weren't allowed in there. So what did you have?"

What was it that made music "the only thing" to do, as Denby states above? Cities like Baltimore and Washington engendered opportunity, which is why both cities had so many in-migrants. Yet, for blacks especially, everything in those cities "was restricted." Opportunity was thus relative to or relegated to the black neighborhoods, districts, and geographic areas—except to work for white businesses or the government. Most everyone seemed to orient themselves so intently around geography, streets, blocks, and areas of town. Andy Magruder mapped a broader history along with his own personal story:

"I was born at 1425 P Street Northwest Washington, which is called Georgetown. I lived on Twenty-Seventh Street, but the intersection [with P Street] was right there. We had up there a small community of black people which they say were the rich slaves—free—because we had a cemetery right up at Twenty-Ninth and Q, which is still there next to Dumbarton Oaks. And they wanted to renovate that property, but this black church on Thirtieth Street said 'No, that's history.' I got an uncle buried up there. He was one of the slaves that they released."

This is precisely what Hayden meant by "territorial history." Magruder described where he hung out in his neighborhood. "Recreations department. It was mostly, yeah, it was during the summer, and because, I'll put it to you this way. Now just listen to what I'm saying. The white neighborhoods was not affiliated with the ghetto recreation centers. We couldn't play ball with them, they couldn't play ball with us. We didn't have anything that invited them to come and play ball with us. But we used to always go to walk and watch them play hoping that we could play with them, on the ball team, yeah. When the ball comes over the fence, at Twenty-Ninth and M. They had the Boys Club there. I wanted to play so bad. Every time a guy knock a ball over the fence I go get it and throw it back, hoping that the coach would say, 'Come on in and try out for the team.' But that never happened."

Was this something he expected to happen?

"I was hoping. I wasn't expecting, but I was hoping. I was hoping. But that's why I say I lived with prejudice so long, and the average guy from Georgetown never—they hoped. They didn't believe it was possible, but they hoped that it would happen. Like I said, that Boys Club was a half a block away from a black theater, the black poolroom, the black barbershop, the black restaurant. But it was a white club, right there. When they got through playing ball, they went up north."

The black side of the city, black neighborhoods, streets, and blocks, sat right up alongside white blocks, streets, neighborhoods, and sides of town. There wasn't a neutral zone, it was sidewalk-to-sidewalk contact and, as Magruder indicates above, an interlocking of racialized buildings with the white Boys Club situated a half block from black businesses.

The vertical, the horizontal, the lines, diagonals and dynamics of the city all provided the framework for youngsters growing up in the city. The areas of the city controlled by whites thus framed—confined would be a better word—the black setting in which group harmony developed on a local level. Singers emphasized their world geographically, in terms of street, neighborhood, or section of town. Each group had their own area. Baltimore was like Washington in this regard and probably like most other cities in the United States at that time. Below, Melvin Coles and George Jackson relate how different vocal groups would come from different sides of town.

Jackson was another second-generation singer; he performed and recorded with a group called the Plants. He was born in 1938, on West Lexington Street in Baltimore. George's father was a Baptist minister, but he had moved to Tennessee and as a result, George grew up in the Catholic Church. He learned about singing through the popularity of Sonny Til and the Orioles.

"Everybody wanted to sound like Sonny Til because all the girls was hollering and screaming."

On the subject of neighborhood groups, Melvin speaks first, followed by George.

"Yeah, the first group I ever knew of, that I actually knew, was the Honey Boys. They were living, you know, East Baltimore."

"Like the Cardinals was an East Baltimore group."
"Yeah. Honey Boys, East Side"
"Sonny Til and the Orioles was West Side."
"Swallows, West Baltimore."
"See, everybody had their area."
"The Vocaleers, West Baltimore."

Everybody "had their area." Young males in particular maintained informally some notion of territory within the everyday life of urban segregation through vocal groups (and, as described below, social clubs). This varied somewhat. Sometimes a group had a particular area which they "covered," wandered around singing or rehearsing, in and out of local businesses, poolrooms or bars. It could also simply mean a group came from, and people associated them with, a certain part of town. Behind much of this segmentation of place were restrictive housing covenants, mortgage "red-lining," or neighborhood steering—all to keep black families out of certain neighborhoods, confine them to others, and divide the city up into black and white areas. One result was that black male vocal groups centered their activities on a particular territory. Surely, segregation was not the sole reason for this, but confinement—this persuasive kind of imageability—had to have played a role. Literature on spatial behavior recognizes the human species as territorial by nature.[1] For young black males who established bonds with each other through music, the racialized street or neighborhood "was a local space containing friends and associates and supplying many immediate needs, functioning virtually as a microcosmic social system" (Dennis 1968: 168).[2] The one consideration that cut across age, gender, and social standing, was segregation.

Segregation determined a great deal of how Baltimore and Washington developed as a home for their citizens, and underlying the strategies to oppose segregation are the histories of African Americans in both areas. Whites in Washington and Baltimore, from the very beginning, sought to segregate and segment neighborhoods by race. Both cities had a longstanding, substantial black presence within their respective borders. Into the twentieth century, both cities had increasingly larger percentages of African American citizens, specific black neighborhoods, and a black history of districts of business and entertainment. There was an economic viability, at least possibility, and a spiritual energy to these public places. In Washington, the largest center for businesses, nightclubs and music, was U Street. In Baltimore the entertainment district was Pennsylvania Avenue (known as The Avenue). Both cities were neighborhood or "side-of-town" oriented. Washington had its four geographic areas of Northwest, Northeast, Southwest, and Southeast. Baltimore had numerous distinct neighborhoods, and three black districts — East Baltimore, West Baltimore, and South Baltimore. In both cities, there were clear similarities in the process of how groups emerged from neighborhoods and engaged with the city at large.

Group harmony was not simply a result of segregation, but there was a dynamic tension, a palpable interdependency between "wanting" to sing, and "having" to sing. Specifically, young singers used urban space available to them to make music and thus define and control that space on their own (musical) terms. These youngsters demonstrated remarkable skill and strategic resiliency in the face of adversity. In order to understand these strategies within the context of the two cities, there are several interrelated factors to explicate. These include the nature of black neighborhoods in Baltimore and Washington, the relative meaning of community, and the relevant institutions, urban networks and channels of movement — the footpaths beneath the feet of black citizens.

City, Neighborhood, Community

The city of Baltimore passed a "segregation ordinance" in 1911. An article in the *National Municipal Review* discussed its consequences.

> An ordinance for preserving peace, preventing conflict and ill feeling between the white and colored races in Baltimore city and promoting the general welfare of the city by providing, as far as practical, for the use of separate blocks by white and colored people for residences, churches and schools.
>
> The ordinance makes it unlawful for any colored person to move into or use as a residence any building in a block occupied by white people. It is also made unlawful for any white person to move into a block occupied by colored people.(Flack 1912: 277)

Postwar group harmony coincided with the increase in the percentage of African Americans in Baltimore, the large numbers of African American families below middle class status at mid-century, and the strict maintenance of segregated neighborhoods. To be sure, this last factor made a lasting impression on a youngster's image of the city vis-à-vis geography and mobility.

The black population of Baltimore was longstanding and significant in number. Before the 1960s, it was predominantly poor and segregated into specific areas that changed over time in response to shifting demographics. According to one publication, "prior to 1955, most of the city's black population lived within 10 square miles in the center of the city from Monroe Street in the west to Broadway in the east" (Nast et al. 1982: 71). A 1935 study commissioned by the Baltimore Urban League states: "More than two thirds of Baltimore's 33,000 colored families live in four of the twenty statistical areas into which the city is divided" (Reid 1935: 15).

In lieu of segregation laws, many cities passed restrictive covenants whereby homeowners in white neighborhoods would agree not to re-sell to blacks. "Neighborhood steering" (by individuals in the real estate business) and "redlining" (by banks and mortgage companies) was common in Baltimore (Nast et al. 1982: 71), Washington, and virtually all places in the United States where race mattered. These practices not only excluded blacks from white neighborhoods, but also whites from black neighborhoods. Although real estate restrictions obtained for some other groups, like Jews and Catholics, racial segregation practices that whites instituted against African Americans were extreme, various, and a mechanism for control. It is no surprise that "neighborhoods" and sides of town became a factor in the development of vocal groups on the street and out on the block.

No doubt all youngsters, both black and white, developed sensibilities that reflected this system of racialized sections of town that designated certain neighborhoods as "bad," or as where one could or could not go. Most youngsters conceptualized their world in terms of race-based neighborhoods and internalized racialized maps of, for instance, West and East Baltimore, even in areas where blacks and whites lived across the street from one another. This was a kind of geographic imageability, racialized and localized.

George Jackson and Melvin Coles tell the story of a particularly tough area of Southwest Baltimore that they were familiar with in the 1950s. George called it Pigtown. "They used to bring the pigs through there, you know. And that's why they got the name. But now Pigtown was integrated part of town, because blacks and whites both lived there."

"Yeah."

George said this was true even in the 1940s, but the area was not exactly what you would call "integrated." It was a tough part of town where both blacks and whites lived, yet clearly drew racial lines. "Well, if you crossed this side of the street, if you crossed this side of the street, that made a difference in the fighting. In the fighting, see. Like the white boys stayed on that side of Washington Boulevard and blacks stayed on that side. Now if you went on that side, or they come over on that side, then you had your fights."

Melvin continued, "You weren't allowed to go across Chase Street; on the other side was basically white people and you could not come up in this area."

And if you went across the street?

Melvin laughed, "Well…"

George said, "You got beat up." And then he laughs, "But you wouldn't get shot."

Melvin explained, "You out of your district."

Youngsters in Baltimore developed their worldview neighborhood by neighborhood, block by block, and street by street. As black families had to live within the social and geographic constraints of the dominant culture, they established closeknit, partially self-sufficient communities, despite economic disadvantages, and music was a large part of a youngster's life in the city. Indeed, Baltimore had a Bureau of Music and a Superintendent of Music from as early as 1915 through the 1950s. One mayor, Thomas D. D'Alesandro, remarked in 1959 that "music was the heart of a city"[3]—a statement of some irony in light of a sentiment articulated by Baltimore native Herman Denby in reference to being young and black in the 1940s—"What else did you have but the music?"

Whereas Baltimore was a city of neighborhoods, Washington was a tale of two cities, white Washington and black Washington. One historian named black Washington "the secret city" because white Washingtonians were "acquainted with only the most obvious facts" about African Americans in their city (Green 1967: vii). Redevelopment in areas such as Georgetown, as Andy Magruder alludes to above, and Southwest Washington displaced thousands of black families, forcing many of them into smaller areas of the Northeast or Southeast and altering their geocentric frames of reference. Washington, in effect, became a city of more clearly configured white neighborhoods and black neighborhoods. As the percentage of blacks residing in the nation's capital grew, so did "the city's discriminatory policies and practices" (Fitzpatrick and Goodwin 1990: 23), especially through the 1940s and 1950s. One would like to think that the municipal control black residents of our nation's capital had grew in proportion to the size of the population, but that was not the case. Even after de jure changes, de facto policies still divided Washington. The "white flight" made the city predominantly black after 1960 (23).

Obviously, an important subtext to the histories of blacks in Washington (and it was true for Baltimore as well) was the "persistent racism and very difficult experiences faced by all black residents" (Borchert 1982: xii) that shaped patterns of social interaction. If anything unified all levels of black society in Washington, it was racism, whose enthusiasts cared little for class, income, or social standing among African Americans. Physical proximity did not always matter. Segregation was as much a construction of the mind as it was of place, and this was not lost on youngsters, as they grew aware of the city around them. Such must have been the case for Andrew Magruder as he hung on to a fence through which he watched the white kids in Georgetown play baseball.

Andy Magruder had a friend named Robert Stroud. They grew up in Georgetown, were lifelong residents of Washington, and sang with the Five Blue Jays in the very early 1950s. Magruder, after the Marines and after his singing career ended, went to work for the bus company. Stroud worked in the post office. They spoke of what the Georgetown neighborhood was like when they lived there and mentioned this fellow "Icky" and how well he sang. Great voice, they said. They remembered him, but had not seen him in many years. As it turned out, in 1990 you could still hear George ("Icky") Tillman singing happy hour at the Market Inn, SW Second and E Streets. He still had a great voice, and recalled growing up during a particular era in Washington. His narration cuts across family, neighborhood, school, and community, and how all of these combine to make the measure of a youngster growing up. Like many others, Tillman never became a full-time professional singer, nevertheless music and group harmony were very much a part of his life in a local sense at a time when the Orioles were just becoming famous.

Tillman was born in Washington in 1933. His family lived between Georgetown and the Mall in the area below Washington Circle, centered on 20th and 24th Streets. "Basically Foggy Bottom," he said, "in that area."

Back in those days, before gentrification, Foggy Bottom was home to a mix of the very poor and the working class, both blacks and whites, at a time when there were fewer and fewer mixed neighborhoods. Much earlier, before and after the Civil War, it had been home to free blacks and then former slaves. Irish, Italian, and German families subsequently moved into the area, but black families were able to hold on there through the 1940s (Fitzpatrick and Goodwin 1990: 265–67). During his early years, Tillman lived in the 2400 block of I Street, in Foggy Bottom. His grandmother lived a few houses away, at 2405 I Street.

"We had a very closely knit family. In those days the houses, people renting the houses, the houses were clean and we had outhouses. Can you imagine that? In a city, they had outhouses, and we had to go to the back-yard for toilets."

What was it that made group vocals so attractive in the neighborhoods?

"I think, first of all, it was the camaraderie that you had with your group that you sang with, and if you sounded good, your peers would like to, I think they wanted to relate to you, to be around you just to hear something that they had heard on the radio by the Orioles, and things like that. And I think knowing you personally sort of put a star in their crown, they say, hey, I know those guys, I mean they're from my school and I know Icky and Boo Boo, or whatever. And in those days people were very poor, a lot of people couldn't afford to buy records, but they could just look out the window or just open the window and hear these four guys out there singing on the corner, singing something you like."

Herman Denby said once that in Baltimore, singing kept youngsters out of trouble. Tillman says something very similar about Washington.

"And let me tell you this, when we sang it was quite orderly. There could have been maybe twenty-five or thirty guys and girls around there. It was quite orderly. They would listen. I really think that it was something for people to relate to, mostly."

Tillman said that he first sang in the fourth grade, but singing as a form of socializing began a few years later, in junior high school.

"We formed a group. We called it a quartet, but the quartet consisted of two quartets. Two groups, so we were about ten guys. And, you know, we would get together and, you'd be surprised. Oh, I wish I'd had a tape recorder in those days, because the harmony was so pretty. I mean it was so pretty."

When Tillman was fourteen he moved out to Anacostia, in the Southeast section of Washington.

"And right away hooked up with a group called the Melodaires. I don't know what happened, we were singing somewhere and they asked me if I would be interested in joining their group. We were the Melodaires and we sang around different places. Sang in a few churches, but it was during the time, during the reign of the Clovers, and we patterned a lot of our song stylings after them."

In the 1980s, Anacostia—the Southeast area of Washington, D.C., over the Anacostia River—was an infamous part of the city that struggled to survive. It was a place where housing developments like Valley Green became "Death Valley" and later, after residents left, "Ghost Town."[4] It was not always so. Fab Fisher wrote in the *Washington Informer* about Anacostia, Icky Tillman, and others of the area. He gives us a good feel for the time, the place, and the sense of neighboring and neighborhood.

The old gang of yesteryears when Carver Theatre, Barry Farms Recreation Center, Lombardi Grill, Doc Qualls' Drug Store and Fab's Photo Shop were the places to be for popularity and excitement. Although those days back in the forties and fifties are gone forever . . .

REAL ANACOSTIANS of yesteryear will remember ICKY TILLMAN as the brilliant young singer who married MARQUERITE BRADLEY (sister of ALICE BRADLEY JONES). ICKY TILLMAN and MARQUERITE moved atop Minnie's Market, C&C Cleaners and Joe Lashley's Barber Shop around the corner from Almore Dale's Market where the J. Finley Wilson Lodge held its first meetings upstairs. Remember?

ICKY TILLMAN'S walking partners then were slick talking SONNY WILLIAMS and fast moving ZEKE BRISCOE plus smooth talking Mike Patterson (Mart Liquors). In fact, Fab Fisher (who was writing in the forties for Nite Life & Gaily News) remembers photographing

ICKY TILLMAN'S first musical group THE MELODAIRES, which came into being in the "du wap days" with popular Anacostians as ICKY, MIKE PATTERSON, ARTHUR GREEN and EVERETTE GREEN. You won't believe this! OFFICER JACK ROY was well known in his day as the bravest Black policeman under FLORENCE MATHEWS in Barry Farms. Jack Roy (may he rest in peace) gave the MELODAIRES a hard way to go. ICKY TILLMAN and his group made no money although Jack Roy had them appearing everywhere for his special occasions. STAN ANDERSON did give the group its first break in Anacostia where Stan was conducting amateur night programs at Carver Theater.

THOSE WERE THE DAYS (in the forties and fifties) when Black and White **Anacostians** were segregated, but they were involved with one another. (*Washington Informer*, May 4, 1989: 18, punctuation and capitalization original)

When Andy Magruder told the story of the Boys Club in Georgetown, he said the white kids, when through playing ball, "went up north." The white children went back not to the same place as Andy and his friends, but to the same concept. They all went back to their respective neighborhoods, home. In some cases, that meant just a matter of a block or a street, but in others, it would mean a whole section of town. On one level, neighborhood simply designated a geographic area bounded by particular streets or landmarks. On another level, neighborhood meant something quite different and less precise, more poetic. It meant a way of life. In this manner, neighborhood could also imply community. Both sentiments served black citizens well during the time of segregation and were the result of aggregate ways in which people conceptualized and lived their lives during those years. On a general level, the history of blacks in cities like Baltimore and Washington helped construct contemporary, though shifting, notions of "black neighborhood" and "black community."

What do neighborhood and community mean? The concepts may be clear in our own minds and in everyday discourse, but if we try to formulate precise definitions, they can be vague. Both terms have varied meanings. To define either is especially vexing because, while "neighborhood" implies physiographical boundaries, it also implies social relations—being a neighbor. The term "community" denotes a geographic part of town, but also strongly suggests human relationships and sentiments. Today especially, the idea of community can cover a wide and diffuse geographic and emotional terrain. Both neighborhood and community exist through good and close human relations, physical and emotional. However, in segregated cities the boundaries of neighborhood and community also had an enforced aspect that indicated a specific place: a black neighborhood, the black side of town, black side of the street. (This "required compliance," if you will, is the precise meaning imbedded in the term "ghetto.") Thus in both Baltimore and Washington, "community" and "neighborhood" were characterized by different degrees of cohesion and by varying meanings, some created from within and others imposed from without.

Locality, a particular section of town, was part of the development of vocal group harmony. For Herman Denby's and Ernest Warren's generation, growing up during the 1930s and 1940s and for Melvin Cole's and George Jackson's generation, growing up in the 1950s, neighborhood and community constituted a collective sense of place and territory. In part, that brought young males together to sing.

When Herman Denby moved with his family from Detroit back to Baltimore around 1943, they settled on Franklin Street in West Baltimore. A few years later, he began to harmonize with friends. They first called themselves the Okaleers, and later signed with King Records as the Swallows. According to Herman, the group spent a great deal of time rehearsing and performing on the streets of their neighborhood. When asked about the war years, Denby touched on the qualities that define neighboring and community. "But there was more togetherness then, than it is now. You know. There were more moral standards then. People respected people then."

The notion of "group" and togetherness as a musical unit was very important to singers, and it reflected values that obtained at home and in the neighborhood. Herman said, for instance, that "hatred" was something just not tolerated at home. "Well, what I think that helped me is, is from my home. It [hate] wasn't tolerated in our house. You know, I couldn't even come in the house and say the word 'hillbilly.' No, no, no. You got a hand across the mouth. You know what I mean? You didn't do this. And we used to hear about like lynchings, and what have you, those types of things. My mother tried her best to keep these things away from us, but we learned about them. You know? But hatred is almost like bred into you, and it's a disease. So you just don't jump up and start hating. You know we used to get angry about it, but we couldn't hate, because it was never taught to us. We, we, didn't know what it was TO hate. We disliked some things. 'Why is it that, that boy's father over there has a job, and he has two and three pair of shoes and I'm standing here, you know, and why should he call me nigger? What is that? WHY?' You know? We eventually found out. But at first we didn't know because like I say, in our upbringing, you didn't bring that home. You dare not have that in the house. And I think that's what helped me."

Despite the racialized world in which Herman lived, he learned from his family an attitude that de-emphasized a person's color in reaction to the negative emphasis that the surrounding city and society as a whole placed *on* color. "When we met Irv [Goldstick], and he was our manager, I just saw him as another man. I just saw him as another man, you know. And then from that I learned, like from my upbringing I learned, I wouldn't care what color you were. You do me wrong; you're a rotten dog, not your color."

Singers brought these sentiments, learned at home and nurtured in the neighborhood, into their vocal groups. Herman put his two fingers together, held them up, and explained. "The Swallows were like this. We were like that. And you had to be like this, or you wouldn't be a group. See, you loved the music, the music had to be right, and, I don't know it, it seems as though if we, if we were together with each other, the music would be the same way. It seems that we thought this way, I don't know if that's true or not. In fact I don't think it probably is. Because I think musicians can dislike each other and still work and make beautiful music. You know what I mean? But WE had this feeling that we had to get along. Like, Earl used to say, there'd be no arguments in this group. There's no reason to argue. Argue about what? You know what I mean? And that was one of the big rules that we had in the group. That we didn't argue with each other. No. I mean, he believed in that so strongly that you would be put off the group. If you did this, you know what I mean? If you continued to start arguments—no, no, no—we didn't argue. And we really never did. We never did."

What Herman said of vocal groups, he also said of the black community. Both Herman and Ernest Warren recalled the community and the ways in which neighboring played out. Herman: "But during the '40s, during the '30s and '40s, early '50s, the black community was—you see how I got my hands now?"

He clasps his hands together. "That's the way the community was. You lived up the street from me and you did something, that man or that woman up there whipped your behind and sent you home. And you know where you went? You went straight home. And we didn't have no telephones at that time, so it was told verbally what you did, and you got your butt whipped when you got home.

"Well let me tell you something. Years ago, black people in the black community were like—

Ernest: "Tight. They were tight."

Herman: "Were like this, you know." Herman puts two fingers together again. "I mean this is moral people I'm talking about. And most people were that. We didn't go out to bother anybody."

For Herman, "family" extended out into the neighborhood, although such sentiments did not necessarily unite all segments of a city's black population. Nevertheless, people would look out for each other across the varied levels of black urban society. The sentiments Denby relates—avoid hate, promote togetherness, look out for one another's children—are evocative, suggestive, and not just an isolated recollection. Melvin Coles and George Jackson tell a similar story about black Baltimore when they were growing up there, a decade later in the late 1950s. They sound remarkably like Herman and Ernest.

Melvin says, "But one thing is, our parents taught us discipline."

George agrees, "Yeah."

"You know, that's what I'll never forget. Some things you just didn't do. You know. You were taught, you were taught not to do. You know a lot of things that, basically, if you knew it was wrong, I mean, if your parents told you not to do it—"

"Yeah."

"And they found out that you did it—"

"That's right."

"I mean let's take, let's say the man, the guy up the street, the gentleman up the street. He's seen you do this thing, this bad, this wrong thing. He would take you and give you a whooping. He would beat you and take you home to your parents, and then you would get an additional beating."

"That' right."

"Yeah, he knew your parents and he said, 'I seen him do this,' and they'll say, 'O.K., we got him now.' And you get two beatings, right?"

"Yeah."

"So, I mean, and so they basically protected each other. But the further you go, even the grownups, the further they went out of their jurisdiction, they had to deal with the same kind of thing we were into."

Andrew Magruder said something remarkably similar about the black neighborhood in Washington's Georgetown of the 1940s.

"It was a neighborhood that I wish could be right here."

Magruder spoke from his home, one day after his fifty-third birthday, in suburban Hyattsville, Maryland, just outside Washington. "When you knock on somebody's door and say, 'Mother's at work, she told me to ask you, can you give me a cup of sugar?' I got a spanking. I got a spanking from somebody else say I should be at home because they knew my mother was at work, and my daddy. 'Hey, you don't belong out here Magruder; you better get your little butt in that house.' Everybody watched out. It's not like that now."

Clear patterns of neighboring obtained when "everybody watched out" in the neighborhood. To use Herman's word, there was a "moral" value system in place. These social principles of right and wrong behavior must have had implications for youngsters who sang harmony, cultivating a sense of "group" beyond merely singing. This was how it became a social activity—and a socializing one as well, because kids learned from it as much as they helped shape it.

Ernest says, "We be there together, and you know what?"

Herman answers, "Let's get us a group!"

Alphonso Feemster (the singer in the Four Bars) lived in the Barry's Farm housing project in Southeast Washington after his family moved out there from his grandmother's place on L Street Northeast, in the 1940s. Although a public housing project (this was the second version, the original housing development came down in the 1940s), Barry's Farm took on the atmosphere of a neighborhood, and a good one.

"The best time of my life, really. I have to say that because everybody in the area—the development out there was fairly new when we moved in—and was really our first real home, you know, where you had your own heat and all the rest of it. And it was a well-kept place at that time. And they had a lot of recreation for the kids, I remember that. We had a recreation center,

which all the kids would get together and you go up and you play games at
the recreation center. You play baseball, and of course we sang. That's
where all the little groups would be on the corner singing, and everybody
wanted to be a group."

When Jimmy McPhail was three months old in 1928, his family moved
to Washington, D.C., from Rocky Mount, North Carolina. Like many
other families, they migrated to Washington to "do better," as McPhail
phrased it. His family settled on the four hundred block of M Street
Northwest, where McPhail lived until he went to college. "Well, it was
between Fourth Street and Fifth Street, on M Street. It was a nice neighborhood as far as I was concerned growing up. Everybody just about had
the same thing; nobody knew they were poor."

McPhail sang in the church not far from his home, at the Gailbreth
AME Zion Church on Sixth Street, between L and M. That was his earliest music experience.

In the house, there were no recordings—this was in the 1930s and
early 1940s—but the McPhails all listened to the radio together as a family.
"Whatever came on that the family was listening to, we all listened to. I
remember, we had 'Jack Armstrong and the All-American Boy,' you know,
you listened to that every day. That was like a little serial. He was, just like
they say, 'Jack Armstrong and the All-American boy,' and that's what it
was all about. You know he had adventures and things, and we just used
to listen to them. And then on Sundays you know naturally we had to listen to church music to start off the day with. That's one of the things that
just happened, you know. My mother always encouraged me, as far as
wanting to sing. I enjoyed it. I learned a lot. I never had music lessons as
such. I never had that, it's just, I guess it's a god gift thing, as far as I'm
concerned."

The four hundred block of M Street, where the McPhails lived, was
about a dozen blocks southeast of one of the large black business districts
in Washington at that time. The area centered more or less at Seventh and
T Streets, just south of Howard University.

"Well see, T Street was the street on which the Howard Theater was
located. Well we would go there on the weekends or when shows would
come into town. U Street was the main strip for black people. That's where
all the movies, well the big movies were located. Like the Lincoln,
Republic, and the Booker T. Yeah, and a few of the clubs, yes. But see, at
that time I wasn't going to any of the clubs because I was too young, but
we would go to the movies and things. And that was the thing to do, that
was where we had to go."

There were contradictions in the lives of youngsters. Though severely segregated, blacks and whites could live, work, and play side by side—and still be separate, as McPhail says. He has some difficulty clearly explaining, as would anyone. "I must say that in my neighborhood, it was a little integration in the neighborhood. Wasn't that much, you know, but it was there. But it was still separate, even though we were there. The kids would play together, but it was separate."

For young black urban males in the 1940s and 1950s, grouping was a common occurrence, whether on playgrounds or streets. Sometimes, as they grew a little older, it took the form of urban associations, or what most folks simply termed "social clubs." Some called them gangs; the distinction was not at all clear. What was clear, however, was that as group harmony formed in the neighborhoods, it often did so within various associations of one kind or another. Singing in general was part of a wider sphere and occurred in many contexts beyond vocal groups—church, school, street, playground, pool hall, nightclub, radio shows, and social clubs. Singing outside of a building, however, points to a particularly male activity—running in groups and maintaining a sense of territory, sometimes informal, but certainly within the large social sphere of strictly delineated black or white neighborhoods, streets, institutions, and establishments. And yes, there were gangs, and young males would run (and sing) just as easily with a gang as they would a vocal group. The irony is that, on the street level, singing was one activity that both participants and the city considered a safe one.

Social Clubs

Herman Denby and Ernest Warren were talking one day about singing and "social clubs"—some knew them as gangs, like the Amboy Dukes and the Vulcans. Herman was talking about this cryptically. "There were gangs, and then there was tradition."

This was the first time that I learned of any connection between vocal groups and gangs in the 1940s. As it turned out, "gangs" and "social clubs" were reversible, sometimes interchangeable names, depending on whether police were looking at young black males making some trouble or an organization of adults. Social clubs were particularly predominant across black America and had begun to take root after the Emancipation.

Johnny Page also mentioned gangs. He sang with a group named the Marylanders during the 1950s. Born in Alexandria, Virginia, he moved with his family to Baltimore when he was about five or six. "My father had visions of better job opportunities. We came and lived with my aunt for a while. My uncle and aunt, said talk to him about how things were here, and they were getting along fantastic at home. And they had luxuries, simple luxuries that a poor person could afford, and we figured that we could enjoy the same things so we came here. It was a later period of time before I enjoyed the music world."

The Marylanders recorded six sides for Jubilee, in 1952 and 1953. Jubilee was the Orioles' record label. Just as the Orioles had listened to the Ink Spots, the Clovers listened to the Orioles, and the Cardinals listened to the Clovers, so Johnny Page and the Marylanders listened to the Cardinals.

"Now Ernest Warren and the Cardinals was my idol. That was the first group that I heard that I really wanted to really be alike. Those guys were fantastic. Lou Karpouzie, who later managed us, too, was managing them at the time. And when I seen him give them cuff links with their initials on it, man that was the greatest thing that could ever happen. They would rehearse along Lexington Street. That's in North Baltimore, Northwest Baltimore, between Mount and Gilmore Street. Every time they came up on Lexington Street to rehearsal, I'd be right there at the window listening to them. I was a little kid. I was a little guy then, you know. Covered a lot of area when I was a younger guy and I did a lot of things that people don't understand about me. But I went through things with gangs and things, you know."

Page recites the names of some gangs he knew. "Well, they had the Nails, the Finals, the Apaches, my gang, the Dungaree Boys, and a lot of interesting young guys that wanted to be macho, you know. I was affiliated with that. I had a gang of my own, which I was the leader because I was the, the best 'knuck' artist, you know. I could fight."

A logical extension of socializing on playgrounds at one age and on the block at another was socializing musically in a vocal group. As local music making extended beyond a city's limits and became a part of the larger, emerging business of rhythm & blues and rock 'n' roll, large touring shows came into theaters and arenas in the 1950s. These shows were, for some, clearly a threat, as one Thomas Rasmusen testifies below. The threat comes from potential violence caused by the very quality that defines the music — emotion — at least according to some white authorities who sought to ban the shows, if not the music. But, there is more than emotion to the story.

It seems that a pivotal link between the neighborhood and the rock 'n' roll shows were local social clubs; some called them gangs. Not only was there a musical link, because the clubs helped encouraged harmony groups, but there was a social link. The social clubs (and singing) were places that would keep youngsters out of trouble. The gangs (and singing) were places for potential trouble. The link between the black male, music, and violence had been in the minds of whites for years. It dates back to bebop, blues, ragtime, and the nineteenth century. The "rock 'n' roll problem" was just another chapter in a longer story. On June 5, 1956, a Washington police captain describes in a letter to his chief an "incident":

> Mr. James E. Whelan, a Guard Officer at the District Jail, 200-19th Street, S. E., reports that about 11:30 p.m., June 3, 1956, while enroute to work driving his 1950 Buick south on 19th Street, N. E. he noticed large groups of disorderly colored teenagers walking north on 19th Street. When at 19th and C Streets, N. E., complainant reports that a group of colored teenagers suddenly and without provocation "bombarded" his car with stones—breaking two windows on the left side of his car, denting in the side of the car and grazing back [sic] of his head. Mr. Whelan stated that the teenagers were apparently homeward bound from a "Rock and Roll Session" at the Armory.
>
> About 11:35 p.m., just five minutes later the same night, Aubrey M. Tolson, Jr., white, 19 years, . . . reported that when at 19th and Benning Road, N. E., he heard a group of colored boys say "there's a white boy" and the colored boys then stoned his 1955 Plymouth sedan.
>
> > Lewis B. Peters, Captain, Commanding Ninth Precinct
> > Metropolitan Police Department
> > June 5, 1956

Two days later the chief received another letter, this time from a police inspector, who comments on the problems associated with rock 'n' roll music:

> The undersigned firmly believes that entertainment provided hundreds of teenagers made up solely of Rock and Roll music provides a media for them to give vent to emotional outbursts stimulated by music which causes a hysteria and frenzy in the manner of the tribal chants and the beat of tom-toms among primitive people in underdeveloped areas of the world.
>
> > Thomas Rasmusen, Inspector, Third District
> > Metropolitan Police Department
> > June 7, 1956[5]

The police took note of black "gangs" and the link that "Rock and Roll Sessions" allegedly had to violence of one sort or another, among white teens as well as black youth. There is here a conflation of three particulars—

the society of black urban neighborhoods and communities, the proliferation of (group) music making on the street level, in clubs and gangs, and the relationship that many whites drew generally between black music, public performance, and violence.

There was a broader issue at work here as well. While rooted in a local event described in the police letter above and an outgrowth of local, street-level sentiments, it outlines a translocal phenomenon. By the mid-1950s, rhythm & blues/rock 'n' roll music was beginning to dominate popular culture and with that, to help support record sales, large touring shows proliferated. Black group harmony was part of this movement. Police and other agencies grew concerned about a perceived relationship between black-derived popular music (the "Rock and Roll Session" that the police refer to, above) and violence. On one level the real fear was race mixing because white teenagers certainly became the dominant consumers of rock 'n' roll, whether the players were black or white, and the early shows, especially in the South, remained segregated.

Similar sentiments—the fear of violence, the black male, miscegenation—were present as far back as enslavement. White anxiety over the black male and his music continued episodically from the nineteenth into the twentieth century. It began during enslavement and continued afterward, embodied in the white minstrel image of the "black buck" and later in the lone, itinerant blues musician, but came to the fore with the introduction of "ragtime" and then "jazz" to general, white (female, in particular) audiences from 1900 through the 1920s (see Leonard 1987). This phenomenon of fear—in stark contrast to the parodying and emasculation of the black male through images of the "dandy" and other Sambo-like caricatures—continued through "bebop" in the 1940s, then rock 'n' roll in the 1950s, and into the late 1980s, with certain rap and hip-hop artists promoting a more assertive type of performance.

Associations that whites especially made from the late 1980s on between black urban youth gangs and rap music (not totally ungrounded) are common knowledge today. In the 1940s those associations were more obscure, but worth noting. There remained an ongoing tension between admiration of, fascination for, and fear of the black male musician for much of the twentieth century. This underlying, contradictory dynamic worked from the highest levels of professional entertainment on down to the street level. Whites could not shake the ambivalence. Was the approaching group of young black males going to sing to you, or cut you?

Back in the 1940s, informal "gangs" were similar to neighborhood or local harmony groups. They were often small, loosely organized and territory-based. To be sure, whites had their own gangs, but there is no evidence that they sang and harmonized. The existence of black gangs was partly an institutional problem. Until the mid-1950s, recreation facilities remained segregated in Washington and Baltimore, and those available to blacks were far from adequate (see Reid 1935 and Landis 1948). There was a proliferation of informal youth gangs as well as youth and adult clubs in Washington as early as the 1920s (Jones 1927: 95). This pattern continued into the 1940s and 1950s.

Baltimore had social clubs as well. In the 1930s, the Division of Recreation for Colored People (which suffered, not surprisingly, from inadequate funding and staffing) promoted 71 "clubs" of one kind or another (Reid 1935: 28).[6] All of these were part of a broader history of African American social clubs and organizations that proliferated after the Civil War. They established an institutional framework for social gatherings away from the church. They also served a social need in the face of segregation and separatism. Black musical associations, formal or informal, were part of this larger pattern of African American social clubs, fraternal organizations, and volunteer associations of one kind or another. The pressures of segregation were no doubt a factor in their growth.

Lawrence Berry, of Washington, said he felt segregation had a lot to do with the proliferation of vocal groups. He remembered that many social clubs and youth gangs were involved in singing. He also recalled the ambiguity of what precisely differentiated "social club" from "gang," because some used the words interchangeably. He insisted that the police would call all black male social clubs "gangs," whether they were or not, and that they were characteristically tied to certain sections of town.

"Every little section of town would have what they called their own social club. If I lived in a certain part of town, all these guys would hang together. And we formed what we called a social club. You had a lot of clubs in this town, and this is how a lot of groups came about, because you played together, you stayed together. This was really a group town."

Why?

"Well, it's back to, I guess, the nature of the city, the way the city is physically made up. Again, back to what I was telling you, everybody is socializing together, and through socializing together you break up into your own little groups and out of those little groups you form a singing group. You have to remember, you're looking for something to do. You talking about a segregated town, so, there were a lot of places that you couldn't go — not that you necessarily want to go, because you didn't even know anything about them. But your part of town became isolated after a while, I mean, you knew every crook and crevice of the town, so you wanted something to do and one of the forms of doing it was to sing."

Along with strong notions of neighborhood and community, young black males articulated a sense of territory and expressed it through groups. The Orioles were a "West Side" group, for instance. Urban geography—what Berry called "the way the city is physically made up"—helped shape the social relations of harmony groups. Sometimes singers met through social clubs or gangs, or larger and more formal associations, such as the Baltimore Boys' Choir. Other recreation centers and social clubs sponsored occasional talent contests. In the case of youth clubs, group singing was a part of organized activity. Vocal harmony groups, gangs, and clubs were part of a social continuum in Baltimore and Washington and constituted social avenues open to both youth and adults. Private social clubs provided entertainment, recreation, and offered a secular complement to church. The ambiguous distinction between the gang and social club points to a value system whereby those whom people saw as "well behaved" were in "social clubs," troublemakers were in "gangs." Harmony groups could have and did come from either.

Data on gang activity and its relationship to singing in Baltimore during the 1940s and 1950s comes from the stories of a few vocalists. Herman Denby belonged to a group that participated in, among other things, athletics. They went as far as registering with the police to avoid being associated with what others (most probably the police) called "gangs." Herman indicates that "you had to be in some kind of gang," and that he first began singing with Earl Hurley (of the Swallows) in a club of some sort. From one side, there was pressure not to associate with so-called gangs. From the other side—you could say the inside, among kids on the street—there must have been pressure to be *in* a gang, or at least act like it.

"You see, like now in the gang thing, the decent people didn't associate themselves with the gangs because it was against the law. See, see, a lot of people don't understand. During the slum area, what I mean, during the slum area of '30s, '40s, and '50s; it's still slums. But I mean during that time, decent people didn't associate themselves with gangs."

Ernest Warren puts in, "They were against it."

Herman says, "In fact, you were taught against this. You don't do this. But you had to go out there among those people, so you had to be in some kind of gang. Like I was in the Vulcans, you know. But we didn't go—it was just that we got ourselves a name and we registered ourselves with the police department so we wouldn't be associated with the other jokers that were knocking people in the head and robbing folk. And we did not associate with anybody that did this."

Herman says, "You understand what I'm saying? We didn't do this. We didn't do this. We told the police, 'We are a group. We specialize in athletics. We sing. And we do this. And we want it to be known that anybody you see with a Vulcan jacket on'—"

Ernest finishes the sentence, "—Is not a hoodlum."

So Herman says, "You see what I mean? That's when I first started singing with Earl. But there were guys, there were guys who did go out, and we knew who they were. That robbed people and mugged people."

Ernest adds, "Well, we had a gang; some of them sang. They [referring to Herman] were the Vulcans. We were a group called the Amboy Dukes, but who knew about us except the ones in East Baltimore. And all we did was have a club and sing. Oh, man, we was teenagers."

Socializing in clubs was an elemental component of black communities and provided a place where groups began singing and harmonizing. The Baltimore neighborhood recreation centers, when they did exist, were places where teens socialized and inevitably would gather to sing. Both Washington and Baltimore had recreation facilities that were, to varying degrees, available for black youth. Through these centers, neighborhood and citywide talent encouraged the formation of group singing. Some singers would put a group together just to compete in a talent show.

Melvin Coles recalled, "As a matter of fact we, it's a recreation center on Eaton Street, right up the street from where we were staying. And we would go up and, you know, attend like talent shows up there."

Like others of that era, Melvin talked about social clubs. "We had a lot of social clubs. Renegades, I could name the Playboys. We had a bunch of clubs. They were in neighborhoods."

Melvin referred to them as "S.C."

"As a matter of fact we would wear the jackets with the names on the back, and they stipulated 'S C,' which was social club. And they would have a different color. Every club would have different color jackets."

George Jackson said that social clubs were marked by which side of Baltimore they were in. "I was on the West Side, he was on the East Side. Yeah."

Melvin said, "I was in East Baltimore."

The sides of town meant territories. "Well that could mean a fight, if you went out of your district. It could mean a fight."

George said that as long as you had someone with you, it was OK, just as Herman and Ernest had discussed for their generation. "But see, when I go to East Baltimore, I would go with him. And like when he come over our way, he would be with us. So that stop anybody from even bothering him. See, that's how we do it."

The police were not the only ones who took note of gang activity; African Americans themselves tried, with help, to tackle the problem in a constructive manner. And the integral relationship between social grouping and singing was evident. During the 1940s, several social agencies made "an effort to convert [juvenile gangs] into socially acceptable groups, or boys clubs" (Johnson 1949: 2). These programs were usually the efforts of African American adults who sought sponsorship in order to help black youth. One agency was the Junior Police and Citizen's Core (JPCC), which organized "choral singing" and "group talent shows" (Johnson 1949: 57–58), the Metropolitan Police Boys' Clubs, and the Recreation Department of Washington, D.C. The JPCC came about in 1942 through the work, not surprisingly, of a black police officer. Oliver A. Cowan, "caught a group of youngsters breaking street lights. He did not arrest them. Instead, they were asked to help him keep the neighborhood clean and orderly and to protect all citizen's property" (Baker Associates 1947: 16).

A group of thirteen women formed another organization in 1944, the Baker's Dozen, "out of mutual concern about the lack of wholesome recreation facilities for Negro teen-agers" (18). The Baker's Dozen developed a program for teens between the ages of thirteen and nineteen. It was the "only agency [in Washington] of its kind and one of the few youth centers with a predominantly Negro clientele" (Robinson 1959: 3). According to Robinson, "as a result of their socioeconomic status, many lower class children resort to informally organized activities where the 'gang' or loosely organized social club is the main type of organization to which they can belong and find acceptance among peers" (56). Even despite the efforts of youth clubs, youngsters often complained of not having anything to do in the evening (Johnson 1949: 64). Gangs and young males in general often hung out in pool rooms, on street corners, in the corner store, around vacant parking lots, and at alley entrances, precisely the same places that vocal groups would inhabit. Harold Winley remembered the Clovers, when he met them, used to hang out in a pool hall near the Howard Theater.

In 1949, there were forty-eight "known Negro boys gangs in D.C. [where] there is often a gang tradition in a neighborhood" (Johnson 1949: 22). These gangs had names like the Vipers, the Cowtown Gang, the L Street gang, the Twelfth Street Gang, the Oilburners, LeDroit Falcons, the Corsicans, and Fat Charlie's Gang (22). Many of these groups sang as a regular part of their activities. In 1949, the leader of the Twelfth Street Gang stated that the group would often "hang out, pat pavement, walk around town…sometimes we'd snatch people's pocket books, slip a drunk, or just sing and have fun" (27).

Four of the Vipers gang members, under the Junior Police and Citizen's Core, "formed a quartette which [sang] at churches and other organizations for the purpose of raising funds to support the club. The quartette is not a trained one and they often give a poor performance, but they are well received" (58–59).

"In the order of their favorite with the clubs, the ten activities in which these boys' clubs most frequently enjoyed are: sports, working together at individual hobbies, club parties, group singing (quartets, etc.). . . ." (90).

Club members clearly recognized and appreciated singing. "In some instances the members of the group tend to identify themselves with one boy who has received recognition as a singer" (91). The talent shows sponsored by some of these organizations were significant for groups around town.

As Andrew Magruder says, "Hey, I'm a tell you something about the Blue Notes. We was the Blue Jays at first, but we won everything in D.C. This was all the city-sponsored talent shows. They got every group from everywhere that wanted to submit your name. Wasn't no white groups. I can't recall one white group in D.C. I know they had them in Philly. And they had them in New York, but no, no white groups in D.C. As far as I know, was not a white singing group ever competed in any contest that I was in in the District."

The dynamics of black communities included the social clubs and gangs and social avenues for expressive performance. Groups and singing played a role in transmitting community norms. Al Feemster said that he was too involved in music to get into trouble (this is a point that Herman Denby also alluded to).

"One day—the first real group that I worked with—we were all going to school. I was still in Langley [Junior High]. And at that time they had social clubs coming out in the black community. They had the Aristocrats, the Jets. Now the social clubs really were, I guess you could say weren't gangs, no. I'm trying to distinguish from the difference, it was more, hey, we send out invitations. We're giving a house party over at such and such an address, given by the Aristocrats. And it was just more of a social club; it wasn't a gang type thing. I had heard some incidents, some kids would get in trouble, there's no question about, even at Barry's Farm. Some kids would get in trouble. But I was mostly into music so much I just didn't have time for that because I was really into music, and I had several friends around. And I hung around with people that were doing the same thing I was doing."

George Tillman did not recall singing in his social club, yet his recollections in other ways were similar to Ernest Warren's and Melvin Coles's, from Baltimore. Of his particular neighborhood Tillman said, "No, we didn't have gangs, but we had social clubs. I was in a group called the Mighty Casanovas. We had white sweaters, and the big thing in those days were, you'd have a sweater or jacket and you had certain colors to identify with the various clubs. The clubs were a good social thing.

"It was good, it kept us together and I think, in essence, it kept us out of trouble, too. Our values were different in those days. We didn't think about stealing, we thought about being the best. If we had a football team we want to be the best. And, I don't know, it was sort of gratifying to me. And when I left Foggy Bottom and moved to Anacostia, and that's when I sort of lost contact with the quartet that I sang with in Georgetown."

Alfred Buddy Slaughter, born in 1927, sang with the Buddies and later, the Cap-Tans. He grew up in what he called the "Capital View" area of Blaine Street, in Northeast Washington. Slaughter came up in the Baptist church and sang in the choir as a child. He said he did not have time for social clubs, although he recalled them. His was the first and only reference to women in the clubs, but here he is talking about adult clubs. "Yes, there was a lot of social clubs. This is like about eight people. Eight men, or either eight women. There was one club in particular, the Esquires, that was one of the bigger clubs. And then the Saints, they were eight policemen.

"They had lots of affairs, like going to the beaches or cabarets, or whatever. We sang on a few of these, too."

The physical shape of the city, for African American citizens, took the form of blocks, streets, neighborhoods, business districts, and other institutions, and was inseparable from the social aspect of life in the city in its totality. This black sphere was the setting for vocal harmony groups. One consequence of this sphere was that young black males grouped in order to sing, whether in a social club or harmony group. Thus singing was the purpose and grouping a consequence. On the other hand, teens ran as a group, social club, or gang. In some neighborhoods, you had to be in a gang, to be "out there," as Herman Denby put it. Thus, singing became the consequence because the groups often sang for entertainment. Either way this constituted grounding for group harmony and it complemented the cultural impetus that encouraged singing and vocal harmony to begin with.[7]

One seemingly impermeable social factor that influenced all African Americans in countless, immeasurable ways was segregation. Another, less obvious, and a far more flexible one, was socioeconomic status among black citizens. A third was the institutions that black citizens created and maintained, such as the social clubs discussed above. The oldest institutions, the most celebrated, and the ones that have had the most influence on black culture and society have been the black churches. For most of the participants in this study, going to church and singing in church was a given—so obvious it was hardly worth mentioning. Most sang in church, a few performed gospel music, and these influences came out in performance style, if not clearly in discussions. In their recollections, the musical influences that participants emphasized included the older vocal group models, like the Ink Spots, Ravens, and Orioles, and the trends in popular music heard on the radio or found in theaters. One institution, however, that many singers did focus on was the pre-integrated black schools. It is a little-researched area of black history, but its influences in the twentieth century have been significant.

Public School

There was strength, integrity, and importance in the black public schools of Baltimore and Washington. No doubt, they were representative in many ways of pre-integrated black schools around the country. The schools administered the educational needs of youngsters, but also served their cultural and social needs. This is true with all schools during much of the twentieth century, but in severely segregated cities, black schools were a special place, a good place, and they contributed significantly to the mix of black urban life. Despite hardships, black schools nurtured and taught well their children. Black public schools were also places where young people learned about and performed a great deal of music, not just the music some stereotypically associated with blacks, but all kinds of music, from spirituals to patriotic songs, pop standards, show tunes, and opera.

Although the central influence on early musical experiences of many African Americans has been the various black churches and music in the home, performers on these pages tell of the public school's importance in their musical lives. The school's influence came quite early in life and appears to have been ongoing, even persistent. This seems especially true for those who grew up during the 1930s, 1940s, and 1950s and attended pre-integrated black public schools. The black public schools in both Baltimore and Washington worked toward and maintained distinction, and more. Duke Ellington, for instance, wrote of the "race pride" in the "all-colored" schools of Washington, D.C., earlier in the century, and the resulting quality of education in those schools. He reminds us of the higher calling of these schools. "Because as representatives of the Negro race," he wrote, "we were to command respect for our people" (Ellington 1973: 17).

The black pre-integrated urban schools were safe havens. For many, school was a place to go, not flee. The schools and their teachers were an extension of home and neighborhood. The black public schools certainly constituted "community" in the full sense of the term, and knowing something about them gives us a fuller picture of the time and place of group harmony.

In the pre-integrated schools of Baltimore and Washington youngsters learned music formally, in classes, or at least had programs for which they learned and performed any number of different types of music. Much of this can be attributed to the strength and caring of teachers, but youngsters used music in a very ennobling fashion, both inside and outside of school. They took what they learned from their different classes, shows, or talent contests and applied it to vocal groups that they formed. They made music in school hallways, bathrooms, playgrounds, and then moved out into clubs and on to nearby street corners. They were not simply passive recipients of music; they were active participants, who used music to advance some semblance of control and order over their lives.

Schools in Baltimore "were of the neighborhood variety" (Nast et al. 1982: 75). That meant schools took students from particular neighborhoods and respective sides of town, reinforcing neighborhood, geographic, and social status relationships that youngsters mirrored in their relationships, social activities, and singing groups.

In Washington, African American communities had the Paul Lawrence Dunbar High School at 1st and N Streets, Northwest, and the Armstrong Technical High School, across the street at 1st and O Streets. Cardozo, at 9th and Rhode Island Avenue, Northwest, was the city's black business high school. The two vocational schools were Phelps, at 24th and Benning Road, northeast, for men, and the Mary Washington School for women. Ten junior high schools and numerous elementary schools were scattered throughout the city (Alexander 1948: 130–32). Washington's black schools were not neighborhood-based, but drew students from all around the city, depending on the student interests, goals, grades, and, as some maintained, social status and color of skin.

The period of segregated schools was one of "blatant racism, exclusion, and inferior facilities" (Billingsley 1992: 172). Yet, beyond statistics, beyond the allegedly pathological, beyond the measurable, there is the immeasurable. There were positive experiences in segregated schools, where dedicated African American teachers nurtured and took care of dedicated pupils. Blacks who attended these schools have said the consequences of segregation for schooling were not always all bad and that something was inevitably lost after integration, not the least of which was direct control over education.

The comments of Mel Lipscomb, who attended and sang in public school in Washington in the 1940s, are illustrative. "We were very fortunate. The best thing that ever happened to us is to have beat the desegregation of schools, as far as I'm concerned. They looked at us as if we were their children, and you just learned."

The scholar Henry Louis Gates echoes these sentiments in a broader context when he writes that in his own hometown of Piedmont, West Virginia, "integration was experienced as a loss. The warmth and nurturance of the womblike colored world was slowly and inevitably disappearing, in a process that really began on the day they closed the door for the last time at Howard School, back in 1956" (Gates 1994: 184).

As people transcended the oppressiveness of racism, so did the black schools. Who could want to relive those years of Jim Crow? Yet, many acknowledge the post-integration changes they felt, as we have already heard. Jimmy McPhail speaks to those same sentiments. "Things got different when they integrated the schools. The values and things were lost. It wasn't the same. We always had aspirations and we didn't mind competing because that was the way life was at the time."

The role of the teacher was central to fostering those aspirations, maintaining that competitive edge. Surely many teachers drew on their own experiences in college, in an earlier era, earning advanced degrees with no place to go with them but home, and understanding what it was like to have to compete with whites for jobs. A good experience with a teacher will last a lifetime.

In Washington, Alphonso Feemster tells us, "Mostly it was music teachers which influenced my life, which you can imagine, because they wouldn't leave me alone. Every program I was on, you know. They would always want to give programs, which kept the kids out of trouble, I felt, because they would get the ones that could sing and always had you doing something."

As stated above, segregated black schools endured gross treatment by the dominant society. Before de jure integration in 1954, they were perennially unequal to white schools in terms of physical space, funding, and expenditures.[8] In spite of this, Washington's black schools were excellent and had truly outstanding teachers.

> Much credit is due the majority of colored administrators and teachers, who in spite of legion discriminatory handicaps, attempted to "keep up"

with the educational standards afforded their white counterparts. While
they were conscious of inequities and inadequacies, their morale was generally high, and their dedication to service was generally impeccable.
(Knox 1957: 8)

Teachers of music in the black school systems were an institution
within an institution. They all had some influence on youngsters in both the
nineteenth and twentieth centuries. They graced history with dedication
and longevity.

George Tillman recalled the first school music teacher that he had in
Washington. "I went to Briggs Montgomery Elementary School and later
on to Francis Junior High. But it was in Briggs Montgomery, 27th and I
Street, Northwest, in Georgetown. Well it's Foggy Bottom. It was there
that I was discovered by my music teacher, whose name was Miss Debruhl.
We had a little boys' chorus there and out of all those guys, and I never will
understand it, she picked me to sing. And of course I had to fight my way."

He laughed. He had to "fight" his way because he simply had no experience singing. "You know, I had no knowledge of, prior to that time I had
no knowledge of even singing. I could have sung, but I didn't know anything about it. But in the fourth grade we had this boy's chorus and every
year we'd have a Christmas program about the birth of Christ and things
of that nature. But out of all these guys—there were about, say about forty
or fifty of us—she selected me to sing a solo.

"But I remember Miss Debruhl. The memory of her will never die,
because of the things that we went through. We were very poor, but we
survived; in those days, you know people helped each other out neighbor-
wise. But I remember specifically one Christmas we were getting ready for
this program, Christmas program, and I was one of the kings in 'We Three
Kings of Orient Are.' I was one of the kings singing one of the parts and
that morning my mother told me I couldn't go to school that day because I
didn't have any shoes and it was raining. I had big holes in my shoes, you
know. But she kept me home and I cried so much and I really wanted to be
a part of that program. And, oh, I guess about ten o'clock that morning this
music teacher came to my house and wanted to know why I wasn't in
school. And so, the lady who was taking care of us said my mother indicated that we couldn't come to school that day because I didn't have any
shoes. She took me somewhere and bought me a pair of shoes that day and
I sang on that program. That's one of the things that I remember about her,
because she cared in those days. And that sort of, I guess that would be the
start of my singing. I guess you could call it career, being a singer."

In black communities, there was reason to persevere and there were elders and teachers to help the children. In addition to the kind of caring demonstrated by Miss Debruhl—she was not an exception but, rather, the rule—the quality of teaching was high in part because many blacks with advanced degrees could not find work elsewhere because of prejudice. What Jervis Anderson wrote about Dunbar in Washington was true for other black schools in Washington, Baltimore, and elsewhere before integration.

> Many of the exceptional black teachers who came to Dunbar had turned to teaching only because there was not much else for them to do. In the early years of Dunbar's history, black college graduates—however well trained, however brilliant—were seldom hired by white institutions in any serious intellectual capacity. Those who were not lucky enough to be lawyers or doctors—and who did not wish to be postal clerks, low-level government workers, soldiers, Pullman porters, or manual laborers—found that teaching was the most distinguished career open to them. (Anderson 1978: 107)

The ones who benefited the most from this situation were the students. The irony was that despite the best prejudicial efforts by white society to undermine "Division II" schools, the same prejudice forced highly educated and caring professionals into the black public school system. Former students all recalled the strength of the teachers in those schools. Jimmy McPhail still maintained vivid memories of his middle school in Washington. "Shaw Junior High School is right there at Rhode Island Avenue and Seventh Street. Right on the corner, Seventh and Rhode Island Avenue, Northwest. Which was a good ground spot for, I mean groundwork for young kids, you know. That was one of the top junior high schools."

What made it good? In the end, of course, it is good teaching that makes good schools and good learning. "I don't know, it just seemed like a, it just seemed like it was nice for me. The teachers were hard workers and they made us compete, you know in classrooms, you know the grades and things like that. That was one of the nice schools."

Melvin Lipscomb and Howard Davis were both born in 1928. They grew up in Washington, attended Dunbar High School, and constituted half of the Dunbar Four, a vocal group they formed while students at the school. They recall their music teachers from as early as elementary school and, like many others, stressed the quality of teaching and the *variety* of music they learned. Aside from what young singers may have heard on the radio, exposure to music of all types in school was significant. It may well have been the most important process in opening up their ears, so to speak, to music beyond church and certainly beyond stereotype — "the spectrum," as Howard phrases it below.

Mel says, "But we had plays even in junior high school, and I guess as long as I've been coming up from elementary school, junior high, and Dunbar, we had tremendous music teachers who were of some renown on their own. A Mrs. Chadwick, at elementary school, at Mott. Dunbar was Miss Europe. Right?"

Howard said, of music material, "Oh we were singing the regular music stuff. Spirituals."

"But we sang everything. We sang spirituals, we sang modern stuff. We sang whatever —"

"Whatever the teachers arranged."

"Yeah."

"Now you're talking about in junior high school, as part of the chorus. Well we would do whatever they arranged and they did the spectrum. From spirituals to patriotic to all kinds of things because that was part of being in the choir. And it was rote; you didn't have music before you. If it was determined that you were second tenor, then you up there with the second tenors, say here's your line. And you rehearsed that, and the first tenor that. Put it all together."

The black schools in Washington had great reputations for their music programs. Jimmy McPhail recalled music and teachers, this time at Armstrong High School. "We had a lady by the name of Mrs. Webster who used to be in charge of choral groups and she taught music there. And we had a man by the name of Mister Amos, who was the band director."

McPhail tells about what kind of music programs Armstrong had at the time, in the early 1940s. A certain number of music classes were a requirement. "And being a technical school guys took different fields and I guess they took music. I was in printing. I took music classes, they were called, more or less, music appreciation classes, you know.

"They did a lot of everything. Miss Webster used to try to expose us to so much music, you know, like operas or things. She would play records, bring music, and then she'd give us assignments to look up these different writers or musicians and we had to bring the reports back to class and discuss them, you know. Then there were times when she would make arrangements for us to go to the opera. Oh yes, we were involved with things like that. Well she was a very earnest teacher."

Out of that kind of musical environment guys put together vocal groups. McPhail's group was the Armstrong Four, and another teacher at the school helped them. "We got together at Armstrong High School. And one of the teachers that really worked with us was Mrs. B. K. Williams. She had a way of promoting things, and we had a big talent show that was so good at Armstrong High School that she took us around to the service bases, you know, like Fort Meade, Fort Belvoir."

Talent shows, which were popular around town, were also popular within the schools. "The people at Armstrong High School, all the talent came from there at that time. We used to go to hospitals and sing, you know. Mrs. Williams tried to get us a recording contract and everything, but it didn't come through."

In many ways, beyond what the teachers did, the school building itself became a musical place, a space to stake out—schoolyards and play-grounds, halls, the boys' room, and of course the organized classes. All of the black schools in Washington (there are fewer sources on the Baltimore schools) had some kind of instrumental and vocal music activities. Anything from spirituals to opera to popular and patriotic songs occurred through either curricular study or programs such as chorus, glee club, recitals, and musical plays, affording students a variety of influences from different musical styles. Musical opportunities depended on the school attended, and music in all Washington schools (both black and white systems) was particularly noteworthy (Pack 1945; Strayer 1949). Vocal music was abundant on all levels. At the junior high school level teachers were "largely left to their own initiatives in teaching procedures and selection of material" and focused on vocal music (Pack 1945: 87). A 1938 study on music in junior high schools ranked Washington first nationally in the development of vocal music in public schools (Doty 1938, quoted in Pack 1945: 14). Another study from the same year concluded that music appreciation classes generally have "a marked influence on the development of taste and appreciation [of music, and that] the junior high school children are offered a variety of opportunities to develop music appreciation" (Murry 1938, quoted in Pack 1945: 16).

In the black school system, music programs varied from school to school. The vocational schools had no specific music programs in place, but informal music making was common. Both Dunbar and Armstrong offered music courses, though Dunbar was "the only one of the three [black] high schools . . . in which there is a required course in music for ninth grades" (Pack 1945: 93). Armstrong, the technical school, had no required music courses, but offered electives such as chorus, music study, music appreciation, harmony, orchestra, band, and piano. Cardozo, the business school, had no music requirement either, but offered electives in orchestra and band and had numerous programs such as music plays and concerts where students performed.

The report of a survey of the public schools of the District of Columbia provides data on music in all of the public schools up until 1949.

> The assembly of music groups and school choruses in the secondary schools of the District of Columbia are distinctly superior in quality and compare favorably with those of any other city. . . . The records for many years reveal that a cappella choirs, glee clubs, and quartets, and band and orchestra instrumental ensembles of the schools have made many note-worthy contributions to the local community. (Strayer 1949: 605)

The Strayer report is for both the black and white school systems in Washington. There appears to have been a great deal of vocal music in both systems. Yet, it is worth noting that the African American males maintained the vocal music tradition outside of the school for, as has been stated, there were no white male counterparts to local, black harmony groups.

In addition to formal classes in school, teachers of music and informal opportunities to sing kept the African American students interested and active, and helped reinforce the idea that music—specifically singing and especially harmonizing—is an accepted form of expression.

Buddy Slaughter's experiences with school programs were typical of his generation. "In school, glee clubs, a combination of a lot of kids, singing different parts. Like a chorus, yeah. Just all kinds of stuff. They had music teachers, you know. And they give you, they find out what you can do first. And they put you in this group and that group. Sing this part and this group sing this part. Like that. Mixed the girls and the boys together."

Alphonso Feemster recalled that his first real experience harmonizing with others as a group came at school. It was the same kind of group that Buddy Slaughter described, the ubiquitous glee club. "And all that come through, I can credit it with my singing in the glee club in school, to help me distinguish the tenor, the alto, which is baritone in a man's voice, you know."

Feemster told of his junior high school's music programs from around 1950 and 1951. "They'd put a program on in the evening so your parents could come to see you perform. It was wonderful back there then. There was always something going on, all the time. And I was always wrapped up in it, in the music.

"We gave a play in school; my music teacher was Mrs. Brown. She was our music teacher at Langley Junior High. She gave this big production play. I was on it, me and my buddy Garnett Brown. He sang baritone, I sang tenor. The name of the operetta was 'El Bandito,' and we took that name and used it as our social club's name, me and Garnett Brown. We had about four or five guys, all from Barry's Farm, everybody from Barry's Farm. Then we formed a quartet. That was our first exposure to singing harmony."

The connection students made in school to music like opera and other European styles broadened their musical outlook and provided the potential to build on pre-existing musical norms learned at home or in church. In general, when we take a close look at the school system and place it within other social activities, it is clear that being musical was an active part of a youngster's social and cultural repertoire. In school, learning patterns often began at an early age, in elementary school, while most often the groups formed later, in junior high and high school. The musical values and tastes acquired during the school years often remained with vocalists long after they left school. Alongside church, the public schools may very well have provided the most important musical influences for these youngsters. Schools are an important focus in any youngster's life, and black youth who had musical aspirations in the late 1940s and 1950s used whatever the schools had to offer. Because many vocal harmony groups were neighborhood-based, youngsters maintained grouping patterns at school. Thus, particular groups or singers were associated with particular schools. For instance the Dunbar (High School) Four and the Armstrong (High School) Four were two very well-known school groups whose singers established strong reputations around town.

Youngsters centered their lives on school. Jimmy McPhail said, "The school for us was the center. And I think at that time we all wanted to go to school because that was the center of life for us—home, school, and the church. And that was it."

The three black high schools in Washington articulated a different status from each other. Each maintained different educational philosophies and, to a certain degree, cultivated different frames of reference. These youngsters, in effect, socialized song partly in accordance with their frames of reference vis-à-vis class status or consciousness as it may have obtained in school. For longtime residents, "status" resided in part in the black high schools. The issue in Washington focused especially on the relationship between, and status of, the Dunbar High School and Armstrong Technical School situated across the street. The two schools maintained divergent educational and cultural philosophies.[9]

Armstrong Manual Training School [constructed 1902] was designed according to the educational philosophies of Booker T. Washington. It provided training for black students in a range of trades based on the belief that "all forms of labor, whether with head or hand, are honorable." The history of the Armstrong complements that of Perry School (M Street High School) [which became Dunbar], each representing a different approach to the education of black students. (Lee 1986: n.p.)

In contrast, Dunbar, according to a 1944 faculty statement, "was to provide opportunity for progressive intellectual development, taking into consideration individual differences" (quoted in Anderson 1978: 96). The implications were that Armstrong was of the hands and Dunbar of the mind. Armstrong was the school that built practical self-sufficiency, in the spirit of Booker T. Washington. Dunbar nurtured the intellectuals, in the spirit of W. E. B. Du Bois. The attendant issues, however, remain far from clear and the best we might do is understand perceptions. In other words, most who recall the two schools will do so in terms of status.

Tex Gathings, a black radio personality in the late 1940s and 1950s (and an acting university dean in 1989) in Washington, framed the issues this way: "Dunbar was synonymous with the elite. If you went to Armstrong you were vocational material, or you had been 'tracked'—that infamous system of the public schools."

Mary Gibson Hundley was a graduate of Dunbar, taught there, and wrote of the school, "Its academic tradition attracted most of the ambitious and promising colored youth in Washington, D.C." (Anderson 1978: 96).

There is nothing to support the assertion that Dunbar actually had better students than Armstrong. Gifted students and singers attended all of the schools. That Dunbar sent forth a stream of successful graduates (carefully chronicled by one Edgar R. Sims and quoted in Anderson 1978: 102) tells us nothing about the social class of its students before they got to Dunbar, or how good Armstrong High School students were. It would seem that the inclination of some was to equate so-called middle and upper class values (in other words, an elite aura) with promise and success.

For instance, "Dunbar's success was also explained by the presence of highly motivated middle class students, who from the outset made up a large part of its enrollment and whose competitiveness helped maintain the high academic standards the teachers set" (Anderson 1978: 107). But weren't Armstrong students (and singers) just as competitive? Put another way, "Dunbar was, in effect, a 'white' school in a segregated system. Washington had a class system among blacks of different shades and economic backgrounds. Therefore, excellence at Dunbar represented the few—the percentage of Washington's black community that was middle class and upwardly mobile" (Dr. Kenneth Clark, in Anderson 1978: 107).

Armstrong, on the other hand, had a reputation for its technical programs, and for its athletes, and thus lacked that "elite" Dunbar status. Andrew Magruder, who went to Armstrong, recalled, "Armstrong had the best athletes." He also maintained that the "lighter skinned" sons and daughters of doctors and lawyers went to Dunbar High School, where "the better looking girls went." Former students from Dunbar echoed those sentiments. Buddy Bailey recalled of Dunbar: "It was just a popular school with a good name. And the pretty girls, they always had the pretty girls. That was one thing, I well remember that part of it."

Mel Lipscomb said, "Now you may not know about this history, but during those days Armstrong was a school that won for the most part in the football and that kind of thing and Dunbar always had the cadet officers and always won first, second, and third prize at Griffith Stadium. And oratory, that kind of thing."

Was that just because of the curriculum differences?

"No, I think it's mainly—well, you know, there are all kinds of things. Depends on what you choose to accept. It all depends how people would feel. For example, they said that if you were the child of a doctor, dentist, you went to Dunbar. Or something like that. If you were of light skin, fair skin, like you, for example, you'd go to Dunbar. Dark skin kids did not go to Dunbar, they went other places. And of course if you were going to be in the trade world you went to Armstrong or what have you."

In their stories, both Howard Davis and Melvin Lipscomb and others comment on the differences between Dunbar and Armstrong. The basic question for vocal harmony is how did one school and its underlying value system affect the sound of a singer or group? Jimmy McPhail acknowledged the differences between Armstrong and Dunbar, yet diminished the significance of those distinctions at the same time. This may have been in part because his group, the Armstrong Four, was the counterpart to the Dunbar group during the 1940s, before the category "rhythm & blues" was established. McPhail pauses to consider whether the "differences" in the schools were real, or perceived. "Well like I said, the school was a central part of our lives, and each school had something different to offer. You went to Dunbar and everything; you more or less would become an educator, doctor, or lawyer or something. Cardozo, it was a business type school and at Armstrong, we were a technical school."

Vocalists used their schools as points of departure for outside singing groups. In Baltimore, as we have seen, specific groups associated with specific sides of town, which is the way the schools were set up there. The Cardinals and Honey Boys, for instance, were an East Baltimore group, the

Orioles and Swallows West Baltimore. In Washington, Armstrong, Dunbar, and Cardozo high schools, as well as Phelps Vocational and some of the junior high schools, all had specific vocal groups associated with them. There was, it seems, a great deal of flow between sanctioned music programs, informal music groups, and neighborhood music making. A few groups centered their activities at school and then developed reputations around town. The Armstrong Four and Dunbar Five came from their respective schools. Most of the Clovers came from Armstrong (the exception was Buddy Bailey, who was a Dunbar graduate). The Lyles Brothers sang at Cardozo, the Playboys at Phelps Vocational, Serenadors at Kelly Miller Junior High School, and the Five Blue Notes (when they were the Five Blue Jays) rehearsed at Francis Junior High, though they didn't all attend the school.

With all of the groups, singing was more than just something to do; it was also a manner of doing something. Group harmony was a style of singing and a style of socializing. Group harmony articulated—constituted—more than associations and identity. Singing was control and vocalists staked out aural territory, if you will, in the society of school, neighborhood, and city as a whole. Singing was a powerful way to establish and maintain one's individual or collective presence.

Lawrence Berry attended Harrison Elementary School and then moved through the Parkview, Banneker, and McFarland schools before ending up at Bell (Boys) High School, just after integration. During those days, in the mid-1950s, Berry maintains, everybody had a group. "If you went to a school, you had a group."

It was, Berry said, "more of a culture or an identification type thing."

In some schools, you had the choice of five or six singing groups. Schools had their own talent shows in which all the groups would participate. "It was just a, I guess a way of identifying ourselves. I don't know, it's kind of a hard thing to say, but I would say it was more of a, it was just a way of being involved, I guess, you know, if you had a group and you was singing. I would form a group and we would start singing. It was always that competition type thing."

The Armstrong Four and Dunbar Five have related histories, having co-existed in the same city during the 1940s. Both groups had similar interests in pop music and were school rivals, as Howard Davis of the Dunbar group recalled. "Somebody came up with the idea to have a battle of the Armstrong Four and the Dunbar Five, at Armstrong. And as Melvin recalls, it was wall to wall, because the people at Cardozo had a keen interest, I mean, they were just nice kids and they knew us from singing. And that place was jammed packed."

James McPhail became the best known of the Armstrong singers during the 1940s. He went on to record and had a professional career on his own, recording for RCA and performing with the Duke Ellington Orchestra. "The kids that were along with us at that time knew us, and we would go to each one of the other schools and perform. Cardozo, Dunbar, you know, they'd have some program and they would invite us over. They wanted us to come."

He remembered the Dunbar group. "Well I knew them. They were sort of like—they tried to be competitors with us. Well, which was real good because they had their school and they wanted to show what they could do. They had a nice group."

While these youngsters sang in school activities or programs, or competitively in talent shows, sometimes the school building itself became a music venue of playgrounds, hallways, and bathrooms. Making music, vocal music and group harmony, was not a solitary enterprise. It was a way to socialize, a reason to socialize, just as simply getting together was a sound reason to sing.

Andy Magruder recreates a scene from junior high school. "I tell you, man. If a guy was to get out of his house and go to school, and you got five guys, one guy goes to another school, this other guy says, 'Hey Mack.'

"We on the same bus, though. But we got to transfer to go to different schools.

"'Hey, we going to have rehearsal six o'clock'

"OK."

"Man, them rascals do their homework. Twenty-fourth and N, which is Georgetown, right by Francis Junior High swimming pool. That's the only swimming pool we had."

"'Alright, man, what's happening?'

"'Ain't nothing.'"

Magruder starts to hum a bass line, and then breaks into a melody.

"'Let's go.'"

One reason Andy Magruder and his group used the swimming pool area to rehearse was the acoustics there, the echo. They sang the building. The school itself becomes part of the performance, a place that could galvanize the social aspects of group singing. Andy and his friends used the school in that way, as part of the performance. There probably is no stereotype more persistent than the image of four or five teenage males crowding together in a school bathroom and harmonizing a song.

Melvin Coles said, of his school years, "I did a lot of singing."

As did George Jackson: "Yeah, I did too."

Melvin says, "Lot of talent shows, we did, you know, like in school."

"Yeah. And we used to like to sing in the bathroom."

"Oh yeah."

"That bathroom had that—"

"We get put out of school."

"—Echo sound. Yeah."

"Yeah, we get put out of school. Yeah, we get put out of school for singing in the hallways."

"Teacher would come in the bathroom, because we was singing in the bathroom."

George laughs as Melvin finishes.

"They wouldn't allow you to sing in the bathroom and walking up and down the hallways, or even in the yards."

But they sang anyway.

Getting back to Armstrong High School in Washington, James McPhail explains how the Armstrong Four started. "Well, like I say, several of us took music appreciation at the time, and I guess we happened just to get together. Like I say, we would go in the bathroom and harmonize."

The effort by one singer to establish something with another resulted in a connection, a call and a response. Singing was not a passive art. Vocalists made subtle gestures toward each other, as Howard Davis recalls an experience in school chorus. "And then you'd hear this guy and you know you kind of lean in, you know, and that might have been the beginning."

He means the beginning of a friendship, of a vocal group. Howard's image of singing—hearing a nearby voice, making harmony and leaning in—is evocative. It nicely illustrates the subtle physicality of singing harmony, and the community of it.

Henry Mont provides a similar example (his stage name later was "King Henry"). He grew up around Lincoln Heights, in the northeast section of Washington. As he tells it, he was in a bathroom stall at Kelly Miller Junior High School (sometime during the 1950s) when he heard some guys singing and "hummed in," as he phrased it. The others stopped, liked what they had heard, and the Serenadors formed, playing initially at a school membership drive. Once again, the school's physical space became a part of the musical process. Henry joined in with his peers, just as Howard leaned in with his, in a kind of sociomusical gesture.

Harold Winley, the bass singer with the Clovers, also recalled the singing that went on in school. "You could hardly go to any school and not hear [singing]. I mean like Shaw Junior High. There's a brother, he still lives on 6th Street, James White. He had a buddy named Louis Day. And there was another brother that played an alto, I don't remember. Louis Day played a tenor saxophone. They were all young guys. Kids, you know. And after school they used to rehearse in the auditorium at Shaw, and the doors would be open so all you do is go up the fire escape and go in. You know. And you hear them fumbling around with their horns and stuff and you just go in and start singing with them, try to do something, you know. Yeah. But there was music in all the schools."

From the perspective of whites, the goal of racial segregation was more than just to set blacks apart; it was to control as well. But it could only work in very limited, specific, and well-defined locations, such as schools, neighborhoods, "whites only" establishments, and the like. Segregation's absurdity becomes apparent when you simply consider the reasons behind it—fear of "race mixing"—and then consider for a moment the physical and emotional reality of cities, the ebb and flow of people who move through town and the lasting images of a place. Washington is, in one sense, a black city. In 1970, its African American population was 71 percent of the total; at the 1990 census, it was 66 percent.[10] That the city is the nation's first city makes that fact profoundly significant. Most national politicians in Washington have never fully realized the city beyond the protected government grounds. In the 1990s, there were still black elevator operators in government buildings—a sight not lost on someone who heard Ernest Warren talk about his days doing that job, in the 1940s. Washington, like the rest of America, still enjoys the transparency of a kind of see-through segregation that we are all supposed to ignore.

Racial partitions placed African Americans into spaces and into categories that became patterns to follow, so to speak. On one level, these patterns literally were pathways—streets and sidewalks that led to African American churches, schools, jobs, businesses, over the tracks or under the highway to sides of town, neighborhoods, homes. This was the physical, visceral aspect to segregation.

On another level the patterns were emotional, perhaps even neurological; the effects remain elusive to quantify, yet obvious enough where a youngster in 1940 would certainly think more than twice about crossing over a particular street into a white neighborhood. The far side of these patterns, these expectations, was stereotype. Whites collectively expected blacks to fall "naturally" into constructed categories of racial behavior, from elevator operators to, of course, musicians.

Racial categories were also maps of expectation for whites to follow, to make themselves feel better, and to internalize better the complexities of race and racism. Whites and others internalized essentialist notions of a homogeneous, even unified kind of American black population and, in fact, made it so because, among other reasons, a racist America looks only at surface features and stereotype in order to determine who or what might be "black."[11]

This point can also be made vis-à-vis how certain aspects of the music industry categorized "black" music has such—a kind of segregation that forced African American music into certain racialized patterns of expectation. Black became a pigment of the white imagination. It was, and remains, another kind of public image, another imageability.

3

Entrepreneurship

THREATENING COURT SUIT—The Twilighters, who recently recorded "Please Tell me You're Mine," "Wondering," "Longing For You," and "Gee, Baby I Need You So," are threatening to take court action to prevent release on one of the records because they are dissatisfied with the background music. Recently featured on a TV marathon for cerebral palsy, they will go on a month's tour beginning Jan. 22 in Vienna, Md.
> —*Baltimore Afro-American*, January 23, 1954

One kid is signed to Mercury, I'm signed (at least for now) to Capitol and there's about two more groups working on their demo. The rest who ain't in college are just sippin' de Brewski, sellin' dub sacks and freestylin' to a gangsta beat. And in the end it ain't 'bout no salary.
> —T-Love, in Cross 1993: 317

Rhythm, Remuneration, and Blues

In the end, maybe it is about a salary, otherwise T-Love would not be talking about who is "signed" and who is "sellin'." Indeed, that could well sum up in two words the fervent hopes of the entire music industry, top to bottom—signed and selling (or better yet, signed, sealed, sellin'). Many of the harmony groups in Baltimore and Washington were of the urban grassroots variety or were not professionals for very long. Indeed, a number of singers will state that they were either interested in "just singing" or wanted to only cut a record, not thinking too much about the money. Nevertheless, there were subtler dynamics at work for many in the 1940s. Music held out the promise of monetary reward if you were willing to do the right things: have the right comportment and repertoire, an appealing style, get correct with an agent or manager, and hang out at the right places, the right businesses—all supported by sound values and a good work ethic. Also, whites generally encouraged black music making by now, the right kind anyway, and so the idea of "make music, but let us control the business side of it" was not lost on very many for very long. Even the most local and amateur of groups did not function in a social vacuum, and noteworthy alliances often resulted. The social milieu that engendered group harmony knits together three themes explicated in this chapter: the entrepreneurial spirit of rhythm & blues and its historical underpinnings in black America, the related notion that black sells, and a revisiting (from the previous chapter) of "the geographic thing," as Tex Gathings phrased it—focusing on the relationship between place and economics in Baltimore and Washington. Along the way, we learn about the work ethic and savvy of young black males of the period, their supposed naivety notwithstanding.

Carroll Williamson tells a story about his band from high school. That enterprise led Williamson and his road partner Howard Spinney to establish Howfum Records. It was a remarkable, albeit brief time in the lives of two young black males who both realized the entrepreneurial possibilities of music while they were still teenagers in the late 1950s in Baltimore. Still

The Twilighters. Left to right, Robert Richardson, William Pierce, Deroy Green, Melvin Jennings, and Earl Williams. Courtesy of the Afro-American Newspapers.

more remarkable was that, in this incident, they realized a couple of subtle things you could do to tweak the potential for success.

"We started playing in a band. One of my partners—I always call him my partner because we did just about everything together throughout our music life until later years—Howard Spinney. Howard Spinney was part of the record company, part owner of the record company. I was in high school with Howard, and Howard came in one day and told me I was going to play guitar. I can't remember what made him think I would play guitar. I never played guitar before. So we went out and bought a guitar, and did a performance almost like two weeks later. My job was to hit three or four notes on the guitar—and I knew nothing about music. I mean I wanted to perform, and as a matter of fact, he and I called the band Lee Carroll and the Imperials. That was the name of our first group. It was called the Imperials.

"Now, you know, it's very easy to call ourselves the Imperials and, I mean, what's a name anyway? We call ourselves the Imperials and then we say we're the Imperial Orchestra, you know, to make it sound big this time. As a matter of fact, we did that. One time we had some music stands made. Now we're just a band, and we had performed behind some other groups. So we what we did was, we had the music stands built, there with the big 'I' on it, and stood behind it, you know, as an orchestra."

Did they have music on those stands?

Carroll says, "Read music? No, we weren't reading any music."

Well, what did the Imperials have on the music stand?

Carroll answers, "Nothing. Just the stand was there, know what I'm saying? We're playing by ear mostly anyway."

There is something endearing, enduring, and tenacious in the image of a young black musical organization putting up music stands with no music on them. And then, there's the name. What's in a name? Nothing and everything is in a name. Bands long ago, black ones included, acquired the tag "orchestra" as a means to elevate their marketing status, that is to say, it sounded bigger, better, fancier, and maybe you could charge more or create a different clientele.

The Imperials fronting with the iconic music stands as well as the orchestral mark would have, by some, been seen as an act of "fumbling amateurs," to draw from a derisive Arnold Shaw (1978: xx). From another critical perspective, however, they were engaging, enterprising, and spirited in their attempt to market themselves. If only for a moment in time, the Imperials were young entrepreneurs, not fully professional perhaps, but entrepreneurial nonetheless. The music stands and the name of the band were two gestures toward establishing some kind of authority in a business sense. That spirit led members of the band to start a record company. The record company is the music industry's warm valley, at once the point of departure and final resting place for popular music making, although business in general, and the business of music (as in record companies) in particular, has been mostly the province of whites, even when black artists such as Duke Ellington were astute enough to cut themselves very good deals. This is a difficult area to untangle, but a familiar story for many because black "success" did not always translate into financial reward. Often success was more in the process, not the result. This is an important distinction to make when you consider the American capitalist ideal: you work hard, do the right things, and you will succeed. The formula does not always work within the context of our racialized state.

Carroll Williamson and the Imperials were trying to gain some control over their music business, as were the Twilighters when they threatened with their lawsuit, but they were also drawing, deliberately or not, from a history of black commerce and enterprise. It is also reasonable to see that what at least some of what black rhythm & blues artists and group harmony vocalists did, even when still young, was to market themselves in an entrepreneurial sense. Harmonizing was something to do, it was a black cultural form, but it also led in the 1940s to the realization that music and rhythm & blues were a business and thus full of possibility.

There is literature on both the entrepreneurial spirit in black America and, according to some, the lack of it.[1] Without engaging too deeply with the argument, we know that slaves became artisans and participated in the business of commerce with much vitality when and where they could, and when and where white society permitted. This readiness and enthusiasm for enterprise continued after the Emancipation for black musicians who pursued the business of making music. Historian Juliet Walker makes a convincing argument for the use of the term and concept "entrepreneurial" to describe the business activities of enslaved Africans and later, African Americans. "Beginning in the 1600s," she writes, "Africans in America, slave and free, seized every opportunity to develop enterprises and participate as businesspeople in the commercial life of a developing new nation" (Walker 1998: xvii).

Walker's definition of entrepreneurship among slaves is precise: "Self-hired slaves who established as sole proprietors and generated substantial profits from their enterprise were slave entrepreneurs." However, setting aside the issue of profit, which, for blacks, racial discrimination mediated, we can broaden the notion of entrepreneurial to mean certain cultural and psychological attitudes and qualities. Green and Pryde (1990: 2, 13) drew from the work of sociologist Albert Shapero to suggest that attitudes include "resilience, creativity and innovation, initiative, diversity"—the same qualities the Imperials and groups like them demonstrated in order to further their music business goals (which were not entirely inseparable from purely musical goals). These types of strategies are remarkable only because, as Regina Austin reminds us, African American "consumption and commerce are in essence considered deviant activities by many whites and many blacks as well" (Austin 1995: 229).

The desire to make music, for a good number of young singers, included the hope for financial success. This adds yet another interpretive layer to the story of group harmony, the business of singing, which has historical underpinnings worth noting. "Making it" is the twentieth-century American dream. We can speculatively add, in light of both terms' commitment to action, creativity, and innovation, that entrepreneurship and entertainment are so close in character that newly arrived slaves would have soon felt their combined musical possibilities. That sensibility continues.

There is nothing in historical records that tells us at what precise point Africans in the Colonies made music for profit from a white clientele, but Africans did make a great deal of music. Music, as a part of the business of entertainment, was one sphere where blacks could and did participate. There was a point in history when Africans made music for (the hope of) commercial viability and thus devised what we can call entrepreneurial strategies—such as were possible at that time. Even black religious music, especially at the point of modern gospel after the late 1920s, became a business to those professional composers and singers who made and sold their music. To the likes of Lucy Campbell, Thomas S. Dorsey, Roberta Martin, and countless others, music was as much a living as a spiritual expression. Certainly there was no contradiction in this, and there was a history behind it.

Eileen Southern points out that "in the North black musicians provided much of the dance music for the Colonies of all classes" (Southern 1997: 43). Although Southern does not discuss any specific economic details of black music making of that period, she does report that as musicians, "slaves were reliable, skilled, affable, and cheap." It is not difficult to see how this established a paradigm in the minds of many whites and blacks alike. Though social dynamics varied between small farms of the Colonies in the North and large plantations in the South, there was much that the institution of enslavement made similar and much that various Africans had in common—music making.

Put another way, one of the very earliest dynamics between African slave and the dominant power encouraged a precedent that blacks entertain (for) whites. Indeed, in the Colonies their musical talents and the instruments they played often identified escaped slaves or those up for sale (Southern 1997: 25–27), uniting in the collective minds of whites the images of blacks and music.

To make any kind of music is, to varying degrees, entertainment of some sort. For slaves it was part of a broad spectrum of interrelated kinds of performances: dances, dialects, displays, masks, and all manner of the verbal arts such as poetry, tales, and storytelling. "Entertaining" functions to both maintain an audience's attention and as a deeper level of cultural communication. As one writer put it, "black entertainers emerged in America virtually simultaneously with the arrival of black people on the continent" (Riis 1989: 3). African slaves drew on what they knew and learned. They maintained their indigenous attitudes because they valued them, as a goal toward which they could aspire in very difficult circumstances, a goal that was important for its own sake, an end in and of itself. But at the same time, these attitudes proved to be valuable in the face of adversity. As a result, African American musical sensibilities, as diverse as they may have been—and as such, an understanding of entertainment in its broadest sense—proved to be a means to an end and surely became a good way to get over on the white man.

In some cases the enslaved no doubt had to make music for whites (because they did it so well) while in others, whites prevented them from gathering to make music (because that could mean trouble). It is reasonable to assume that Africans (slaves or free) soon imagined the power and possibilities of making and controlling music during the Colonial and slave periods. This was not a new idea either, especially given the role historically of professional musicians (not to mention market and business activities—see Walker 1998: 1–31) of every sort across West and Central Africa. During and after enslavement, the profusion and proclivity of black music making fueled its social acceptability among whites. This, in turn, led to a kind of social channeling and outright stereotype fed by prejudice and white expectations that blacks do and would make a lot of music. A very broad, socially constructed race issue here cuts across truth, authenticity, and stereotype.

When Herman Denby asked, "So what did you have but the music," he referred specifically to social restrictions white society placed on young black males in Baltimore during the 1940s that made finding some recreation difficult. In a sense, though, he could well have been making a sweeping historical generalization about the correlative relationship between white society and the African's role in shaping American popular music and the role music had in shaping black lives. Blacks who trained in other areas but were musically skilled often turned back to music to earn a living because of limited opportunities in those different disciplines. The orchestra leader Fletcher Henderson for instance, whose college degree in chemistry did him little good when he moved to New York in 1920, turned to music. If he could not sell his abilities in one chosen area, then he would fall back on music and sell that—his personal failings as an astute businessman aside, for the band still had been a profound success. A person, after all, had to put food on the table.

As indicated above, to some observers and participants of the time, a record producer in the 1950s could simply "buy off" young black male singers to record for a new suit of clothes. Some—including singers themselves—asserted that they were not all that interested in money at the time or simply did not know any better. They were, after all, still youngsters. Just the thrill of making a record was supposed to be enough of a reward. Although there is truth in these observations, most singers at some point began to think about remuneration, especially given the success of popular black entertainers at the time. As they first circulated beyond home, out on the block, and in the neighborhood or school, they probably thought more about singing than money. But, as they moved beyond those spheres, to other ones around the city, and learned of the older, successful groups, surely the notion of making music and money became apparent. It would have also become obvious that there was a strong relationship between black America and the entertainment industry, for better and for worse. Surely, it was a way to make a living, but it must have become obvious that whites stereotyped black musical proclivities and controlled and limited social mobility in other pursuits.

At the same time, as they grew older, these singers typically had to have day jobs of one kind or another. Two things resulted. Most developed and maintained a good attitude about work, and they encountered through local jobs both black and white businesses that supported music making in a myriad of ways during the rhythm & blues era. These, combined with the remunerative attitudes about black music making on the part of performers and other, served as the entrepreneurial (and integrative) underpinnings of group harmony.

In black areas, local businesses and business people were inseparable from the families, neighborhoods, and the communities at large. This interrelationship refers us back again to the complex and varied urban affinities out of which rhythm & blues group harmony emanated. For just about everybody involved, and at a time when budgets were very modest, there was a bottom line to the music industry measured in money as much as in talent, performance, and style. Singers quickly learned this value.

Ernest Warren was twenty-two in 1951 when he recorded with the Cardinals for Atlantic Records. "Little bit of money for recording was good because, hey, you going to record a song and a man going to pay you too? That was very exciting, you know, during that time."

While younger singers did not always think much about money at first, it frequently had a way of dropping around, literally, and exchanging hands anyway. At some point in time, some groups would find themselves doing things—developing a broader repertoire, for instance—to increase earning potential. Singing and harmonizing thus became more than just something to do, it became a way of life that included, inevitably, the happy possibility of "making it." It seems that just under the surface floats the idea of making music for money.

For example, if a few vocalists gathered in a public space to sing, then not much later someone inevitably would come along and throw down a few coins, whether the group was looking for it or not. This is an old story in black America and practically a stereotype as, for instance, Louis Armstrong recalled singing for pennies as a child in New Orleans. These kinds of occurrences, incidentally, were city things. The mythic, West African-tinged "crossroads" may have had importance as a place of power in the starry dark nights of the rural south. In the city, though, the street corner was both the figurative and literal place of power, and had no direct rural counterpart. It was a place full of people where young men could congregate and make something happen in the 1940s and 1950s.

Buddy Bailey, who was born in 1931, used to hang out on the street with friends in Northwest Washington. They would play homemade instruments and harmonize. They were not really looking for any money at first, but people would pass by and drop coins. "We were around twelve, maybe thirteen, and people would throw us change, and stuff, you know. . . . Different people would just stop. We'd just entertain ourselves. We were really doing it just for the, I guess, the love of it."

For the love of it, yes, but there was nothing stopping them from picking up loose change and turning entertainment and love into a little bit of commerce as a group takes shape.

Jesse Stone was, among other things in a lifetime of music, the seminal writer and arranger for Atlantic Records in the 1950s. He was skeptical of any "entrepreneurial" interpretation of group harmony (ironic for someone who was in the music business himself for his entire life). Instead, he taps into the black experiences of singing because " 'you want to,' you know," as Buddy said, for the love of it.

Jesse Stone said, about young singers, "Because they were doing it more, like, for the enjoyment. They did that like years ago they used to have barbershop quartets in schools, colleges, and whatnot. They didn't do it for the money, they did it for the enjoyment, you know, the kicks they got out of it. Show off at parties and all that sort of stuff. It's the same thing these kids did. They'd get on corners at night and just sing and draw a crowd and people will throw maybe a few quarters on the sidewalk for them to pick up and all that sort of stuff. And that was kicks for them, you know. But they never thought of doing this for a living or becoming famous or anything like that. It was a way of self-entertainment, that's what it was. They used that because there was a lot of other things they couldn't do. The way prejudice was you weren't allowed to go in certain places for enjoyment and so this is what had to be done, they did something for their own enjoyment."

Stone reiterates points already made in these pages, for instance, about singing because there were limitations to what you could do back in those days. Others, however, recall the entrepreneurial spirit of group harmony in ways that Stone does not—to sing, draw a crowd, and have people throw down money, even if it was only "a few quarters." At some point these men did indeed think about singing for a living and becoming famous, especially after the Orioles hit. When Buddy Slaughter attended Washington's Armstrong High School, he sang first with a couple of friends. Then they formed a singing group called the Buddies. In 1947, he left for New York. His view was a common one from the perspective of singers. "We wanted to make it big. That's how young people be, you know, going to New York to make it big."

Herman Denby, of the Swallows, said his inspiration to do music for a living came from watching successful groups at black Baltimore's famous Royal Theater. "Every time I went to the Royal Theater and saw those people, who were on stage, I felt good. I was there. I was there with them, you know. I identified with this. That's what I want to do."

Ernest Warren suggests that initially singers were just interested in singing, not money, but as they grew older, they learned some things about the outside business interests that looked to make something off the groups, and in turn helped make the groups. Ernest spoke in his typical, direct way. "Yeah, well it was hard. The only reason we made it and, a few other guys like us, is because people interested in making money in the entertainment field, and when they found something they thought they could cash in on they grabbed it. And most people our age that came up now have been, were being used, because we didn't know nothing about it. The only thing we wanted to do was sing, but then as we got older we learned too late then."

Ernest had in mind the realization that, for some, the financial success of rhythm & blues occurred at the expense of the creators and performers of the popular style that the industry constructed as "rhythm & blues." This admittedly was a complex situation. Ernest specifically was recalling an effort by a number of artists from the 1950s and 1960s to get Atlantic Records to recalculate its royalty payments, which they did.[2] In the early years, industry practice did not (nor does it now) always benefit performing artists (especially blacks) equitably and some, like Ruth Brown, worked for years to get her proper payments.[3] Ernest Warren, like his contemporaries, was keenly aware of the issues that defined the romance between the marketers of black rhythm & blues, like Atlantic, and finance. Rhythm & blues was, after all, a business, with the product good, commercial music. The irreducible fact was ultimately to make money for producer and performer alike, thus the real issue was *fairness* in profits and payments. On this point, Ernest strikes a gracious balance between the intimations of half-baked, if not fully cooked, books from a long time ago, and possible legal recompense in the 1990s. The acknowledgment is that in the 1950s Ernest and a lot of others just did not always think to ask the right questions. There is in his words justifiable pride.

"Ahmet Ertegun. He's still the president of Atlantic. And I don't know where he is, if I did I could give him a call or a letter and I'm sure he would respond, but it's not that important to me. He heard and he knows that I'm living so if it was anything that he wanted with me he would contact me, you know."

The system is just this way. If you are going to make popular music beyond your basement, you have to think about selling it. You have to think about the marketplace, and that gets us back to entrepreneurial spirit. The point here is that young black male singers engaged with the business side of making music in subtle but meaningful ways. There was also significant overlap between making music, living and working in the city, and the small businesses in the city—all this in the wider context of rhythm & blues as an industry.

Only recently, a black music style (specifically rap and hip-hop) emerged with an explicit, direct tie to business possibilities or tie-ins, like fashion. It is however, impossible to consider the place black music has had in American culture and society without considering the broad economics of that place. Black performers generally have always been aware (or became aware) of the racialized economics of their work and their music. The music business, as commerce, was a system that did not work to a black advantage and whites used "blackness" to their own economic advantage. Most African American musicians, on almost any level, would have to consider options in response to those economics. Those options included serving both black and white audience needs, material selection, performance style, and, especially in the rhythm & blues era, local business connections of one kind or another. It is with this commercial, economic perspective in mind that we consider three interrelated narratives that connect rhythm & blues group harmony with individual entrepreneurship, work ethics, and the general scope of black music and commerce.

The opening of this chapter briefly outlined the first broadly historical narrative. It tells us that for a long time, Africans and African Americans practiced entrepreneurial skills—the lack of large profits notwithstanding. This activity constituted a point of departure from which singers could pursue specifically the business of making music. That impetus, however, was also rooted in how vocalists put into singing and integrated into their groups an attitude about life that came simply from the things they had to do away from music to survive—work and hold jobs, for instance. In particular, singers maintained a relationship with local businesses, many of which sponsored music making in myriad ways. Also important is the work ethic that youngsters put into their singing, brought into their groups, and maintained throughout their lives as workers at these businesses.

As we shall see, many of the singers from Baltimore and Washington talk about day jobs with local companies and businesses that supported local music in numerous formal and informal ways. Sometimes an employer would give singers who worked for them time off to pursue their music, and then hire them back. Local businesses also maintained radio programs through sponsorships, advertising, or even paying disc jockeys. They sold records and advocated local artists, and occasionally sponsored or managed talent shows, contests, or the groups themselves. There were also countless clubs in Baltimore and Washington, and two famous theaters that were a part of a professional circuit—the Royal in Baltimore and the Howard in Washington—all part of the networks that connected venue, musician, management, and financial backers. In both cities there were companies, businesses, businessmen and businesswomen, music people of all kinds, and assorted activities with which vocalists came into contact. For singers, it meant at the very least exposure to the business aspect of music. At best, it fostered and furthered an atmosphere of entrepreneurial opportunity.

A second story is about both blacks and whites who pursued the business of specifically making (and in some instances, constructing) black music ("black music," of course, variously and not always very precisely defined). They did this most often in the kinds of alliances that popular music making, beyond just singing, requires. For instance, there were alliances between musicians and producers, or between managers and vocal groups. For groups the players away from the microphone could be women (writers, producers, and managers—see below), thus the social dimension doubled with informal alliances between black and white female and male. All these intersections occurred in the city, in urban areas, and through myriad enabling ways of which singers took advantage.

Friends, family, people who wandered into a performance, liked what they heard, had a connection to make, something to offer. It was the racialized aspect, however, that resonates most tenaciously and in both directions. Whites, for instance, could work the business of creating black music in relative social isolation, away from African Americans (their music style, of course, excepted). The now notorious white cover versions of black rhythm & blues and rock 'n' roll of the 1950s tell us that story.

For African Americans, however, there was no working too far from whites because whites owned the industry, institutions, and financial structures. Blacks have also had to consider white expectations. The process of successfully making music includes meeting not only one's own creative needs, but audience expectations as well. Black public figures—not limited to singers or entertainers—have confronted the racial and political implications of social contact with whites and over the years designed, devised, and initiated strategies toward success and acceptance (or avoidance, which is sometimes not such a bad idea). But for entertainers it is an old story—you make music for yourself; you make music for white folks.

Vocal groups took initiatives and commonly sought out and worked with managers, producers, writers, radio disc jockeys, investors, and hangers-on of every sort. Many but certainly not all were white. Much of this activity simply has to do with the vagaries of the popular music business. Some had to do with the white businesses in black neighborhoods. Some also had to do with the difficulty black business people had in breaking through color barriers. There are no data to suggest that vocal groups intentionally sought out white managers over black ones (or the other way around). In the presence of a white-dominated industry power structure, however, considerations of color would be inevitable, whether black groups went to work for a white manager or a black manager sought a record contract for his or her group.[4]

A third, connected, and larger story here, taken up below centers on the understanding that "black sells," and this phenomenon contributed to the whole music entrepreneurial ethos, especially during the postwar rhythm & blues era and later. When Hazel Carby (1998: 1) writes of today's "multimillion-dollar international trade in black male bodies," she taps into a very old thing that has been over the years modernized, post-modernized, rationalized, rectified, refined and rarified. So what has changed?

During enslavement black female and male bodies were literally sold, with at first little mind paid to the intellectual property that Africans cultivated and maintained, except that which would directly benefit the system — knowledge of crops, farming, or other trades and crafts. During enslavement whites began to understand black "culture" as something marketable, even vaguely mysterious. This first took the form of images (mostly visual, often distorted through caricatures during minstrelsy) and eventually, of course music.

Most recently, as Carby rightly asserts, "Nike" and "Hollywood" market in the black male body — all over again. The relationship between music makers and other participants, however, is not simply one of exploitation and trafficking. It remains far more nuanced, perplexing, and, to varying degrees, one of transaction, exchange, and mutual benefit between parties.

The point here is a consideration not of music as a framework for black business per se, but of blackness as business — specifically as a framework for making commercial music. This, in fact, was the whole reason for rhythm & blues. It is a well-known story. The phrase (and the concept) was an expression that Jerry Wexler, then a writer for *Billboard*, conceived in 1949 to reflect changes in postwar black popular dance music. He simply wanted to give it a name and replace the trade name "race music," which the industry had used since 1920 to catalogue nearly all recordings made by African Americans. The term "race" had originated among African Americans, who used it self-referentially long before whites adopted it. Many by 1949 thought it too deprecating for commercial use. "Rhythm & blues" thus replaced "race" as a catchall term for African American recording artists and music. R&B became a market category that quickly developed into a marketing strategy and, eventually, a full-blown performance style (unlike "race music," which never was a manner of performance). The result (if not always the intent) was to segment, separate, set apart, and set up black music. To "set up" as in a bit of a swindle, yes, but also to put up on a pedestal. The swindle had to do with the music industry initially classifying most if not all African American performances and recordings as "black," thereby creating the need for a rhythm & blues category. There was no such thing as "white" rhythm & blues in 1949. There were exceptions, but simply put, if you were black, you were rhythm & blues; if you were white, you were "pop."

That was the swindle. The pedestal side was the white interest in black music, the need to learn (about) it and, in some instances, to make it (perform as well as construct and control it). Categories of black music were white inventions, and their need to create "blackness" has always had much more to it than simple separatism. If an artist did not conform to what the industry expected a black artist to sound like, then whites easily became unsettled, confused, and even a little nervous. In fact, the whole subject of black music—to make it, sell it, construct it, deconstruct it, or just try to understand it, takes us into a confusing, convoluted realm of irony and of white making.

We find blackness—a social and cultural construct—as a modern framework for making both mainstream and "black" (that is, marginal) music. Such was the world in which rhythm & blues harmony groups found themselves in the late 1940s and early 1950s. It is a fascinating web of racialized intrigue, but not an easy one to untangle.

"That blackness is most black, brother, most black . . ."[5]

Many African American performers reached deep into the pockets of Tin Pan Alley, aside from its being a dominant sound and a sound musical structure, because they simply liked the music and its sentiments. There is no denying the appeal of standards and no denying anyone the feelings imbedded in the songs, as Buddy Bailey said.

"There was something about the lyrics, you know, the meaning. They were meaningful to me. They told a story. Great love songs."

The music of some vocal groups of the late 1940s and early 1950s was quintessentially conventional, especially when we listen today. The Orioles, Cardinals, Five Keys, Flamingos, Moonglows, and numerous other groups dug into sweet ballads and performed standards extraordinarily well. That fact made little or no difference to the categorization of black performers, but it meant much to the record industrialists interested in cultivating an "authentic" (read ghetto) black sound.

Jimmy McPhail knew that story. "See, after I got out of college and started recording for RCA Victor, they at that time felt that all black singers, RCA Victor thought that all black singers were rhythm & blues singers. I was a ballad singer, but they felt, you know, because you were black you were rhythm & blues."

McPhail's comment can mean two things. A vocalist would either sing what and how he or she pleased, but be classified rhythm & blues anyway, or simply conform stylistically to what the industry thought rhythm & blues should sound like. This industry conception probably began with what Jerry Wexler presumably heard when he coined the phrase in 1949. Postwar popular black dance music was something of a departure from swing offbeat phrasing. Instead, you could hear in some arrangements an increase in sharply attacked backbeats. There was a proliferation of small ensembles, as in jump bands, gospel-based vocals, and edgy lyrics. Wexler must have also heard blues structures or something vaguely "bluesy" in sound and feel, at least with some performers. Overall the sound was more emotional, whether the song was up-tempo or slow; beyond these imprecise indicators, quantifiers are pointless. Yet, there was then a very strong element of ballad singing in material classified as rhythm & blues because singers like Jimmy McPhail liked standards. The term conflated style and category. It reflected changes in postwar black popular music, at least according to industry ears, but also was a catchall phrase for any type of postwar black music. The details of black music definitions seemed to matter on one level, insofar as the record companies tried to define or construct black music. Yet, those same details did not matter at all on the level of category: anything and everything black became "rhythm & blues."

There were two reasons to categorize black music at all. Economically, rhythm & blues was a marketing category and a marketing strategy — its point was to sell records and to make money. Socially, it meant distinguishing, discriminating, and constructing a frame to contain African Americans and things that they do and create. The idea did not originate among African Americans. The point always bears repeating that categorization of music was just another way to categorize the human beings that made the music. Had white people accepted Africans and then African Americans and not attempted to own, control, and categorize them, the notion of "black" would be far different from what we now know. The category of black music was a setup to sell and to control. Whites in the nineteenth century created and manipulated black images ranging from subtle to the most pernicious, exaggerated stereotypes through minstrelsy and advertisements. From and through these images, whites sold ideas, racist ideals, products, and eventually music. It's another old story.

White, public interpretations and then manipulations of black images and sensibilities increased with the growth of white minstrelsy after the 1820s and black minstrelsy after about 1865, when many whites came into contact for the very first time with (stereotypical) images of African Americans or African American performers. Music became a conveyance through which entertainers and musicians, both black and white, would market "blackness," despite, or more likely because the term was concretely exclusive, but elusive in concrete meaning. It meant, in fact, different things to different groups—and it still does. The point here is not to try to define "blackness," but to understand that the concept retained salability from both black and white perspectives. "Blackness" maintains to this day a variety of cultural meanings that depend on viewpoint, period, and linguistic means of transmission. "Black," the word and the idea, over the years carried different political weight as well, as it translated African, Ethiopian, Negro, Colored, Afro-American, African American, and back to black again. Black is power, it is sublime, and it is implicative and carries the weight of historical associations. It can be wonderfully nuanced as well as forcefully direct, which made it fine company for music. Ironically, for all the disenfranchisement over the years in America, "blackness" in particular ways is cachet and cash under white circumstances.

Through entertainment especially, blackness became a means to economic enterprise during the development of capitalism in the United States as the nation industrialized during the nineteenth century. In music, blacks came to provide the labor, as entertainers and blackness became, in the entertainment world, a kind of cultural capital that held earning potential for those who could embody it. By the mid-1890s, black musicians slipped into the role of potential entrepreneurs by virtue of the economic viability of their music making and the use of that music by themselves and whites. Ragtime, after about 1896, was arguably the first African American music style to enter the popular and remunerative mainstream, in direct alliance with publishing, piano rolls, and other facets of the emerging music industry. Eventually, inevitably, a reciprocally beneficial (if, importantly, uneven) relationship developed between the popular entertainment industry in the United States and the African American composer, musician, and performer—though black composers like Shelton Brooks still had difficulty getting their material sold and performed by whites (where the money was). Despite this, by the twentieth century, popular music making was one of the few areas where white society acknowledged black adeptness and encouraged black participation, at least up to a point. At the same time, though, whites tried to copy and capitalize on black styles through the trade names they propagated: ragtime, blues, jazz, swing, rhythm & blues. Why pay the brother when you can play the other?

After Emancipation African Americans tried to capitalize on their own vernacular entertainment through minstrelsy, ragtime, blues, other forms of stage entertainment, and the public performances for whites (such as the Fisk Jubilee Singers). Though remuneration was rarely equal to what whites received, black performers obtained a limited amount of prestige and currency among whites. Black musical skills also furthered the marketing and mythologization of the black musical mind and body. It was precisely those circumstances that furthered opportunities for black musical professionals in the twentieth century, coupled with the interest that whites had in black images—sound, visual, or otherwise. These circumstances were part of a large economic sphere whereby any number of industries, from music to food, used black images to advertise and sell to whites (and much later, to blacks).

There is truly an ironic if not slightly absurd twist to this. Black vernacular images (constituting, from the dominant culture's perspective, the socially "marginal" in America) became part of an unconscious strategy to define the center or mainstream in two different and opposite ways. The more black images pervade white society, the clearer the distinctions between white and black and the wider (whiter) the divide between "us" and "them." With black as a cultural ingredient, white is that much whiter. It was Lucius Brockway's black finger-dipping that made Liberty Paints Optic White the white that was right—"If It's Optic White, It's the Right White").[6]

Yet, black images (sound or visual), in a way, eventually socialized and acculturated whites, once they could get past the stereotypes. It was acknowledged for years that white artists who performed black music — Paul Whiteman, Benny Goodman, Elvis Presley—"opened doors" for the acceptance of the black artists whose music they emulated or learned. Black images, black culture, took whites closer to black sensibilities and thus ever so slightly began to blur the distinctions between black and white in relation to the American cultural whole. The enigmatic absurdity of all this is nicely crystallized by Granda (1992: 12–13) in her telling of the origins for the Aunt Jemima image. Originally an 1890 minstrel poster of a white male in "drag" and black face, Aunt Jemima came to constitute an important advertising strategy. "Through her blackness, Aunt Jemima signified a collective sense of Whiteness" (13). Thus, white use of blackness could either blur or simultaneously make clearer lines of distinction between black and white.

Musically, in the early twentieth century, we find a similar use of blackness by seminal mainstream and popular performers such as Al Jolson (1886–1950) and Sophie Tucker (1884–1966). Both Jolson and Tucker, early in their vaudeville careers, drew on an older white minstrel tradition and flirted with blackness to varying degrees as they established their mainstream personas. Jolson wore blackface as he "played" at being a black entertainer singing, wide eyes, white lips and all, about Mammy,

Swanee, and Dixie. Tucker, whom black entertainers knew as generally benevolent, nonetheless performed blackness through her vocal style and her professional associations, especially with the T.O.B.A. circuit.[7] In her early vaudeville stage shows, for instance, she used "picks," that is, young black singers and dancers hired to round out her show (Stearns and Stearns 1968: 80). She also employed, for a period, the black songwriter Shelton Brooks, who composed a number of popular songs, including "Some of These Days"—a Tucker standard—in 1910 and "Darktown Strutter's Ball" in 1917 (Southern 1997: 351).

Al Jolson and Sophie Tucker illustrate the complex interrelationship between black, white, making music, and the attendant economic (not to mention psychological) implications. This has much less to do with black and white music per se than with the construction of blackness, marketing it, and the reciprocal effects on performers. What we discover here is a broader issue, a wide-ranging recirculation and interdependence of musical ideas between blacks and whites. Both Jolson and Tucker were accomplished stage performers and exquisite interpreters of popular song. Although there is no way to measure it, they must have had at least some influence on any number of performers who followed them, even the ones you least suspect.

Al Jolson was not a great singer, but he had the ability to put a song across in a great way that perfectly fused melody and lyrics. Despite this, in some ways, he was the antithesis of African American artistic and performance (not to mention social) ideals despite (or because) his embodiment of them on stage. Through his black persona, he became the consummate mainstream performer, the popular white ideal of twentieth-century entertainment before the rhythm & blues era. Though he established his act during the vaudeville era, he crossed over to Tin Pan Alley and film and continued to be popular through the 1940s. His influence resonated past his death. For instance, in 1917 the composer Jean Schwartz wrote a song specifically for Jolson. With lyrics by Sam M. Lewis and Joe Young, "Rock-a-Bye Your Baby (With a Dixie Melody)" was a latent minstrel ode of plantation ideals, from a white perspective. The song became one of Jolson's signature numbers. When Jolson sang the song, he often improvised lyrics, sometimes spoken, to include references to Old Black Joe, a character from nineteenth-century minstrel songs.

During the last half of the nineteenth century, and early into the twentieth, it was common for black artists to perform and record minstrel and "coon songs." Black composers like Ernest Hogan wrote some of those songs. Involvement by blacks was not necessarily an endorsement of the sentiments of the song, as some black artists would "double voice" and change lyrics and attitudes to fit a black perspective, depending on the audience. Yet, those songs and their original sentiments crept further into the twentieth century and into the consciousness of America. Jolson's song spawned other interpretations years later, from Judy Garland to Wayne Newton and Connie Francis. The Supremes, Aretha Franklin, and Sonny Rollins also recorded the song. When later performers interpreted it, they certainly had a choice over material, but the song had long ago entered the mainstream. Whether black artists realized the deeper implications of the song, we do not know. The material, though, clearly had an impact on another generation of singers after Jolson, including African Americans. Aretha Franklin once performed the song on a mid-1960s television program called *Shindig*, a show that always seemed to feature a predominantly white, teenage audience.[8] She played piano and gave the song a rocking, soulful, gospel turn. Was it ironic? Perhaps, but only in that Franklin most likely did not give thought to the racial politics of the song (as we might today). Why should she have? The point was that the song was mainstream and open to musical interpretation. She could sing almost anything, make it sound great, and make it her own, completely turning the minstrelsy around, if not correcting the references. She also made her material sound "black," and one selling point of Aretha Franklin to white (and black) audiences was the "blackness" in voice, that is, her powerful, gospel-like interpretations. The original selling point of "Rock-a-Bye" was the meeting of blackness and mainstream, through Al Jolson and what he had put into the song with his contrived black stage persona.

These kinds of interchanges—for they were more than just intersections—have varied over the decades, and both blacks and whites have been part of the process. They ranged from the "theft" of black style on the part of whites on the one extreme, to "covers," emulation, or genuine interest on the other. They also include "selling out" on the part of blacks (at least some might call it that). Aretha Franklin poses a challenge to interpretation. Did she sell out because she performed a minstrel song on a white television program? Or did she demonstrate her poise and integrity because she did a gospel interpretation of a minstrel song despite—or because of—the white audience?

Whatever the answers are to these questions, behind these musical exchanges are two economic motives. Whites "blackened up" their performances, at first literally, then stylistically to add an element of exoticism to them and because they realized that blackness "sold" as well as rocked. African American performers also realized that blackness sold. They also "mainstreamed" (you could say toned down) or otherwise altered their performances or material selection in part to cross over into a more economically viable (white) market and meet audience expectations. You could argue that Aretha Franklin did that perfectly with "Rock-a-Bye," where she performed "black" enough to meet white expectations, but picked a mainstream song so as not to scare people. Economics and exoticism are not the only reasons for the confluence of black and white, but these in particular are deliberate and conscious strategies.[9]

Historically, whites who learned black music, or may have mocked it at one time through minstrelsy, did so not out of necessity (unless you consider the deep, psychological pathology of white minstrelsy necessary). Slaves though, needed to learn aspects of their captors' culture in order to survive. The whole dynamic of "struggle" has fed the energy and stamina of black styles. Put simply, if whites "acted" black it was because they wanted to. If blacks "acted" white, or acted in any particular manner toward whites, it was because under innumerable circumstances they had to, and that became one of the defining aspects of African American culture.

The dynamic of whites flirting with color began in the nineteenth century, was pervasive in popular culture by the end of the 1920s, and continued through the 1950s and beyond. The 1920s through the 1950s gave us the Three Kings, Whiteman, Goodman, and Elvis. These performers internalized blackness to varying degrees and played their interpretations of black music for the white public. While earlier white minstrel players and later vaudeville performers like Jolson maintained only a superficial connection to black music, Whiteman, Goodman, and Presley played the music with no resort to the vulgar mask that Jolson wore. Paul Whiteman was the self-proclaimed "King of Jazz" and said he made a "lady" out of it, implying that jazz was a whore before he came along. Benny Goodman became the "King of Swing" by 1935, and then came Elvis Presley, the "King of Rock 'n' Roll."[10]

Because it served to blur the distinction between mainstream and marginal, even as it reinforced that distinction, "blackness" became a deliberate and constructed category, albeit often rife with contradictions. African Americans worked to establish a professional class of entertainers toward the end of the nineteenth and into the twentieth centuries. The record industry after 1920 fueled the business of making black music, by both African American and white performers. Black music contributed powerfully to the growth of that industry, to the whole entertainment industry, in fact, through ragtime, blues, and jazz, black sound and visual images, were broadcast and popularized on records, over the radio, and through film and television.

White America's palpable ambivalence toward black culture crystallizes this contradiction. On the one hand, there seemed to be an interest, sometimes fascination, with the exoticism of blackness. On the other hand, antipathy and fear of black America was evident in what reactionaries wrote (and what the mainstream may have felt).[11] Conservative white America's biggest fear was race mixing and miscegenation—the great white wail about the black "race," a concept it invented in the first place! Yet, white society bought (and buys) deeply into blackness through the very culture it criticized (and criticizes). This occurred through ragtime, jazz, swing, rhythm & blues/rock 'n' roll, and assorted pop artists and other consumer/consumable products—not the least being rap and hip-hop's culture of posture, attitude, clothes, and shoes in the 1990s.

Black music, even in its variety, helped define essential aspects of mainstream American popular culture. It also served as a frame through which all Americans viewed themselves, each other, and the world, and in particular, a frame through which African Americans viewed themselves and society around them. The singers of group harmony recognized the popularity and possibility of black music in the context of white society. They also inevitably would have grasped the interrelationship between black and white music, between, say, mainstream, standards, and the blues. Vocal groups like the Ravens and jazz performers made that last relationship—between standards and blues—clearly heard if not always entirely understood.

The popularity of black music, as it manifested on the radio, in the form of records and recording stars, and through film, contributed something important to black society as a whole. This was what an earlier generation called "race consciousness" and "race pride." Eileen Southern, writing about black concert artists, states that they were "race symbols, whose successes were shared vicariously by the great mass of black Americans that could never hope to attain similar distinction" (Southern 1997: 408–9). What was true for some during the Harlem Renaissance a later generation shared, only by then young people were able to think they could attain the success of others, especially in the realm of popular culture. There was always, in a word, possibility.

By the 1940s, young black singers looked to the success of older black performers and figured out that there were things they could do to also be successful. Established performers served as good entrepreneurial role models to follow for anyone looking to enter the American mainstream.

Group singing was one entrée into at least the potential for music and free market enterprise. Underwriting the development of postwar group harmony was the potential for two parties to seize that entrepreneurial moment and assume the risk and responsibility to manage the enterprise of making black music. There were the singers themselves, and then there was an assorted group of local and long distance businessmen and women, managers, agents, and record people of the period.[12]

With this in mind, let us return to Jesse Stone. "Everybody," referring to vocalists, "that was in the business seemed to be in there not for the money, but for the enjoyment of doing it, you know. They liked what they were doing and they enjoyed rehearsing as much as they did working in, you know, up on the stage in front of people."

At first glance, perhaps, they were not in it for the money. But in the details, we understand a little more deeply the intricacies of "making it" in music. "They were young kids and they just, they were enjoying themselves. Most of them, those groups that I had, they weren't dependent upon those groups for a living. They were shining shoes, in parlors, you know, waiting tables, washing dishes. They did a lot of other jobs, you know."

Stone said that when he got to them, "They didn't know anything, and they had been as singing, you know, passing the hat on the street sometime or something like that. And they thought that they were moving up into the business, you know, going up a step higher than where they had been. Some of the guys who worked in a shoeshine parlor they used to sing while they were shining shoes, you know. And the people would give them a little extra tip or something like that. That was their approach up until they were contacted by somebody from Atlantic Records or some other record company. Then they were willing to do whatever they were told, you know."

Stone supports the assertion that these youngsters had, at the very least, a healthy work ethic and were good at finding jobs. He also maintains that young singers had little if any business savvy and put their fate in the hands of others, like him. Yet, in spite of his assertion about the kids being there "not for the money," his suggestion that they were indeed thinking about "moving up into the business" is revealing. He also substantiates that people would give money to the singers—certainly a strong incentive to think about the relationship between singing and making money.

When Stone contends that the singers "left it all" up to him about what material to sing, he articulates the attitude of a real industry insider. But that did not necessarily mean he was in complete control because from the perspective of young recording artists, "willing to do whatever" you are told is just as good a strategy for success as any, given the circumstances.

What were they supposed to do, tell *him* what to do? A group that acquiesced to the type of sound a record company wanted it to have provides a good example of ambiguity at least, if not something more revealing. Who is "in charge" remains arguable, simply because the singers often did what they wanted to do, or what they *had* to do to get where they needed to go, at least in the short run. That most often meant listening to what music professionals told them. Thus, the other side to Jesse Stone's narrative is the less-acknowledged business savvy that some groups did demonstrate. Although vocalists rarely if ever got rich from singing, you cannot fault them for trying. Many of these kids thought the right thing to do was to find a manager or, if found by one, listen to what he or she told them. Often older musicians would offer advice, not specific musical advice necessarily, but business strategies. Vocal talent was always abundant, but the groups who succeeded knew or quickly learned what to do with that talent. Herman Denby and the Swallows listened initially to older voices—musical and otherwise. This brings us back to the subject of standards and material selection, which was as much a business decision as a stylistic one.

"But see, we were around older musicians and they taught us. You know, 'learn everything. Learn everything.' You know like, at that time they were called standards. You know, 'learn them.' It was a good thing we took that advice because when the Swallows first started singing—you probably won't believe this, but the first thing I sang was country and western songs. I used to imitate people. I could do that when I was very young. I used to imitate people, you know. And our manager, the jobs that he got us, were in white clubs. And when we found this out at first we said, 'What are we going to do there?' "

The Swallows, however, learned suitable material and took the steps necessary to keep working. "And that happened before we did black clubs. We did that before we did black clubs. We went along with it because you don't know what kind of job you going to get. And wherever you are, be able to work. See, that's what we were taught. Be able to work."

It made for sound business practice. "At the time we didn't particularly care for it. We saw, we saw the logic in it, you know. And we wanted to sing. You know. We wanted to sing. So we really accepted it. And then later we saw the benefits from it. Like, like we did the tune that did fairly well, 'Tell Me Why.' No black group was singing that song. Blacks weren't singing that, you know. 'Come On a My House,' I used to sing that. In fact I used to sing that song and it did so well in the clubs somebody, I think, I can't remember what record company she was recording for then, but I met Rosemary Clooney. They brought her to the club to hear me do that song. I sang it after she recorded it, but I was doing it so well, this record executive got her and brought her to the club to hear me do it. You know. And she, and she had to laugh. It was a popular song, and like I say, with the flair that I had for imitating people like that, and I used to sing it with the, with the, Caribbean accent, you know. And it went over big. That's when I met her. And we were a good group. The Swallows was a good group. What you hear on the records is not just what we did. You know? We did, we did all types of things."[13]

The manager of the Swallows was Irv Goldstick. "He heard us one night and he said, 'Come up and see me.' He had a record shop on the corner of North Avenue and Druid Hill Avenue, and he had told us to come up see him and that's how that started."

Herman laughed at the irony. "And we started working these clubs, and when he [Goldstick] found out that I could sing country and western songs, [he said] 'Do that,' you know. And I mean, I was called all kinds of names, you know what I mean. And at the same time people would come up and give us money to sing the same song again."

Herman's experience and his recollection speak the enigma of African American life, the public life. White folks called him all kinds of names and yet they went up and paid him to sing some more.

It is clear from the singers that many groups wished to move beyond amateur status and make some money, for it was quite simply one function of making popular music. It is that inevitable drive toward economic spheres, toward professional or semi-professional status. Eventually for some, that drive points toward producing your own material and maintaining control over your own artistic trajectory—in a word, success (which for many of us is just another word for control). And here is the catch in which African American performers found themselves: by playing their musical hand, so to speak, young black males played into social channeling and stereotype. By accepting the standards of the popular music industry, that is, doing what was necessary to succeed and move beyond a niche or "black" category, singers confronted the "selling-out" stereotype or the "not sounding black enough stereotype." This was not a new problem. Nevertheless, vocal groups had little to lose and much to gain through singing and through trying to do things—pay attention to style or material, for instance—in order to succeed. This was not necessarily an imperative with all groups, but certainly with many, and their strategies for success were all very similar.

Groups worked toward a good sound, either a completely original sound or, more likely, a sound that would remind listeners of an already popular one. They tried to have an appealing look, the right material, a good manager, and venues at which to perform. Beyond the strategies for the right sound, singing became a strategy itself. Singing was a means to gain access to the mainstream, the center, what America was supposed to offer. The mainstream, as a point of view, surely is one of the goals of assimilation. It is also part of where all in the popular music industry look for remuneration and acceptance (authentication). Mainstream appeal sold records, and that is precisely the point of the popular music business—popular acceptance, success, and record sales. Though a particular style or category of music begins on the marginal fringe, the eventual destination becomes the center, through one means or another. The whole phenomenon of rhythm & blues constituted two points of view that were both a part of, and apart from, this mainstream.

Rhythm & blues as a category began as a niche market for music initially aimed at "black taste." This was not at all a precisely defined concept, an essentialist one in fact, but one the record industry advertised and aimed for nonetheless. It was also a market to which white youth could and did travel, in the manner of earlier generations. They did so to flirt with the difference, hazards, or exoticism of blackness, of dance, and of sexually edgy themes (e.g., Wynonie Harris's 1947 "Good Rockin' Tonight," later covered by Elvis Presley, and other songs like Billy Ward's "Sixty Minute Man," 1951). This movement was part of the mainstreaming process. It was almost as if rhythm & blues as a musical racial category was also a social space through which one could move in two opposite directions at once—away from as well as toward the center or mainstream.

Vocal harmony repertoire expressed a related duality, almost certainly an intentional one. Most of the vocal groups by the early 1950s maintained a mix of pop ballads and blues-based or jump novelty tunes. The Ravens established a kind of paradigm by peppering their mostly pop song list with an occasional blues number. They recorded "Write me a Letter," which happens to be an outstanding boogie blues performance, alongside material like the "The House I Live In" (unworldly patriotic) and novelty songs like the Yiddish "Mahzel."

"You got to have a little mahzel, because mahzel means good luck, and if you have some mahzel, you'll never never ever get stuck."

The Ravens also recorded, probably in the spirit of Paul Robeson, "Old Man River," and songs like "No More Kisses for Baby," with its jive-spoken introduction. Pianist Howard Biggs wrote many of the Ravens arrangements from the period 1947–1950, when the group recorded for National.

Although slightly formulaic, they were snappy, well conceived, and marvelously executed. On the business side, their style and mix of material was varied just enough to give them a broad, mainstream, crossover appeal.

Just as the Ravens looked to earlier successful groups—the Ink Spots, Mills Brothers, and Delta Rhythm Boys—vocal groups that came along afterward looked also to appeal to a market as broad as possible, in the spirit of mainstream pop, and as narrow as possible, in the spirit of a black rhythm & blues, vernacular sound. In almost all instances, groups combined musical approaches to one degree or another in order to expand their potential. The result from all of this was a range of related styles that makes rhythm & blues quixotic and has deeply resonant social implications. Harold Winley, the bass voice for Clovers, mused about the "Greatest Group of Them All," as the Ravens were known: "Too black to be white; too white to be black."

It is an observation that analyzes more than the music, for it reminds us of the starkness, the social realism of racial categories in the first place.

The Ravens and some other groups were particularly good at maintaining a stylistic middle ground. Despite a varied repertoire that alternated between, say, blues and standard ballads, their performance personas were strong enough and consistent enough to tie the material together in a stylistic unity. Some other, less successful groups simply dichotomized their repertoires in an extreme manner. One example can illustrate this point.

A relatively obscure group from Washington, D.C., the Cap-Tans grew out of another Washington group, the Buddies. For a period in the 1950s, they recorded for Lillian Claiborne, who also managed them. The group recorded two songs in particular, "Goodnight Mother" and "Feel like Ballin' Some More," around the same period.[14] They performed the former in a sweet Ink Spots style, complete with a talking chorus and a patented Mills Brothers guitar introduction. The feel also reflected lead singer Harmon Bethea's earlier experience with the Progressive Four, a gospel quartet. The performance is a quiet and reflective lullaby, where the term "mother" is also a substitute for "wife."

On the other hand, "Feel like Ballin' Some More" was an up-tempo jump shuffle that musically mirrored the title. This time the lead switched to Sherman Buckner, who had a higher and lighter voice than Harmon Bethea, and the group added a full rhythm section with horn accompaniment. This is a hard-driving jump number with a reverse call-and-response structure. Its structure, ironically, was the Tin Pan Alley 32-bar, AABA form, utilizing the venerable "rhythm changes."[15] In the A section of the song the background singers are answered by the lead voice and the whole group sings the one-line refrain (which is the title).

The Cap-Tans in their contradictory performances illustrate how groups dichotomized their repertoire to vary it, to appeal to trends in black popular music, to mix pop material with novelty numbers, and to draw on an old pattern of offering suggestive and sexual material in song. The latter topic is widely covered in blues and folk music histories and was understood keenly by the historian Lawrence Levine (1977). The sexual innuendo of African American expressive culture was, if not appreciated by, certainly capitalized on by the white-controlled record industry that encouraged the production of such material.[16] At the same time they found it objectionable and tried to "clean it up" in white cover versions.

The whole notion of a rhythm & blues category, as it originally emerged, was as contradictory as the Cap-Tans' song repertoire seemed. The concept went in two directions at once. The designation replaced "race" as a catchall term for black popular music (you might also find "sepia" used occasionally in the late 1940s), but it also described a new sound, reflecting the movement in black popular music away from "swing" in the late 1940s. Any way you say it, "rhythm & blues" was racially delimiting. There were no white rhythm & blues artists at the time, just as earlier there were no white race artists. Rhythm & blues was similar to other terms meant to segregate, separate, and displace, in this case black music and musicians away from the "pop" (white) category.

At the same time by virtue of being popular music, that is, commercial, the aim of rhythm & blues was to sell and to cross over, if possible. That was how the industry increased appeal, sales, and profits, through crossover appeal. Crossover simply means you expand your base and reach a larger, wider (whiter, in this case) mainstream audience that usually translates into more record sales. Group harmony singers held out the possibility of escaping and assimilating into that very same mainstream, thus increasing the potential for a group to make money. One point to the whole "rhythm & blues" marketing category was to sell. The ever-present hope for so many singers (and the record people, if recording was involved) was that they could convince someone beyond a narrow, exclusive category to make a purchase. Thus, rhythm & blues was a strategy as well. Rhythm & blues was commercial music and really, that was the whole point of the concept to begin with, social precedent of separatism aside. To profit you must sell, to sell you must market, to market you must categorize, and to do that you must first define and name what it is you have to begin with.

Jerry Wexler, who came up with the term rhythm & blues, joined Atlantic Records as a partner around 1953. He was a forceful promoter and producer for the next twenty years. Wexler was down to earth and direct about making commercial music. Oddly—or maybe not so oddly—

his sentiments worked well with black performers who would do whatever it took to put a song across—all, in a sense, were entrepreneurs. Wexler, unintentionally, but honestly here, personifies the American popular music industry, in a typically (for New York) cynical flavor. According to him, the taste and flavor of popular music remains inseparable from its commercial viability.

> I dug cross-cultural collaborations and craved commercial success, which is maybe why Ahmet and I got along so well . . . we lusted for hits. Hits were the cash flow, the lifeblood, the heavenly ichor—the wherewithal of survival. While we couldn't divorce ourselves from our tastes and inclinations, neither could we deny our interest in income.
>
> Consequently, the term "commercial" was not a pejorative for me . . . If "commercial" meant a song with a strong hook, an inviting refrain, melodic variety, and rhythm pattern with a walloping bass line—well, give me commercial and lots of it. The merry jingle of cash registers was music to my ears. (Wexler and Ritz 1993: 91)

By the early 1950s, "rhythm & blues" started to become a more discernible style and not just a strict marketing category for black musicians. It also became more commercially viable, thanks in part to record people like Jerry Wexler, Jesse Stone, and groups like the Clovers. This transformation, not coincidentally, began as white consumers began to understand the music and white musicians—Bill Haley, Elvis, et al.—started to learn and record it.

Vocal harmony records in particular moved away from some of the pop ballad interpretations of the late 1940s, and by 1953 a more assertive, danceable sound prevailed. Ballad singing never went away, but the performances certainly took on a more emotional quality with many of the younger groups.

What emerges in the story of young black vocal groups is that they worked at their music making with the business side of it in mind. At the root of this lies the history of the commercialization of black music and the impetus behind "black sells" in this society. Overall, there was an entrepreneurial attitude about rhythm & blues, from the perspective of those singing as well as those helping to produce or finance the music.

There was a range, however, of singer participation in the business of making music, from grassroots amateur to semi-professional and professional. Some singers effected an easy transition between music as an avocation and music as a vocation. Others did not. Most often, there was not a clear distinction between singing "for a living" and singing for the fun of it, for recreation. Singing, as we have seen, for many participants was more than just something to do. It was a way to go through life, but that did not always mean you worked at it as a job all of the time. The earning possibilities were always there. However, as anyone will tell you, it was difficult to earn a living making music. That does not mean you could not, would not try. The interest in money was always there, if not from the singers initially, then from other interested parties. Some of those other interested parties turned out to be neighbors, of sorts. The relationships forged between singers and their groups, and the businesses around them, well expressed more of the entrepreneurial aspect of rhythm & blues group harmony. The larger picture, once again, shows us how hard people worked, not only to make the music, but to maintain families. One of the primary reasons for black families to move from rural areas to cities like Baltimore and Washington was the promise of jobs, and a strong work ethic obtained in most families. Men and women needed to work, and that impetus resulted in a shared dynamic that developed between young singers, local businesses, employers, and the surrounding community.

Work, Jobs, Businesses

Men of Ernest Warren's generation (he was born in 1929), as they grew up, found that at a certain point they had to begin earning a living. Child and adult in those days did not yet have the in-between liminal space of "teenager." By the time some of these guys were in their early twenties, they already had families. If it were not to be in music, then work would have to be at something else. Often those spheres intersected, overlapped, and most men, like Ernest, had strong work values that carried over from one realm to the other. Ernest explains: "See, we never was without work. Whenever we came back to this town right here, if we didn't have no bookings or whatever, we had jobs that we could go back to and work.

"I was an elevator boy at that particular time. And then, I had two guys working in the same place. They worked at Epstein's, but when I went in the army and came out they were working at Capitol Records distribution over on Madison Avenue, and one still worked at Super Music.

"We went away on a tour for six months and come back we had our same jobs. Yeah, we worked. We always worked."

Ernest was unapologetic about what he had to do in postwar Baltimore. "I was an elevator boy. No sales at that particular time, they had special sales people and that was a predominantly white store. And they started hiring blacks, but I was an elevator boy—a good elevator boy—me and a friend of mine; my wife's sister's husband. But we always worked. Always worked. If we did a tour for six months and came back, we never walked the street."

Ernest said that the people at Epstein's Department Store where he worked knew about his music. "They knew. They knew, because see, like, I worked across the street from Super Music and one of them worked for Super Music. He had a loudspeaker outside his store and they used to play our records hundreds of times a day.

"And when time come for us to go we would, you know, we was good workers and we wasn't no bums and they let us go and come back. If you can make it, make it. If you can't make it, come on back to work."

Ernest touches on a variation of what is no doubt a very old story for many mid- and late twentieth-century musicians. It is the need to work, to make some money, to support yourself, your family, or your music. The flow between day job and music job rings as true in the 1940s and 1950s as it might today.

"Everybody knew us in this town and they never knew that we didn't have a job, whether we were singing or not. You know, so it was no big thing or embarrassment or they wasn't surprised, you know it was like, 'Them guys always work.' You know.

"One thing I can tell you in 1955, believe it or not, there were thirty-three babies between five of us, so, we had to work. You know, because if we hadn't of worked you know where we would've been, been over there with the city people" (the 1950s version of welfare).

"So we worked and did what we were supposed to do, moving here and moving there. It was a hard life, but I enjoyed it.

"We were doing, we were doing all right for being young guys. You know. Nobody never got in trouble. They took care of their obligations. Everybody did what they were supposed to do in this group."

Johnny Page, who sang with the Marylanders and the Stylists, also maintained a day job at a place where the owner let Page work around his music career.

"I was working for the Calvert Rug and Linoleum Company. I was a porter, part-time salesman."

Sam Ross was Johnny's boss. "This Jewish guy, but he was a very good friend of mine. He was the manager of the store at the time and he encouraged me. He let me take time off to go to my shows and everything."

Not all employers let singers come and go as they pleased. Buddy Slaughter, of Washington, says, "Job off and on, trying to sing. You know. I was government, and I lost that by traveling. I went about it the wrong way, I didn't take a leave of absence, like the rest of them did, you know. I was too anxious. I went about it the wrong way. And I was working private industry and back into the government, and oh it was something."

The Four Bars of Rhythm were a Washington group. At the time they were active, from the mid-1950s through the mid-1960s, Alphonso Feemster worked day jobs. One was at Morton's Department Store (Seventh and D, Northwest), in the warehouse and shipping department. Morton's was one of the Washington businesses that sponsored a radio talent program. Feemster also worked at the Navy Department and then the Commerce Department. The other singers also worked near Morton's.

"All the while now I'm singing, still singing, working day job at Morton's, right. Eddie Day worked at an old mattress factory around the corner from Morton's. Melvin worked in there with him. We were all in the same area.

"Perry [Van Perry, their manager] and Eddie. They some kind of way got to Jerry Blaine was the guy's, the president's name, of Jubilee Records. And they invited us up. Took off from work, stayed a whole week."

Did they mind over at Morton's?

"No. Told them what I was doing; they encouraged it. And we went up, and of course we had to perform for them and then Jerry said O.K., I'll sign you to a contract. And he gave us a date and everything, we had to go back, and that's when he got Sid Bass and got his orchestra together for us, and got us studio time."

The thread of these narratives is that many of the singers had strong work ethics that carried over into music and then back again to day jobs. They tried to work as musicians, that is perform, whenever and wherever they could, like all good artists.

Jimmy McPhail of the Armstrong Four said, "We did a lot of things, though. There was a fellow lived in Alexandria, used to come and pick us up and take us to his—they had a clubhouse over there—and he would take us, oh, maybe every other weekend or something and give us five dollars—not apiece, the group! He used to take us over there and bring us back. It was something. It was a private club. See, in Alexandria you didn't have nightclubs as such, and especially they weren't integrated. And they had this particular club [the Departmental Club, a black social club], and this is where we would go to entertain their members and things."

Like McPhail, Alphonso Feemster explains how connections helped get his group work—somebody knows someone who knows somebody else. Youngsters *worked* at getting music work.

"A girl that I went to Langley [Junior High] with knew I sang a lot. Her brother was interested on forming a group. Her brother's name was

Alfred Jackson. He's worked a lot in this metropolitan area, too, as a single and with groups. So she in turn gave him my telephone number. He called me one night and said, 'Hey, I want to start a group called the Velveteers,' and we got together and started working, working with those guys. And they come out of Northeast, over on Collins Street, Northeast . . . all of them in the Northeast area. And I was the only one from Southeast area. So I started with them, and he had to come and ask my mother for permission, because I was a baby. I was young. They were all older than I was.

"We did all the latest stuff that come over the radio, and we did some original things that Alfred would write. He did most of the writing. Some of the things I can't even remember now, but we never really made any records with that group because by that time Eddie and Melvin come out of the service, and they were looking to form a group.

"We just sang on the corner. And we worked at some old road club down not too far from the area where they lived at. And we never really did anything big, you know, with that group. But we sang a lot and, you know, sounded pretty good." Later, Alphonso sang with the Four Bars.

George Jackson remembered working at a shoe store with a friend, another singer, in Baltimore. "It was me and another fellow."

His name was Ralph Bickers. It sounds like George and Ralph established a quid pro quo with a local shoe store—they "advertised" the store's name, by using it as the group's name, in exchange for free shoes.

"He's deceased now, but we had a duet, me and him were singing duet. Just two of us. The Manchesters. Manchesters, after this shoe store that was on Hal Street during the time. And they supplied all our shoes free. I was willing to try anything, you know."

The initiatives young black males took to make music, combined with serendipity, were an elegant extension of other aspects of their lives. There was much in the way of flow here, between home, family, church, street, school, neighborhood, and the city at large—life's lattice. Likewise, the entrepreneurial imperatives of group harmony were inseparable from (and occasionally integral to) the business activities around town, especially in the black business districts. These were areas of enterprise, economics, and interaction. They were territories made necessary by segregation. They were zones of possibility and profit for black-owned businesses. They were zones of profit and possibility for black citizens who worked there. They were also areas where white-owned businesses profited, and also provided jobs, services, credit, and products of every sort to black citizens hemmed in there. It was at best an uneasy set of circumstances.

The Four Bars of Rhythm. "Armstrong Grads—The Four Bars of Rhythm, a group that is developing as a headliner, are all graduates of Armstrong High School. They have cut on records an original composition called 'Wish You Were Near' and 'Daddy, Cool Breeze.' Perry Sprigs, employed at the recorder of deed office manages them. In rear, from left, are Eddie Day and Alphonso Feemster; in front, from left, are Francis Henry and Melvin Butler." Photo dated January 30, 1954; courtesy of the Afro-American Newspapers.

Well-known white-owned establishments in Washington—Morton's Department Store, Quality Music, Super Cut-Rate Drugs, among others— sponsored and encouraged not only singers, who sometimes were their employees, but black music and entertainment also. These businesses were located in black business districts and had a black clientele. They helped promote music through radio programs and amateur shows. And as the guys above pointed out, their employers would let them come and go; they encouraged their careers in that way.

On the one hand, one could argue that white-owned businesses brought essential goods and services into segregated black neighborhoods. On the other hand, one could also argue that the system that made neces- sary segregation in the first place—racism—also prevented the flourishing of black capitalism and businesses. Under those circumstances for the white businesses—and this extends to most in the popular music busi- ness—there was never any clear boundary between fortuitous geography (for whites), stark, racialized necessity, sound business practice, self-inter- est, selfless good will, and even paternalism. It was not just one simple dynamic.

> We took care of the people, you know, we were their friends. It wasn't the typical white man taking their money and running. (Alan J. Bloom, on Super Cut-Rate Drugs)

Although the white-owned businesses had their specific roles there, the black districts were also fundamental zones of enterprise for black-owned businesses that served the needs of black consumers. Citizens were protec- tive of that, too, and no doubt wished to preserve the economic viability and aesthetics of black-on-black business, even while civic groups worked to eliminate Jim Crow in Washington. Published directories from the 1940s helped guide black consumers to black businesses. James T. Terry published the "Metro Glossary Business—Professional and Service Direc- tory" in 1947. The two-dozen page pamphlet grew to 130 pages for the 1948 edition and became the "Dee Cee Directory." It sold for a dollar.

The Baker Handbook was similar to the Dee Cee Directory. James H. Baker, of Baker Associates, a public relations firm in Washington, compiled and published it in 1947. The purpose of these directories was clearly to advocate and (in a somewhat understated manner) to urge black con- sumers to patronize black small businesses, and thus to help the growth of a black business class. The Baker Handbook points out, with no commen- tary, that a full one third of Washington's citizens (in 1947) were black.

Such a fact and its implications tug at the long-held belief that African American consumer power can be potent economic as well as political power. Black businesses and services in black neighborhoods were almost exclusively for their own citizens. Then, of course, white businesses situated themselves there also. That whites occasionally sought out black entertainment and traveled in those areas was not an issue. Blacks, however, could never travel the other way, into white entertainment or business areas. One-way was what Jim Crow was all about.

The very general sentiments of black Washington held that, as Lawrence Berry said, "You had everything you wanted" in the black neighborhoods. "We were comfortable with what we had." Yet, no one except perhaps whites took comfort in segregation as either theory or practice. Activists on the one hand tested discrimination, but there were also those who clearly were protectionists—it would be a stretch to call them separatists. They worked to promote and preserve black-to-black enterprise within the larger, white-dominated capitalist system. There was no contradiction in these two circumstances either, but rather a mix of (one could also say tension between) old-fashioned African American practicality and principle. The development of a strong black business class, supported by black consumers (not necessarily to the exclusion of white ones), was part of the self-sufficiency ideal articulated by Booker T. Washington and much debated by others. Whether folks really wanted to go into white establishments was not the point, but rather whether they *could* go. The point was freedom of movement, obviously, when, for instance, whites frequented the Howard Theater to see black talent, ad libitum, but blacks could not even come close to entering "white" Washington's downtown theaters or restaurants.

Black neighborhoods in Baltimore and Washington varied in degrees of care and comfort, prosperity and poverty. Nevertheless, they remained extraordinary places where businesses of all types provided a living framework along with home, church, and school, around which music making occurred. Until the 1968 riots, 14th and U Street and 7th and T Street Northwest were two centers of commerce and social life for much of black Washington.

In Baltimore, the Pennsylvania Avenue business zone served the black communities and those whites who wanted to visit the clubs and theaters there, like the Royal Theater, through the 1950s. This area went into decline during the 1960s as residents fled the urban core. Another, smaller entertainment district, known informally as the Block, centered on East Baltimore Street and went into a "seedy" decline by the 1950s (Nast et al. 1982: 265). These were not the only areas, but the largest, most concentrated, and certainly the best known. It was entertainment and culture, but it was also about business. Buddy Bailey, though from Washington, remembered The Avenue in Baltimore.

"Well, Pennsylvania Avenue was like a showcase. This was the end, you know, the living end, and everybody who was anybody wanted to go to Pennsylvania Avenue. Pennsylvania Avenue in Baltimore was clubs, night life."

Nearly every city and town in America where there is an African American population has or has had that one area, avenue, street, or section where you could find black entertainment. In Washington the U Street corridor, constituted the premier black commercial district centering on 14th and U Streets, Northwest, through the 1960s. U Street catered to an established black clientele, as opposed to the Seventh Street area, which was the "soul street bustling with southern rural immigrants" (Fitzpatrick and Goodwin 1990: 177).

Buddy Bailey recalled, "Yes, well here we had U Street, right along that corridor between Georgia Avenue and Sixteenth Street. It was full of clubs and lounges. I remembered the [Club] Caverns, Eleventh and U. You went down, it's like a cavern, you know, you go down the cellar, and they had all these crystals, shingles, or whatever you call it, like in a cave. It was real pretty. And they had shows there."

After the Show

V I S I T ! ! !

CLUB CAVERNS

U Street at Eleventh

"The Rendezvous of Washington's Socially Elite"

WINE—DINE—DANCE

A Private Club—Members Only—Be a Guest

Become a Member

Brownie Combs   **Alonzo J. Collins**

(advertisement, 1948 Dee Cee Directory, 97)

You could find some of the best-known postwar black clubs along or around the U Street corridor. The Republic Gardens, at 1355 U Street, had "floor shows" on Friday, Saturday, and Sunday. Club Bali was actually at 1901 Fourteenth Street, around the corner from "You" Street, as it often appeared in print. There were also small places down along Seventh Street, like the Old Rose Social Club, near T Street, around the corner from the Howard Theater.

Buddy Bailey remembered, "Black clubs, yeah. 'Sepia,' they call it. The hot shows, you know, and this, the dances, the whole bit. Of course, we had lots of white fans that would come there to catch the shows. You know real music lovers never cared about the complexion. They went for the music."

"Real music lovers," indeed, never cared about complexion. In segregated Washington at the time, white patrons would visit the black clubs (just as they did in other cities). The system, however, did not work the other way around, real music lover or not. Black groups that specialized in standard material, however, would perform in white clubs, like the Blue Mirror downtown. During the war years and afterward, many of the white clubs were out on Connecticut Avenue. Note that when Buddy mentions Connecticut Avenue, he states he "read" about the clubs there. Folks would refer to U Street as "the black Connecticut Avenue" (Fitzpatrick and Goodwin 1990: 177), indicating its social status.

"And I would read about Connecticut Avenue. I can't think of the name of those clubs now, but they had a corridor along there, had some very famous—Stan Kenton and people like that. They had the big white groups, bands. Washington was a, it was a great show town during the '40s. Yeah. Between 1940 and I would say '55."

Tex Gathings was one of the first black disc jockeys in Washington. He started in 1946 as a "Sunday morning part-timer," with WOOK. Gathings had a keen sense of place, what he called the "geographic thing" that he maps for us. "The geographic thing—1836 Seventh Street, Northwest and the 1832, I can picture it clearly. Across the street directly, the barber shop. Next to that physically was a very popular photographic studio. On the corner is Gene Clore's Restaurant. On the corner on the same side as Max Silverman's, the very famous, or infamous, Old Rose Social Club, which was an after-hours joint on the second floor. Around the corner on 7th Street, there's the old theater, the other movie theater. On the south side of the street was Miss Mattie's Restaurant, the poolroom, then the Howard Theater, which is at the corner of Seventh and Wiltberger.

"Across the Wiltberger Street was the Stage Door which was owned by a man named Herb Saunders, his son and I were very very dear friends for many years. Behind that immediately was the All Sports Club, which was originally owned by a black aviator of World War One, Two fame. That became Joe Hurd's All Sports Club, which was operated by his wife May after Joe died. All of the latter three, the Old Rose, the All Sports Club, in addition to Lindsey's and 652 Newton, were *the* after-hour places in Washington, plus the Bohemian Caverns where the majority of black music, per se, really developed. It wasn't at the stage of the Howard as much as it was in places like this. Six fifty-two Newton, Billy Simpson, Lindsey's—Charles Lindsey—the Old Rose Social Club, Herb Saunders, where you could have music, entertainment, from eight, nine o'clock at night until the sun came up in the morning. These were the places that were wonderful in terms of the music and the interactions."

Harold Winley of the Clovers also remembered the Old Rose, from the same neighborhood where the group would hang out. The place was full of what today a businessman might call synergy, and the Clovers used it for their own aspirations.

"Things started happening, you know. We went by the Old Rose, Seventh and T Street, an after-hour club from the '30s, '20 and '30s. The best I can understand it; I know it was the '30s. That was owned by Herbert Saunders, who owned the Stage Door, who built the Stage Door, that building right across from the Howard Theater right now. He built that, and Buddy and them had been up there before. And this is a club where all the great entertainers used to go, after their shows. The people I met there, man. Unbelievable. I met Louis Armstrong there. Louis and Lil Armstrong. I met Wynonie Harris there. Earl Bostic. The Ravens. You name them.

"It was a beautiful, long room. And they never had no trouble in there. We used to go up there and say, hey, that's nice. We ended up being the janitors. Mac was given a job as a janitor there. We all helped clean up. And with everything, you know. You sing a while and if they needed some ice you'd help the girl and do the—it wasn't a thing where, hey, you know, do this so-and-so. It wasn't a thing like that. So, and the next morning at eight, nine o'clock you might, you know, hit the man for some car fare to go home. If there wasn't no money, we'd walk from Seventh and T out to 513 D Street, Southeast. We done that a couple times. Singing all the way."

Andrew Magruder also recalled black businesses during the 1950s, from the perspective of a Georgetown resident. "Mott Theater. Twenty-sixth and M. That's the only black theater we had over in Georgetown, right across from Chestnut Farms milk dairy, and that was the best milk in the world. That was a movie house, it was the only place we could go, unless you went up on U Street, and that's big time. You only go up there on Sundays. You know, after you go to church, then mom will give you your money, you catch the streetcar. You had streetcars here then. You ride up there and you see all the big time guys, with [watch] chains on."

In Baltimore, as we have seen, the place of music and society was Pennsylvania Avenue. The way the Swallows' Herman Denby describes it, the Avenue had different sections, different types of entertainment, and different sensibilities that shifted from block to block. "They were predominantly black clubs, but a lot of white people came to have fun. You see there were sections—we were talking about how bad it was. There were sections where the street was bad. And if you wanted a fight you knew where to go to get one. You know what I mean? Yeah, but I mean like, where the clubs were, you never heard of anything about people fighting. They went to have a good time, you know? Well we used to go to the Royal Theater and we would listen to the band."

This was around 1945. It must have been easy for a youngster to get to see a show, for theaters such as the Royal and Howard ran live all day and into the night. The Howard, for instance, could have as many as "four shows a day—at 2, 5, 7:30, and 10 p.m. with a midnight performance on Saturdays" (Fitzpatrick and Goodwin 1990: 157). Can you imagine today that much live music in one place running all week, all year round?

The point, for Herman and other young singers, was to go to the shows, hang out and have fun, and to watch, listen, and learn. This was part of the process toward professionalism. "And your group, I mean your associates were interested in what you were interested in, you know. Listening to the harmony and listening to the sounds that the band made. And then we would leave and try to do it with our voices."

In addition to theaters and clubs, black business districts maintained a variety of other music-related enterprises that sold music merchandise of one kind or another, as shown in the list below.

The black business districts were places where both African American and white businesses musically maintained an interest. The small businesses were a part of what Nelson George calls the "rhythm & blues world." For him the "core" included independent record companies, black radio stations, black disc jockeys, mom and pop retail stores, and live shows (George 1988: 29).

In Baltimore and Washington, this R&B world was nuanced in a biracial way. Any clear notion of black economic self-sufficiency blurs with the juxtaposition of two famous white-owned establishments and a mostly black clientele. Near the corner of Seventh Street in Washington, at 624 T Street, the famous Howard Theater remained a black entertainment landmark from 1910 through 1970. Around the corner on Seventh Street was Waxie Maxie's record shop, which Max Silverman opened as Quality Appliance in 1938.

Black-owned Washington businesses that specialized in discs and record players or relied on music as a secondary source of income (Baker Handbook, 1947; Dee Cee Directory).

David's Radio and Music Store, 1928 14th NW — Home of the latest records.
Deanwood Music and Hardware Shop, 4802 Deane Avenue NE.
Edward's Music Store, 814 4th St. NW.
Frank's Radio Laboratory, 907 U St. NW — Type Records — Popular, Classical, Jazz, Blues, Spirituals. "If it's been cut, we have it."
Langstow Radio and Record Store, 1545 7th Ave. NW.
Langstow Studio Music and Appliance Co., 2403 Benning Rd. NE.
Modern Radio & Music Company, 407 L Street.
The Music Box, 2131 Georgia Avenue, NW.
Northwest Novelty and Amusement [Record] Co., 1003 U St. NW.
O'Meally's Novelty Shop, 231 Florida Ave. NW. Cards, Stationery, Gifts, Records.
The Platter (Music & Appliance Co.), 409 Florida Avenue, NW.
Record Shop, 1112 Colonel Road, NW.
Rip's Record Center, 1545 7th Street, NW.
Service Music Co., 1233 U St. NW, 718 4th St. SW, 1715 1/2 7th St. NW.
University Studio, 1839 7th St. NW

Here was an admixture of economic possibilities and social realities that resided in the cultural and economic interdependence of retailers and residents. The irony here deepens our sense of the complexity of these urban landscapes, where we find two sides to the story of white-owned businesses in black neighborhoods. One was that these places siphoned off business from African American establishments. The other was that they provided commerce and services to those areas. Either way, there was a power to these places realized both by singers and by those who wanted to be in business. Businesses large and small had a significant impact on group harmony in particular and the enterprise of popular music in the late 1940s through the mid-1960s, as Nelson George illustrates. However, it is not sufficient to say simply that business helped "make" black music. It worked the other way around as well, where the impact of a black music style determined the economics, large and small, of various forms of white commerce.

Morton's Department Store — the same place where the Four Bars' Alphonso Feemster worked — sponsored Jack Lowe's amateur hour, and that was how the Clovers found their bass vocalist, Harold Winley. They met their manager through Max Silverman, the owner of Quality Music — the House of Hits — which later became Waxie Maxie's.

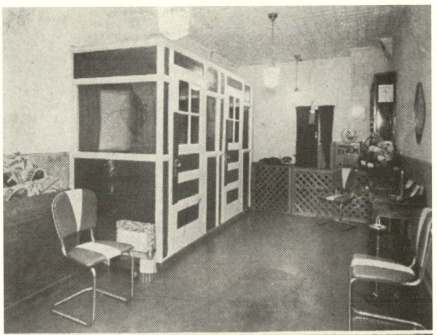

Northwest Amusement Co. Author's collection.

Quality Music Co., 1836 Seventh Avenue, Northwest, 1948. Courtesy of the Afro-American Newspapers.

Silverman's store was also the place where young Ahmet Ertegun went and acquired black music recordings. It was the cigar smoke and schmoozing at Silverman's that led the Clovers to their manager and, ultimately, to their contract with Atlantic. The musical dynamics of Washington and of Silverman's led Ahmet Ertegun, in a circular sort of way, to start a record company, Atlantic. That in turn led Ertegun and Atlantic back to Silverman's and to the Clovers.

White-owned businesses like Quality Music on Seventh Street in Washington could have displaced similar, black-owned businesses. There is no way of knowing now. Silverman, with the location, the goods, prices, and whatever else consumers found appealing, clearly brought something dynamic, perhaps even transformative, into that neighborhood.

Alphonso Feemster explained that, for Anacostia residents, Waxie Maxie was the place to get records. "Well, we would mostly get it from Waxie Maxie, places like that. We would have to go uptown, of course, to get those, because out in Anacostia I don't think it was—there might've been one or two old record shops that I don't really remember now. But I know most of the kids would get all their records from Waxie, you know mostly. Anything new come out, you would hear it on the radio, of course, with your deejays, and then you go buy the record. Then the stars would eventually show up at the Howard Theater, and you go to the Howard Theater to see them perform."

In Baltimore, Epstein's department store, where Ernest Warren worked, as he explained above, was right across the street from Sam Azreal's record store. This was how the Cardinals met their first manager. One member of the Cardinals worked at the music store, which became a reason for Ernest to hang out there. "Super Music. Right there at 570 North Gay Street. Yeah, used to go down—one guy worked for him and I worked across the street directly in front of him. I was over there throughout the day. Lunchtime, dinnertime—all year. Wasn't buying nothing, just hanging around there. And he had a guy worked for him called Goody. He knew how to put things together so he could record you and we did a couple recordings. Yeah we hung around there for a long time. Yeah, yeah, he [Sam Azreal] got interested. And he was the first one to get a piece of us."

Melvin Coles also hung around Super Music. In those days, some stores had a booth in which you could cut a cheap recording. "When I was in high school I was playing with a band, we called ourselves the House Rockers, Jerome Scruggs and the House Rockers. We did a lot of things around, you know like fraternity dances and stuff like that, and we played around town. There was a place on Gay Street they called Super Music, but that's been years ago. We would go down there and he would spin a disk. Anybody could walk in and, you know, it puts you back there in a booth and, you know, you just go and do what you know. That's the way we got the demos from, and so we went down to Super Music and we did that disc and sent it to New York. About a couple of weeks after that they called us up and told us to come on in for a session."

This was with Bobby Branch. A manager drove them up to New York. He was a Baltimore barber by trade. "He would go to New York and he would, this cat, he had a good gift of gab. Yeah, we called him Fats. Well his name is William Elliott. Bill Elliott.

"He knew a lot of people in New York City and he would just pal around with those guys up there in the entertainment business, and they would say, 'Well send me a demo up; let's hear the guys.'

"We'd go up with him a couple times and we would do a couple of tunes and the guys would say, look, give me a call in about a week, you know, see what we can do, see if we can set up anything."

Melvin never asked for details. "Man, I didn't really care as long as, as long as we were going to record I didn't even care. Back in those days, you know, you wanted to be on wax that bad. Teenage Records, so they eventually sold the tape to RCA Victor."

White businesses large and small were strategically situated in black neighborhoods and intersected with young singers in large and small ways. Small business owners who encountered singers would sometimes become managers of vocal groups. The manager of the Clovers was a shop owner, as was the manager for the Cardinals and the manager for the Swallows. Johnny Page rehearsed with the Marylanders right on the celebrated Pennsylvania Avenue. That was because the group's manager, Paul Fleschman, owned a shop there. "Well, Paul Fleschman had a record studio on Pennsylvania Avenue, and the 1300 block where the Royal Theater was, directly over across from there. So we had the third floor all to ourself."

Despite the numerous small, black-owned Washington businesses dealing in record discs, and some white-owned establishments (like NB Records, see below), two white-owned establishments became the major players in town. One was Quality Music. Alongside Silverman, there was another name situated famously between black consumers and the black business district and the business of making and selling (primarily, but not exclusively) black music. This was the Feld family. Unlike Max Silverman, who remained a local phenomenon, the Feld store moved into an ever-widening music, entertainment, and professional sphere that culminated with their purchase in 1967 of the Ringling Brothers Barnum & Bailey

Circus. In 1989, Alan Bloom was an executive with the circus and maintained a rich perspective on the history of the Felds and things related. His association with the family goes back to the 1940s, when his brother worked for the brothers, Irving and Izzy Feld. Alan eventually followed. The Felds owned the Super Cut-Rate Drugs at 1108–1110 Seventh Street, Northwest, right at the heart of the business district there.

Irving Feld was born in Hagerstown, Maryland. His family relocated to Baltimore and Irving found work at a cosmetic firm. He got to Washington as a salesman, selling patent medicines and cosmetics. The original Cut-Rate drugstore was first a warehouse for his sales route. According to Bloom, Irving started the store in 1940 with the intention of serving the black community. During the decade, Super Cut-Rate Drugs became a multi-purpose pharmacy crowded with, as the window announced, perfumes, liquor, toiletries, sunglasses, stockings, a soda fountain, and records. The front marquee happily announced "luncheonette." Bloom insisted that it was at the behest of the NAACP that Feld installed a soda fountain

Super Cut-Rate Drugs, 1108–1110 Seventh Street, Northwest, 1940s. Courtesy of the Afro-American Newspapers.

inside the store, after which patrons began asking for music. As it happened, Max Silverman's Quality Appliance and Merchandise Company stood nearby on 1836 Seventh Street. According to Bloom, Silverman rented an area in Feld's store where he began a small record "department." After about six months, he moved out and began to sell records in his own store, which eventually he turned into Quality Music. Irving Feld then also started to sell records in Super Cut-Rate Drugs, at Max's former record counters. That store on Seventh Street eventually became the first of numerous Super Musics.

The disc jockey Felix Grant heard a more detailed version of that story. The Feld brothers initially gave Max Silverman a triangle in the corner of the store for records. "There was so much traffic back to the corner they threw Maxie out and decided to sell records themselves. That was when the record counter came out to the center of the store."

Both Silverman and Feld were shrewd businessmen and provided a range of products to keep customers coming back into their stores. Records, however, became a focus for both as they established business and personal relations with customers, musicians, and other businesses. For instance, Super Music purchased airtime from radio station WWDC—four hours per weeknight and an hour on Sunday. According to Bloom, the radio station paid the disc jockey, the store paid the station for the airtime, and the record companies paid the store in merchandise for getting their records on the air.

"We programmed all the music," Bloom said. "We played what we wanted to have on the station and then the record companies used to pay us for getting time on the radio. They didn't pay us in cash, they paid us in records. We would generally pick [to have played on the air] what we thought were going to be hits, and we didn't think were going to be hits. And if a record we had played on the air a couple times and started to sell we would continue playing it, and if it didn't, we would cut it off."

Jackson Lowe was one of the disc jockeys from WWDC who, according to Bloom, was part of the above arrangement. So was Jon Massey, one of the postwar African American disc jockeys in Washington. Massey, incidentally, also did the window at Super Music for a couple of years, from seven to eleven at night (WOOK's Al Jefferson did the window—called the "goldfish bowl"—over at Max Silverman's Quality Music). Super Music also sponsored an hour's gospel and a half-hour "hit-parade" on Sundays. The main advantage for Super Music in purchasing airtime, obviously, was to promote their own products, including rhythm & blues music shows, which they began around 1949.

Super Music and Quality Music sponsored radio shows and hired local disc jockeys to broadcast from store windows and advertise and promote their stores and favorite records. They sponsored talent shows, promoted musicians, and ran specials to keep business flowing. They used to empty their warehouses of unwanted products by packaging records for Saturday and Sunday sales selling them, five for the price of one. The trick was that customers could only see the top of one record and the bottom of another. They would buy the package without knowing what was in between.

In 1946 the Felds opened a second store, Super Music & Appliances, at Thirteenth and H, Northeast. It was next door to the old Atlas Theater, where the Felds found Arthur Smith, the blues singer, whom they later recorded doing his "Guitar Boogie." This particular store had white customers from its neighborhood and thus sold a variety of music styles. A white disc jockey in the window, Connie B. Gaye, later owned radio station WGAY in Washington. In 1948, the Felds opened yet another store, Super Music City, on F Street downtown.

With the success of Super Music, the Felds expanded their entertainment world to include music promotion and production. They began locally at first, with Sunday night dances at Turner's Arena in Washington, at Fourteenth and W Streets, Northwest. Turner's Arena originally was a boxing arena built by Joe Turner in what at the time was a residential neighborhood. In the 1940s Super Music cosponsored Norman Granz's "Jazz at the Philharmonic" at the U-Line Arena, on Third and M Streets, Northeast. The U-Line was an old icehouse that eventually became the Washington Coliseum. They tried other ventures as well. One time—this was around 1950—the Felds leased a boat, the *Bear Mountain*, for summer Sunday night cruise shows on the Potomac River.

The company also had two record labels for a short while in the 1940s, Super Disc (jazz, blues) and Quartet (gospel). Also, according to Bloom, the Felds held interest in a record distribution company sometime in the 1950s that eventually one Harry Schwartz bought out; it became Schwartz Distributors. Bloom also mentions a local group named the Skylarks, whose lead singer, Bobby Cooper, worked in the store (and who later recorded "Glory of Love" in 1951 for Decca). If that were not enough, in 1947 and 1948 the Felds promoted gospel shows. They also recorded and worked with the world famous evangelist, Elder Lightfoot Michaux, in his yearly Baptismal at Griffith Stadium in Washington.

Beginning in 1950 or 1951, the Felds looked beyond the Washington area. They worked with Tim Gale of the New York Gale Agency in producing large, touring variety shows. They formed a partnership in 1952 and by 1956 Super Enterprises, as it was called, had a great deal of what industry insiders like Bloom called "rolling stock," in the way of large touring rock 'n' roll shows. Buddy Holly, the Big Bopper, and Richie Valens were all part of a Super Enterprises show when they died in a 1959 air accident in Iowa.

The incident related in the previous chapter, where a number of black male teenagers caused some trouble after a show at the armory on June 3, 1956, came after a Super Enterprises show. The show was Super Enterprises' "Biggest Rock 'n' Roll Show of '56." It included a mixed array of attractions and, to its credit, had both black and white artists. The headliner, though, was a white group—Bill Haley and his Comets.

The metamorphosis of Irving Feld and family, from cosmetics sales to Super Enterprises, says as much about the man's entrepreneurial spirit as it does about the interrelations of black and white Washington and free enterprise. Much of what Feld accomplished, from the period of his drug store through the rock 'n' roll shows, he did in black neighborhoods, with black consumers (perhaps complicitly), or through black music. What Feld's story illustrates is really an African American issue: black America was not only a consumer group, but also a resource for these white businesses. On the other hand, record stores and other businesses such as Super Music and Quality Music in black districts played critical roles in marketing and mediating, if not actually making, black music. You would not call it a partnership, but it was a vital interdependency.

This brings us to another aspect of the story, the actual making of the music. Here the record company was the object of affection and entrepreneurial interest during the rhythm & blues era. This was because consumers wanted to buy records, artists wanted to cut records, and everybody wanted to make money. If singers on the street exclaimed, "Hey, let's get us a group and record," then folks of every stripe would say, "Hey, let's put up some money, start a record company, have hits, and make money." It was a challenge to go very far in the business, no matter which end you were in. Making and selling records successfully seems to require a near perfect blend of art and business, creativity and control. The growth and innovations of postwar popular music were partly the result of the now famous "independent" labels scattered around the country. Certain cities— New York, Chicago, Los Angeles, for instance—were more central to recording than others were. Smaller centers for rhythm & blues recording included cities like Cincinnati, Cleveland, and Houston. One studio in Washington was American Recording, out in Alexandria, another was U.S. Recording on Vermont Avenue, a third, later, was Edgewood, also on

Vermont Avenue, Northwest. These were probably the three most used and independent facilities in the Washington area. There were several smaller places as well, like Tru-Tone Recording, on Illinois Avenue.

Local vocal groups that received recording contracts most often traveled to record in other cities. The Orioles, Clovers, Cardinals, and Swallows went up to New York or out to Cincinnati, where their companies had their own studios. Some groups went up to New York to use independent studios, like Bell Sound. Both Baltimore and Washington had a number of corner stores where kids could make an acetate disc for a few dollars. Radio stations could cut discs also, and occasionally a group would make a demo that way, but these two cities were not recording centers.

Baltimore and Washington had an abundance of black talent, but they did not have any significant presence of record labels. Nationally, there was a paucity of black-owned labels, as you would expect. In Washington, however, there were at least two small black-owned record companies—June Norton and Chevis Parham's Pam-Nor label, and Theodore Gaffney's Flayr label. York Records, also in Washington, was white-owned, as was Lillian Claiborne's "D.C." label.

In Baltimore, the Marshall label was white-owned, but there were two black-owned labels, Jordan and Howfum. These were among only a handful of very small, locally owned independent companies that recorded vocal groups and other regional talent during the 1950s and 1960s. Most were start-up ventures, family owned, and a way to capitalize on the growing popularity of vocal groups and other popular music.

Generally, the smaller labels simply brought a group into a studio and recorded them, without too much rehearsal or arrangement. There was no production technique as such, no attempt to construct an identifiable sound, as was the case with Atlantic or King Records. You can hear that on the recordings themselves. It is a candid sound. It is indeed ironic that what some larger studios conceived and constructed as a so-called "ghetto" sound was not that at all. The low-budget recordings of neighborhood companies achieved that without trying. The larger independents like Atlantic in fact produced a more polished cleaned-up version of the neighborhood counterparts, who by not "producing the material," maintained a rough edge to the sound, which today is an aesthetic savored by fans and record collectors.

It is difficult to say with any certainty how the few, very small labels in Baltimore and Washington functioned. Their success on any level is a debatable question. Certainly local groups and local record companies combined to create, for however short a period, a local music business environment.

Rarely was it a step to bigger things. Most local groups remained that way. Even less certain is whether, in Baltimore and Washington, there was any kind of definable regional sound. Most likely not, although some record collectors may argue the point.[17]

The local record companies were remunerative in neither Baltimore nor Washington. They came and went quickly. Yet human, business, and musical relationships that those enterprises engendered speak to us about black-on-black relations and white / black relations as well—not to mention women and men, young and old, teachers and students, businesses and lay persons. These small "start-up" ventures may have begun as an attempt to make money, but often there were quieter, deeper things at work too.

Lillian Claiborne was an enigma in the Washington and Baltimore area. She was a well-placed producer and manager, based in D.C., who recorded or represented a number of black male vocal and instrumental groups in the 1950s and 1960s, among them the Cap-Tans, Harmon Bethea and his Octaves, the Capitols, Frank Motley & His Crew, TNT Tribble. She worked with dozens more over the years.

According to Claiborne's attorney, her husband had left her money that she put into her interest in music, which dated back to the 1940s.[18] Her interest as a white female in black music remains unexplained. Many of her recordings went unreleased or were out for only a short time. As with any small label, distribution was always a problem. Claiborne was also friends with June Norton, the co-owner of Pam-Nor, another small, local Washington label that put out just a few sides in about 1953 or 1954 that featured the Four Men, a harmony group, and the Three of Us Trio. Norton also managed a group called the Jaguars for a short while in the late 1950s. Her music business partner for a time was Chevist Parham, who later kept the company by himself, as the Pam label.

People around Washington still know about June Norton, a gracious and beautiful woman. She sang professionally for a short while around 1950 and later did some advertisement modeling. She was, in 1989, one of the few African American women still alive that had any direct connection with recording harmony groups.

"I was working for a while with the National Security Agency and I had some lulls in my career, and that was a job that you had to use so much of your energies because it was that type. It demanded so much of you. And I had talked with a friend of mine name Chevist Parham. We decided wouldn't it be wonderful if we could get together, he said, there's so much talent around here, and it was. And I had been introduced to him by Jon Massey, he was a disc jockey, and he was a composer, too, and a singer, and he introduced me to Chev. So he said, why don't we try to get a record label going? I say, you think we can do it? He said yeah, we put what money we have into it."

This was in 1953. It is difficult to say if Miss Norton threw in with Chevist to nurture talent, which she mentioned, or to make money. She probably also wanted to just remain involved in music, for she did say she had some "lulls in her career" (presumably her singing career). In all likelihood, it was a combination of all these reasons. The economic motive for starting up a record company was probably there because it took money to begin, and cost money to continue. It stands to reason that no one gets involved in the recording business as a strictly charitable gesture. However, there was much benevolence in black communities, and musicians were always helping other musicians, especially younger ones.

"Yeah, and we were able to get the label and we rehearsed. Mister Tildon at Republic Gardens [on U Street] allowed us to use his upstairs to rehearse free, because we were on limited means, you know."

They learned as they went along, like many of the other independent labels of the time. They began with just two groups, the talent that they had in mind before they started up the label. "Well, we got to know enough to be able to get the label and we knew enough to get the master. Of course we didn't broadcast so much that we had a label because we didn't have the money to do everybody, but we knew that this was a very—these two, if we could make it with them, we could expand—with the Three of Us Trio and the Four Men."

Miss Norton laid out on a table some sheet music she still had after all these years, with Charles Kelly's songs. Kelly was the saxophonist for the trio. On the music paper were the names, along with C. E. Kelly, of Eddie Perdue, Samuel Mercer and the Swanns (spelled that way), and Robert Brown. She no longer remembered who those others were—they may have been the Four Men—or why the names were on the music. She brought out a 78-rpm disc of the Four Men, the harmony group she worked with, and contemplated the contemporary competitiveness over old records, especially black group harmony from the 1950s. She took a hard line with reissues and seemed protective of the performers' property rights.

"I've had people try very hard, who are into the record business up in Silver Spring, to try to buy the stuff from me and I know what they do is make a master of it and the people who are on it will never get a dime. And it'd be just out there and they'd call it something else."

Miss Norton broke some color barriers during the 1950s, especially when she filmed some local, Washington television commercials. She once tried out for a job at the Shorham Hotel, "Long before the lines had broken. And I was the only fly in the milk."

She said that, in the end, she lost all the money she had put into Pam-Nor, maybe it was a thousand dollars or so, but losing the money forced her out of the business while Chevist Parham continued for a while with just the Pam label.

The only two groups Norton recorded were the Three of Us Trio and the Four Men. The Four Men made only a few sides, now rare and difficult to find. One of the songs they recorded was "Drink Everywhere They Go." The group sings in an old, Ravens style, but without the strong bass. This particular side was a boogie-woogie, piano-heavy 12-bar blues. In a way, it reminds you of the Ravens' blues "Write Me a Letter," although not close in quality.

The stories of Lillian Claiborne, who was white, and June Norton, who was black, give evidence of the involvement of women in the array of group harmony music and business participants. Many women, black and white, worked with male groups. Locally in Baltimore, for instance, Deborah Chessler (white) managed and wrote songs for the Orioles (see chapter 4), and Zell Sanders (black) worked with the Plants.

George Jackson said the Plants formed around 1956. They met Zell Sanders (she was the "S" of J&S Records, out of New York) at the Royal Theater one night during a Five Keys show. "Zell was a sweet person. Her and Hot Rod [Hulbert, the Baltimore disc jockey] went to college together."

At the time, she managed her daughter, Johnnie (Sanders) and Joe (they recorded "Over the Mountain"). As George relates it, Zell Sanders heard the Plants singing out in the alley behind the theater. She asked the fellow at the door who was singing and then invited the group into the dressing room and asked to hear a couple of songs. They did a couple of Moonglows songs, and she later contacted them to record. Sanders was from New York, and also managed the singer Baby Washington and the group the Hearts ("Lonely Nights," on Chess). Zell wrote to George and the Plants and brought them up to New York to record six sides in 1957 and 1958, on the J&S label. According to George, Sanders managed the Plants for about four years, until the group disbanded.

There were other professional relationships between women, both black and white, and black vocal groups. Mary Osborn helped with the Marylanders, Bea Tibbets managed a group from Washington named the Coolbreezers, Erthaline Lee managed the Jets, from Washington, and helped them record a couple of sides in 1953 for Eddie Heller's Rainbow label (Goldberg et al. 1976: 4). In New York, a songwriter named Esther

Navarro managed the Cadillacs and lists as a co-author of their biggest hit, "Speedo." Ruth Bowen, the wife of a later member of the Ink Spots, Billy Bowen, managed the bandleader Earl Bostic, as well as singer Dinah Washington (George 1988: 72–73).

In Washington, singer Jimmy McPhail recalled that his high school typing teacher tried to manage the Armstrong Four.

"You know, when we were in high school—the Armstrong Four—Mrs. Williams tried to get us a recording contract and everything. But it didn't come through. Blanche. Yeah, we used to call her BK. Well that was her initials, you know, B. K. Williams. She was the typing teacher at Armstrong, but she just had a way of promoting things. She just had that knack. And she was a real personable lady, for us, you know. She tried to book us everywhere and take us everywhere, so we could be exposed, you know."

Howfum

One of the most engaging stories about young black male musicians as entrepreneurs comes from Carroll Williamson. Carroll was born in Baltimore in 1937, which puts him a fair decade behind the Orioles, Cardinals, Clovers, and Swallows. Carroll was the next generation, his aspirations those of youth not yet made cynical. The way that Williamson describes himself and his partner, they sound like genuine operatives—optimistic and enterprising. Williamson's story, while not entirely about group harmony, nonetheless says as much about possibility as about what became unfulfilled during the rhythm & blues era.

"I was born in Baltimore, as a matter of fact it's only, I guess, five miles from—I never lived more than five miles from where I was born. I was born in Baltimore City. I lived there until I was about four years old and moved in Turners Station, which is about five mile toward Sparrows Point, and I lived in Turners Station until about fifteen years ago.

"I was influenced by music at that time because my mother and father were pretty young people, and I can remember at four years old hearing music by Nat King Cole, you know, 'Straighten Up and Fly Right,' and things like that. My mother, come to think of it, was a teenager herself at that time. Looking back now and counting the years back, I never saw her as being a young person, but she was a young person and always loved music. My family lived in Turners Station and we always had record players, we had all these big seventy-eights, things like that. Music was just a part of us."

Turners Station, just east of the Baltimore City line, lies between Dundalk Marine Terminal and Sparrows Point, home to the Bethlehem Steel Company. It's a small curve of land tucked into a corner on the Patapsco River, near the entrance to Baltimore Harbor. Port neighbors to the east are places with names like Coffin Point, Clement Cove, Cattail Point, and Peachorchard Cove. It is a place with an endless array of bays, boatyards, coves, creeks, canals, and points. Back in the 1940s Turners Station was home for workers of the steel mills and the shipyards in and around Sparrows Point. These temporary developments for workers during the Second World War ended up as permanent homes for black families. Carroll calls it the "ghetto" of Dundalk. The area is down below Dundalk Avenue, adjacent to Main Street.

"Dundalk was a pure white neighborhood and somewhere to the south of that, to the southeast of that, we had a place called Turners Station where all the blacks lived.

"It was a pure black neighborhood. You didn't bring people from Dundalk, which had a nice big, grand high school up there, to our little high school. But it was perfect because we had a very, very good high school."

Williamson—his nickname had been "Little Bubbles"—graduated from high school in 1955; typical of the pre-integrated black schools, the black faculty was rich with talent and dedication. "As a matter of fact we had, I think, on our teachers' staff we had more master's degrees and Ph.D.s than most of the white schools then."

In high school Carroll was not yet a musician, but he and his friends listened to the first generation rhythm & blues performers. "My favorite group was the Dominoes. Some of my friends' favorite groups were the Swallows, and everyone just loved the Clovers. But I was a Dominoes man because I thought Clyde McPhatter was the greatest singer in the world. And that was one of the, kind of the arguments, like you argue about sports now, you know, who had the best bass. Who has the best bass, what group has the best lead, and that kind of thing. But my favorite at that time was the Dominoes."

When Carroll finally got involved in music he began to make contact with singers from Baltimore proper, and some familiar names appear. By this time, the latter part of the 1950s, many of the original groups had broken up and singers were trying to maintain careers (and group names) by going with the younger, second generation players.

"It was only a little while after I got into music I met most of those guys. See, I met Money [Johnson] who played guitar and sang with the Swallows. Sonny Til [of the Orioles], I had the band in Turners Station and wound up doing some background music for Sonny Til when he went out on his own. So I played with them. And there was a fellow by the name of Lou Karpouzie. Lou Karpouzie was from East Baltimore, he was, I don't know, Italian or Greek or something like that, and he used to book a lot of bands and things around. He managed the Cardinals. So that's how we actually hooked up with the Cardinals one time, we played with the Cardinals on some performances.

"Don't forget now, we were kids from Turners Station and what we heard on the radio, I mean we didn't know where these people were from. As a matter of fact, I didn't know until later that the Swallows were from Baltimore. I didn't know that, I mean this come across on the radio here. And the Clovers, I didn't know until later on that the Clovers were from the Baltimore-Washington area."

Sometime in high school, Carroll and Howard Spinney formed the Imperials. "Howard, he got me interested in doing that, when I bought a guitar. And from that point on we started to actually get into music very seriously and we started playing around and became pretty, pretty good. Became pretty good as unpolished musicians. And from that point on—I'm summing the music part now—from that point on we started getting very good musicians in that group, you know, learned from people who actually studied music. And Howard and I were more or less like head of the group. But to get the record company started—we were always interested in doing something like that."

The business connection for these guys was a disc jockey on radio station WITH, Jack Gale. "Howard recorded for a fellow in Baltimore named Jack Gale. His thing was, now Jack Gale worked on a radio station, but Jack Gale also played music. And he called himself the Hound Dog because he go, 'Owwwwwwww,' like that, every time he come on the station. He was white. See, at that time, on the radio station there was another fellow by the name of, he spinned a record for me, I got to think of his name there. But he was on WITH and he used to do Cupid's Corner and stuff like that.

"Well, anyway, Howard and I did this duet together and we all always thought about getting our own company together because we read that the Spaniels, the fellow who owned that label also took one artist and started his recording company. Now we didn't know how he did that, as a matter of fact, we had a fellow who couldn't play drums that well, but he was one of our friends. And I remember one day I gave him a quarter, I say make a telephone call to someone and find out, and get in touch and find out how he did it. I mean we must've been around sixteen years old at the time, because I was interested in how he did it. But anyway, when Howard made that recording with Jack Gale he came back with the format of how it was done. He said you record people, you carry them to New York and you, no, you carry them to New York and record them, and then you send the masters off to RCA somewhere to have the masters cut."

Howard Spinney also had a group at the time called the Howards, and they had made a recording through the graces, once again, of the disc jockey Jack Gale. Disc jockeys were true mediators in the rhythm & blues era. "Anyway, he came back with the idea and we said, 'Well, let's do the same thing.' First we tried to record some of our own songs, and I think, I'm not sure how it happened, but we did something called 'The Baltimore Serenade.' We said that if we called it 'The Baltimore Serenade' people in Baltimore will like it. And come to find out, Howard played it again to find out exactly, but there's a melody that's, it's copped directly from another melody. So it wasn't our music anyway. It was an instrumental we did, and we had a fellow by the name of Percy Brown who blew the saxophone. Percy Brown at the time was I guess maybe about sixteen, seventeen years old. But he was the fellow who knew music pretty well."

An outgrowth of all this was the start of the record company. "Now what we did was, when we started out, we started out—the name of the group is called Howfum. 'HO' was for Howard. 'W' was for Williamson, and 'F' was for Felder, a fellow by the name of Gratis Felder. And 'U,' I'm not sure, I think you need another vowel, put it in there. But another was a white fellow, the only white fellow in this group was called Mike Mitchell. Mike Mitchell was a saxophone player. Gratis Felder was not in the group at all, Gratis Felder was just a friend who we thought maybe had, in a business sense, would be a good business man. Howfum is the name of the record company. The musical group was called the Imperials."

As they all left high school and moved into the working world they remained in the area and used their own money to keep the record company afloat. "Mike Mitchell, he got into the group as being a sax, he was our saxophone player. He seemed to be like he could carry on some duties as part of the business. That's how we got him in. No one had any money. We did it out of our pockets, really. As a matter of fact, that's why we went broke because I think somebody got laid off or whatever. I was working, I was basically working. I was working down at Sparrows Point Shipyards at the time, and I had some savings bonds. I would cash my savings bonds to do a lot of financing, and they had the odd jobs."

Some of the others in the organization were more than part-time musicians. "So they were more into music. Gratis Felder was doing some work;

he worked for some guy down Baltimore Street. Ben Segal, I think it was, Ben Segal had a book store down there and he did some work for Ben Segal in some of his other stores. Mike Mitchell at the time was just playing music. And I'm not sure whether I got laid off, whatever. Anyway, funds dried up, so I had to keep financing through those savings. And I got to a point where I said, no, that's enough of that."

As Carroll, Howard, and the others began the record company, they found some office space. The collective thinking was along the lines of the Imperials having music stands. It was fronting, yes, but one essential aspect of being a business, is looking and acting like one. "We decided that we needed a place so we can bring people in, you know, so we can be legitimate. Our idea was if you have an office, people respect you more, that kind of thing. And we needed it too, because the office was full of our records. That was our storeroom."

They found some space on Park Avenue, in Baltimore. "We set up shop in Park Avenue. I remember that was a good ring, you know, a place on Park Avenue—Four seventeen and a half Park Avenue, because it was like a storefront that was partitioned at the doorway, and we had 417½. That's where we had all our equipment. We had a mimeograph machine. My father had a mimeograph machine. I carried that to the office. My wife did all the ledger work."

The record company used the Imperials as a kind of house band to back other artists as well as to perform on its own. They also learned how to book time at a studio. "We did all the recordings in Bell Sound, in New York, in New York City. We went to New York and recorded. Howard lived in New York for a while, for about a year or so. It was word of mouth, more or less, that it was a good studio. And it was. It was a very good studio."

At first, Carroll and his company made dubs in Baltimore. "We did some dubs and things around here. There was a place on, I think it was on Pratt Street, it was a little studio, but it wasn't big enough to do bands and things like that. A lot of people did do dubs and carried them to other places.

"We went to Bell Sound and Bell Sound I think at the time was about, it went about sixty dollars an hour, something like that. And what we tried to do, when we went up there we went up there with the band and whatever groups we had and everything. We tried to do it in one take. As a matter of fact we didn't have time to, we didn't take time, we didn't take time because it was money, to go through it and say, 'we'll try it again.' Only thing we did record over again was when we had the mistakes. You would make a mistake you say O.K., cut it. Try it again. Or on the very first take, the guy's trying to get a level, so he'll go maybe a few bars into the song and then you straighten it back out.

"We used the studio engineer. We didn't have anyone sitting in on our behalf. This fellow knows what he's doing, he's running the studio. I remember we were very, very green, we didn't know that kind of stuff was done. I guess if we had stayed in maybe just about five more years we'd probably start taking over a little more of the operation. We knew more about how the business end of it would work. We just went there and, you know, we were at their mercy. As a matter of fact, we didn't know. We really didn't know that you were allowed to be in there" (in the control booth).

"They treated us very well, like I say. I can't remember being mis-treated. They were very patient. Of course the longer it take, the more money they make. Small operation as far as we were concerned. But we thought that was one of the better sounding places."

One of the performers Howfum tried to work with was, of all things, a folk singer. "At one time we had, she was a white girl. Her name was Bobbie Martin. Bobbie Martin sang folk songs. Mike Mitchell had a friend that worked at Fred Walker's Music Store, and Bobbie Martin was introduced to us. And we had decided not to carry her up there [to the studio] because we were concentrating on the rhythm & blues and rock 'n' roll and that kind of thing.

"We went to Bell I guess about four different times. The Antwinetts, I think it was the very first group that we recorded. Young girls, twelve, thir-teen, fourteen years old."

When traveling up to New York to record, they pared down their numbers. "We did have up to twelve pieces a little while later. We started having horn sections and stuff like that. But the thing is that was only for performing. For recording, we never used that many people. And, face it, to go to New York, we only had maybe one or two cars at most, you know. Trying to get up there, I'm talking about people packing the car trying to go up the turnpike just to make a recording. You had to have somewhere to stay; it cost money, you know."

They took the master tape home after the recording session. "It came home with us. Yes. Yes. All we got was the tape. Now the master was pressed by RCA. We called RCA and told then we were sending something to them and we told them what we wanted from it, and they gave us our copies. I think at the time you had to have a minimum of a thousand copies, well let's put it like this, to make it cost effective. Well, a thousand copies, we ordered a thousand copies and then after that you order lots of five hundred, if I remember correctly. These at the time were forty-fives."

Howfum left the masters in RCA's possession and never thought to ask RCA to return the tapes. Carroll tried to get information on the tapes once, but didn't get very far. They also realized that they needed to publish and copyright their material. "Now we need a publishing company, O.K. We just say O.K., we need a publishing company. So we published the songs."

The publishing company Howfum formed was C&H, registered with BMI. Howard Spinney still was with BMI in 1990, but under Regent Music. Spinney wrote two songs, "Lola" and "Mimi Girl," for the Howards, which was before Howfum. Carroll and Howard also wrote for the Imperials and the Imperial Orchestra.

Another group that Howfum recorded was the Magic Tones, who came out with a version of a previously recorded song, "Tears in My Eyes" (b/w "Spanish Love Song") in 1957. "The Magic Tones walked into the office; word of mouth that we were recording people."

They also had signed to record the Antwinetts, the girl group, and a single. "Antwinetts was our star group. We kind of liked Antwinetts because at the time girl groups, it was very catchy. The things the Magic Tones were doing was very indicative of the '50s, but at this point right now we were ready to leave the '50s. The sound is a little more lighter, you know you had the girl groups and things like that. In the early '50s I can't remember any girl groups. So, the Antwinetts, the Antwinetts, that was our star group. We sold more copies of the Antwinetts that we did the Magic Tones. Antwinetts was on our label, on Howfum label."[19]

Carroll Williamson explained how the company's "distribution" worked. "Now it's another fellow that came and started working with us when we let Mike Mitchell go. What he did was take our distribution, he was in charge of distribution. What he did was take our records around to the different stores. For a certain percentage for the stores, they would keep our records on the shelf. Howard, Gratis, and I carried them around to the different [radio] studios."

Carroll and Howard carried their records around to various stations, as far out as Annapolis where a black DJ out that way, Hoppy Adams (WANN), gave them "more play than anybody in Baltimore did." Hot Rod Hulbert also played their records.

"And what we did was, like I said, we carried them to the radio stations and asked them to play our song. And for the most part they were nice enough to play it, whether or not they really like the songs or not. But Hoppy Adams really did. He really liked the song, he played it quite a bit."

Howfum wrote its own artists' contracts, and here Carroll says something startling. "I guess we could have been considered crooks if things had turned out the way, if we had enforced all the things that we had on contract. Because not only did we, we had the record company. We had the publishing company. We had managerial rights on the groups. "We were their managers. We were their managers. If they had gone somewhere else and recorded, done anything else, we had a contract that said we were their managers and we get a percent."

Who wrote the contract?

"We did. I'm not exactly sure how binding the thing was, but we wrote the contract.

"I thought it was fair, because what we did was what we saw other people do. We knew that for a record, that the artist would get so many pennies per recording. And I think it was no more than about, was it, three or four, five cents? Something like that, I remember that. And I know that most groups had managers, O.K., and that management fee was about 15, 10 percent. I'm not sure exactly what it was. And so we had a percentage of that. It was just that we had a percentage of the person such that no one else can come in and take over that person, [such] as a recording company and managerial rights. But the contract itself was fair."

Like all businesses, no matter the time or place, the Howfum Record label needed to attend to the business of business, which they could not do. "Yeah, as a matter of fact, that's how we went out of business. At the end of the year, we got this thing. We had to pay inventory tax. I never heard of inventory tax, no one told me about inventory tax. We had every record that we, you know, as a matter of fact I think we just recorded just before that. Had an office full of inventory, I mean for us, and we had to pay inventory tax on it. We couldn't pay that, we couldn't even pay our rent. Just dropped everything. As a matter of fact we ducked out."

That was an inglorious end to a dramatic idea. "Inventory was lost, confiscated. We never got inventory back. I tried to find—that company's out of business. The building itself is torn down."

The owner of the building, not the city, ended up getting the inventory, along with everything else in the office. "I was concerned about our typewriter. Our little mimeograph. We had some pictures on the wall of all the artists. That's gone. Our records. We had a picture taken of everyone."

In spite of losing Howfum, the Imperials continued as a band until Howard Spinney started playing with other artists in the 1960s. Carroll worked a day job and continued to play local clubs through about 1980. He left the shipyard, Bethlehem Steel, in 1964, to work for Western Electric.

He attended Johns Hopkins and Morgan State, and ended up as a computer specialist for the Social Security Administration.

One song on the Howfum label, "Tears in My Eyes" by the Magic Tones, endures for collectors and fans of the era. It remains a qualified gem of local, late 1950s group singing. The song captures in spirit, sound, and circumstance the poetics—if you are inclined toward nostalgia—of what that era meant. Even a bad recording 50 years later can mean a good memory.

As Carroll remembered it, the Magic Tones came looking for them. "The Magic Tones walked into our office; they come in our office really because we didn't have a song writer. You had to have an original song. We thought it ['Tears in My Eyes'] was an original song [it wasn't].

"I mean, they were older than us, you know. We thought we could bring someone else along and they were older than us. And if I remember correctly, I kind of felt like, we must be good that they'll come to seek us."

The Magic Tones were a little-known Baltimore group that recorded four sides for King Records, released in 1953 and 1954. Their most memorable recording, however, at least today, was their 1957 Howfum "cover" of another extraordinary recording of "Tears in My Eyes." Another obscure Baltimore vocal group, the Baltineers, first recorded the song a year earlier in 1956 for the Teenage label. The bass singer and guitar player for the Magic Tones, Eugene Hawkins, said he wrote the song, but the copyright belongs to Percy Cosby (presumably one of the singers of the Baltineers) and William C. Gordon. Gordon also owns the song's publishing company—Jeepster Music—as well as the Baltineers' record company in 1956, Teenage. Gordon, also known as Bill "Bass" Gordon, recorded with the Colonials for the Gee label in 1954. He began the Teenage label in New York in 1955. The label, black-owned and operated, was one of the rarities among the independent labels in the mid-1950s.

The Baltineers, who recorded four sides for the label, must have been among Gordon's very first recording artists because the master number begins with TA-1000 [Teenage 1000] (Ferlingere 1976: n.p., Gribin and Schiff 1992: 165). Gordon said that his partner at the time, Eddie Shaw, handled promotion and management. They apparently had been down to the Baltimore and Washington areas once or twice in the late 1950s to record, probably at U.S. Recording in Washington, but he did not recall where the Baltineers recorded. Gordon did remember, however, that he came across the Baltineers through "Charles Taylor and the Royal Crown Carnival," but that was all he could recall.[20]

Melvin Coles said that he was in New York when the Baltineers recorded "Tears in My Eyes" (b/w "Moments like This"). He confirmed that the session was put together by Billy Gordon of Teenage Records, with another Baltimore group, the Jolly Jacks. (The Links, another Baltimore group, also recorded with Teenage.) The Baltineers, especially in that recording of "Tears in My Eyes," are a group remote from the rhythm & blues mainstream, save for the record collectors today who savor their sound. Gene Hawkins of the Magic Tones said that he knew one of the singers in the group, called "Cat Eyes." Apparently, some also referred to this singer as "Billy Grey Eyes," presumably because he had one "bad" eye.[21] Melvin Coles and George Jackson said they remembered the Baltineers and two brothers, Joe and Percy Cosby, who sang in the group. One of them, Melvin says, "was blind in one eye." One of the other songs the group recorded was "Joe's Calypso." The truth be told, no one really seems to know much about the Baltineers, except the intangible wonder in their recording of "Tears in My Eyes" and a bit of the elusive mystery of the group. A few collectors have the original recording, a constructed sound document that at once deepens the mystery and lessens it. As with the Magic Tones, the Baltineers constitute a fleeting glimpse—a fleeting sound—of vocal group harmony on a very local, urban grassroots level. In this particular case, we have little else but the vagaries of the music.[22]

In the coming together of these two versions of "Tears in My Eyes" in 1956 and 1957 we have something of an epiphany. The moment—albeit a long moment—comes just as group harmony was peaking as a rhythm & blues phenomenon. It comes just after rock 'n' roll derivatives were tumbled around with enough of a guitar-based sound to alter the sound of American popular music. It comes about as two African American-owned record companies are trying a start at a tough business. The two recordings also demonstrate the Janus-faced nature of (black) popular music as it looked in two different directions in one performance—a pop ballad style, and a harder-edged gospel and blues sound. The Baltineers and Magic Tones, two little-known Baltimore groups, recorded the song slightly differently, although both drew deeply from the lyrics with an impassioned delivery. They drew from a varied mix of pop and blues. The recorded performances also reveal differences in production, the Teenage version smoother, more "polished" than the Howfum records, which has a raw urging to it. The Baltineers version was lighter, with the lead's obviously young, delicate voice maybe in the style of a Frankie Lymon over insistent piano chord triplets typical of the period. The Magic Tones sound slightly older and the lead sings in a falsetto just barely into that range. His voice cracks in places. They also use the insistent triplet feel, but the tempo is slow and heavy. Both groups use a prominent bass obbligato—almost like two leads—but the Magic Tones bass singer, Gene "Hawk" Hawkins, sings in a wide-open style that equals the passion of the lead. The poem is poignant, if simple; the poetics of the performance more complex.

The Magic Tones version begins with a short introduction of falsetto voice that alternates between two high notes, the last one sustained—B-A-B-A-B-A-A-A—then spirals upward to form a chord with the other voices. A fan of this particular song, the record collector, dealer, and historian Les Moss, first played the recording for me. Before it started, he said the introduction sounded like angels descending from heaven. It's a terrific description, and maybe even true, given how long ago it was when the group recorded.

In the modern world, to write a good song or to sound good meant more than just composing or singing well. There are other factors and more to the story. You had to be an activist of sorts, and during the period of group harmony, activists of sorts were young, some old, black as well as white, women as well as men. We are not talking about political activism in the usual political sense of the word, but something closer to attitudes that ignored, rubbed against, or went around prevailing social or racial conventions. Also, importantly, they enabled the circuitry and channels of city life. This tells us simply what musicians and entrepreneurs (and ethnomusicologists) have known all along—there is no such thing as "the music itself."

4

Mediators

"In those days, once a disk jockey laid off of it, that was the end.
They were THE connection."

—Deborah Chessler

The vocalists of group harmony maintained an effective if not always compelling role in their own direction and development and by no means did they work alone. They forged alliances outside family and church, worked with others, and in the process drew from their immediate surroundings and beyond. This chapter focuses on those other alliances, the variegated relations between group harmony and local radio and disc jockeys, and a ubiquitous group of music professionals comprised of agents, managers, arrangers, and producers.

It was something of a complicated, curious interplay because the power and influence flowed both ways. These young black males had as much of an effect on the world around them as their world had on them. Their world may not have been that large, but as singers developed their style and performed and recorded, and vocal music made its way on to recordings and the radio especially, the black voices of group harmony sounded beyond the immediacy of just one city. Their collective musical influence since the late 1940s has been more than persuasive.

Radio was very much a part of helping to broadcast that sound and, conversely, was very much a source for and influence on singers as they grew up and developed their musical skills. In addition, because radio and DJs in particular played a vital role in the music business and in local communities, the character of the radio industry and the characters on the radio help us to further understand the intricacies of group harmony development and rhythm & blues more generally.

The other group with whom singers worked—agents, managers, arrangers, and producers—was important as well, especially when you consider, once again, the business aspect of the music. The more astute arrangers and producers in particular helped to cultivate a sound and take it to market through recordings and live performances. The individuals that worked most closely with local groups were managers and agents, many of whom were area businessmen and women, but often part-time amateurs in music. The full-time professionals of music production, which was a field in growth and transition in the 1950s, were arrangers and producers who would get involved with singers when they prepared to record, especially for some of the larger independent labels, like Atlantic and King.

The relationships between singers and these various mediators with whom they came into contact were for the most part unstructured, fluid, flexible, mostly informal, sometimes fruitful, and occasionally rife in contradictions (as for instance, who might be "in charge"). It is problematic that information about those relationships is incomplete. Still, what we glean from personal accounts is instructive, and tells us that group harmony would not have developed as a rhythm & blues *business* without the work of the aforementioned professionals. The fact that all of these participants, singers included, interacted within a loose, urban framework established a working environment in which the musical and entrepreneurial attitudes of rhythm & blues had an opportunity to flourish on stage, in stores, on records, and over the radio airwaves. Over time, the sound saturated popular music. With this information, we can more fully understand the personal relationships, the give-and-take, that underpinned the music and the racial dynamics of the period.

Radio / DJs

One set of individuals to encounter group harmony and musicians of all kinds were disc jockeys, and this opens up a much larger issue for discussion here. While disc jockeys of the late 1940s and 1950s for the most part played a minor role in the development of vocal groups per se, they were major players in the development of rhythm & blues as a radio phenomenon. They also helped to make radio in general an integral part of a young person's life, at a time when radio programming was much less specialized than it is today. Beneath that story is the emergence of the black disc jockey in the 1940s and the interplay between their on-air style, the white-owned media, local businesses, black music, and black audiences.

The shifting soundscape of radio and its vitality began with those who played records on-air as much as it did with the discs themselves. DJs were the original mediators. They were instrumentalists even before cutting, scratching, and hip-hop. Black disc jockeys, and some white counterparts, in particular worked to develop black oriented radio and a distinctive on-air style in the late 1940s. At the same time, the emergence of postwar radio played an indispensable role in the development of rhythm & blues, which fed back to influence groups on the street, increased the popularity of rhythm & blues and probably of radio programming in general as well. Radio also affected singers in several important ways, from mediating influences to promoting careers. A broader issue here is the role of radio in the context of American popular music after the Second World War and its role in arbitrating "black" and "white" styles.

Radio since the 1920s had been an agent of change, an actor in the development of the music industry as well as popular culture. The rhythm & blues era brought the record industry more in tune with the business of popular radio and much closer to two important markets—the emerging teenager of the 1950s, and African Americans.[1] Radio helped get rhythm & blues music out to what became its core audiences.

The predominantly white-owned radio industry reached into black communities, once it realized they were there, in active and engaging ways, both economically and socially. We can say the same thing about the radio industry as we said about white businesses in general. There was never any clear boundary between serendipitous geography, stark, racialized necessity, sound business practice, self-interest, selfless good will, and even paternalism. As radio, however, began to reach out to black audiences as a targeted market, black music in general became more a part of what came over the radio, regardless of audience. This simply was a result of the growing popularity and marketability of black rhythm & blues.

At the same time that radio ownership increased for African American families in the 1940s, radio station owners—all in Washington and Baltimore at that time were white—made gestures toward black listeners through programming, sponsorship, and on-air personalities. The modern, postwar challenge for stations was to appeal to a black listenership, to get that market share, but without alienating whites. Before that period, the stations all but ignored African Americans as a specific target audience, save for religious programming.

Young singers often learned songs from the radio as they heard not just religious music, but popular secular styles as well. At the very least, they became familiar with what was popular during the period. They musically socialized as much to the radio as from other sources, and ended up hearing a range of radio programming. In Washington, James McPhail said that his family had a radio, but no records.[2] "Whatever came on that the family was listening to, we all listened to."

A generation later, in the 1950s, also in Washington, Al Feemster said of his vocal group, "And we did all the latest stuff that come over the radio."

Ernie Warren in Baltimore remembered how he first learned pop songs. "Well, it was just something we picked up. You know we used to listen to music and records. There was a group that used to come on the radio every morning at six o'clock called The Trumpeteers. Yeah, spiritual group. Two songs used to come on at six o'clock in the morning, and the second voice was Jan Peerce. You remember "Bluebird of Happiness." We just started from things like that."[3]

Part of the Orioles' popularity had to do with the radio. Their first big success was on Arthur Godfrey's radio program, and then they hit big in 1948. Herman Denby and his group, the Swallows, knew some of the members of the Orioles because they all were from West Baltimore. The Swallows at the time were still mixing their ingredients and had not yet begun to cook. They noted with much enthusiasm the older group's success. One indicator was what came over the radio.

"We liked them, so then we changed our thing and started sounding like them, because we liked them. We were singing already then, but you see, like, what happens is like, you walk the streets and you hear different things. You hear radio. And well you didn't like the whole song but there was a part of it that you liked, so you took that and imitated it."

Herman Denby heard a variety of styles on the radio, including country music singers. "You listen to the radio. You heard them, you know. And my favorite was Lefty Frizzell. There was a singer named Lefty Frizzell. He, he had his own group, but he was a popular country and western singer, you know, and I used to sing a lot of his songs."

For this generation of singers coming up in the 1930s, like everyone else, radio must have been something special. Rather than taken for granted, it must have been highly valued and a real focus of family entertainment for those who had radios (and shared theirs with other families). More than likely youngsters would have been interested in almost anything that they heard at that time, which may account for their varied tastes.

What came over the radio in the mid-1940s, at least in Washington, D.C., came from a combination of large and small stations. The major network affiliates were WORC (NBC), WTOP (CBS), WMAL (ABC), and one of the more popular stations in town, WOL (Mutual). In addition, Washington had a classical music station owned by the *Washington Post*,

WINX. Two independent stations were WOOK—a very popular station—and the smaller, WQQW.

> A Sunday afternoon program entitled "Classics of Jazz" is the work of Charles Parker, who's heard from 3 to 4 p.m. on the Sabbath over station WQQW in Washington. He's a Supreme Court messenger and collects records as a hobby. (*Afro Magazine Section*, March 5, 1949)

Another Washington station that went on air in 1941 was the independent WWDC, which broadcast pop music of one kind or another, 24 hours a day. Joe Katz, an advertising executive from Baltimore, owned WWDC, at Connecticut and K, Northwest, according to the disk jockey who once worked there, Felix Grant. WWDC was, by day, a predominantly "white" station, and by this, Grant meant that the music played was for "mainstream" tastes. During the evening, however, the station allowed more "race" and jazz material.[4] Either way, it was typical of the kind of station Washington residents, black or white, would have listened to in the 1940s.

At first, there were mostly only white people on-air, and some of them initiated "black" programming. Washington's Jackson Lowe, for instance, had a very popular talent show on WWDC during the 1940s that, by his own admission, African Americans relished with particular zeal. Lowe also made noise around the city as he began to give black artists some general airplay alongside Perry Como and Doris Day. Later, after stations integrated, that happy task fell to the emerging black radio personalities of the mid- to late 1940s, but especially after the transition from "race" music to the "rhythm & blues" category in 1949.[5] The black DJs were real heroes and true activists who first conformed to convention (they had to *not* sound black), and then resisted it mightily.[6] Radio in the United States was never the same after black DJs came into their own. The spirit of DJs and the radio industry as a whole had a significant effect on popular music in general. As Maurice Hulbert says below, DJs in those days could choose what to put on the air. There were no "programmers" who determined play lists, at least not as we know them today on commercial stations.

Black DJs also knew well the varied tastes of their black audiences and introduced to the public a distinct black style of on-air talk that was a combination of jive, rhyme, time, affectation, and warm affection for the listeners. It was all show with lots of flavor. Lavada Durst, who went by the name "Dr. Hepcat" was one of the first black DJs in central Texas. His on-air

style was typical of the period, though a few years behind the East. He published a slim book in 1953 on his vision and version of "jive talk." He presents the material as a kind of language primer, and "schools" the reader with
an introductory example.

> In spinning a platter of some very popular band leader, I would come on
> something like this: "Jackson, here's that man again, cool, calm and a
> solid wig, he is laying a frantic scream that will strictly pad your skull, fall
> in and dig the happenings." Which is to say, the orchestra leader is a real
> classy singer and had a voice that most people would like. For instance,
> there was a jam session of topnotch musicians and everything was jump-
> ing and you would like to explain it to a hepster. These are the terms to
> use. "Gator, take a knock down to those blow tops, who are upping some
> real crazy riffs and dropping them on a mellow kick and chappie the way
> they pull their lay hips our ship that they are from the land of razz ma
> tazz."
>
>   Now we have some people of class visiting your city and you want to
> take them to hear one of the country's leading orchestras. You want
> everyone to put on their tuxes and visit the outstanding night spot. *Let all
> the ickies drape in shape and fall from the pad hip to the tip and most mad. We're
> going to dig a cat that will make you mickey mouse rock the house, and the goon
> leave Saskatoon, you can believe this kitty is ready, willing, and able. He's just like
> the man in the casket, dead in there.*" (Durst 1953: 1, emphasis his)

Radio stations woke up to an African American market, particularly as
these early black radio personalities (and the whites who, sometimes with
less flare, played black music) plied their wares. They in turn nurtured a
clientele that consisted of listeners as well as businesses. Through the disc
jockeys, stations developed relations with local commerce, especially the various stores that sold records, appliances, or clothes, and could afford to sponsor programs, and maintained an indispensable closeness with local residents.

Radio at that time, as a business and as a form of entertainment, prescribed music style and taste as much as it reflected it. Radio helped establish what became popular, and this had a considerable economic side. It
also placed a lot of power into the hands and mouths of savvy DJs. In
addition, and aside from their on-air style, the local black DJs, along with
a few whites like Jack Lowe and Felix Grant, worked the neighborhoods
with a combination of self-promotion and honest, civic responsibility. They
made friends in the neighborhoods, pushed local talent, and promoted
whatever they had to, whenever they could. They were visible and approach-
able in those days—walking, talking entrepreneurs of their own talents and
of current popular culture.

Although there were a few very early pioneers, like Jack Cooper in Washington, it was not until the mid- to late 1940s that black personalities were able to break the on-air color barrier in numbers. Washington disc jockeys like Tex Gathings and Harold Jackson began on the *Washington Post* station, WINX, bought by Richard Eaton in 1950, before they moved to his WOOK station. Cliff Holland, another seminal black disc jockey in Washington, started in 1947 broadcasting every night on station WOOK (*Afro Magazine Section*, March 5, 1949).

Jon Massey also began his long career at WOOK. The *Afro-American*, in its inimitable style, ran an article about him.

> Life never becomes dull for Washington's newest disc jockey, Jon Massey, WOOK morning man.
>
> The ole conductor on "The Uptown Special," heard daily from 6 to 10 a.m. and Sundays 6 to 12 noon, already has more radio time than his fellow platter spinners—26 hours per week. For good measure he doubles back on Sunday for a half-hour recorded program in the afternoon.
>
> Massey's day begins around 5 a.m. and usually ends around 10 p.m. After arising he takes a quick shower and shaves, gulps down a cup of black coffee and then drives to Silver Springs, Md., arriving in time to warm up the controls and start his program's theme song, "Take the A Train," spinning by 6 o'clock. (*Afro-American*, 1949, no month given)

In 1950 Massey moved to station WWDC and took over the weekly amateur hour that the white DJ Jackson Lowe had begun, by his own recollection, in late 1941 or early 1942. The sponsor changed from the original Morton's Department Store, to Marvin's Clothing. Massey also did early (1947–48) television broadcast work from the Howard Theater.

Tex Gathings, Cliff Holland, Harold Jackson, and Jon Massey were among those who were able to come into their own during the period after the war as radio stations developed specific local programs aimed at African Americans, but they could not have done it without establishing alliances. Local businesses sponsored, supported, and capitalized on the effort by purchasing airtime or even paying disc jockeys for specific programs linked to a business or store.

Tex Gathings described the relationships that, after the late 1940s, began to include television as well as radio.

"But the truth of the matter is the way things went in those days, places like NB Records bought thirty-minute segments, morning and evening. Nate and Norman Bernstein. They had a combination record store, drug store-cum-variety store, as was the enterprise owned by the Feld Brothers,

Israel and Irving, who had the same thing, Super Music and Super Drugs, also in the upper part of 7th Street. Their empire expanded at a rate that was phenomenal to the point that, in the late seventies, they bought Ringling Brothers Barnum & Bailey Circus."

Gathings laughed at the thought. "But each of these record stores, drug stores, variety stores would buy fifteen or thirty-minute segments. Like in the morning, there was the NB Gospel Hour, morning and evening, fifteen, thirty minutes. In the afternoons, there was the NB Blues, which was thirty-minute segments. In between you had, quote unquote, shows where the disc jockey or air personality within the constraints of the music available played what he or she desired. Every now and then, you'd have an eleven o'clock or a noon gospel show operated by people like Francis White, who's deceased. Her successor was a woman named Lucille Banks Rodgers, who I understand is still active. Because you see, much of the Sundays were small churches, black churches, who paid dearly for their air-time. We only carried one free-church broadcast, and that was the National Presbyterian Church, which Mr. Eaton carried as a prestige item."

Richard Eaton owned WOOK at the time. Gathings provides a simple answer to why Richard Eaton, radio stations in general, and other local businesses took such an interest in black communities. It was partly the same reason why businesses and individuals had taken such an interest in rhythm & blues harmony groups.

"Greenback dollar bills. This was a market segment that was untouched and most people were afraid of it, you know. The big station in this city, the two big stations in this city were WOL and WWDC. They were not about to alienate the majority of their middle-class white audience, or even the other classes, playing too much of this, quote unquote, race music. But then when the population shift began, because remember, we're talking about an era in which there are two public school systems, officially called the 'A' system and the 'B' system. I'll let you guess which was which."

He laughs again. "It was an idea who just needed somebody with either the courage or the courage born of desperation to take advantage of it, and he [Eaton] did. But you must understand all these stores—NB, Super, Quality Music, which was Max Silverman's operation—were dead in the heart of the predominantly black neighborhoods. You know all of these stores existed between the 600, the 700 block of Seventh Street, Northwest and the 1800 block of Seventh. And you see the 1900 block of Seventh brings you to Florida Avenue, I mean the Florida Avenue, U Street changeover, juncture. So, these were a matter of being smack in the midst of a particular market, so, why not. That's easy to understand."

It was simply "bid'ness is bid'ness"—and fortuitous geography?
"Precisely."

Back in those days, the best radio personalities became consummate professionals. They were entertainers, and as such, actors. They were also actors as decision-makers, in a larger social and entrepreneurial process. They were agents, they were happening, they made things happen in that they would facilitate for favors or profit—bookings, represent performers, whatever. They were also agents, as those who exerted power and influence. They were music mediators—transmitters, promoters, reconcilers, interveners, and interviewers. They were intermediaries between disc, group, song, management, record company, and public—they were operators. They were music critics and cultural critics of the time, not to mention keen social observers, chroniclers, interpreters, and oral historians. Black deejaying was hip long before hip-hop. They were a gas. They were cool.

Baltimore, in 1949, had only one black disc jockey. Chuck Richards, a former singer with the Fletcher Henderson Orchestra, was on station WITH. "He gives newscasts and conducts a record program," wrote the *Afro Magazine Section* (1949: 3).

The other large station in Baltimore at the time, WSID, became more of a black-focused station, according to Maurice "Hot Rod" Hulbert. Hulbert came to station WITH in 1951 from Memphis, and was one of the city's earliest black radio personalities. Nationally, Hulbert was among the first of the original black radio "pioneers" (George 1988: 43). He was very clear on what integration meant to radio stations at that particular time.

"It was the best thing that ever happened to them, and in so doing it was the best thing that happened to a lot of black people. And, in fact, it was the best thing that happened to the industry for black people because at that time there were very few black stations with personalities because there were no stations. You would hear some quartets, you know like on Sunday and things like that. But the only recording things were 'The Wings Over Jordan,' things of that nature. Then it began to open up wide and then it began to blossom all across the country. You know what I mean, the success of that station. So that's how I came to Baltimore."

Some of the other black radio personalities in Baltimore after 1950 were Bill Franklin of WSID, who, along with white station manager Mary Osborn, managed the Marylanders in the early 1950s. Paul "Fat Daddy" was on WSID, as were Paul Johnson, Billy Fox, Kelson Fisher, and Douglas Henderson. Most if not all black disc jockeys of the 1940s and 1950s (and later) were involved with the African American communities in a variety of ways. Baltimore disc jockeys, like their counterparts in Washington and most other places, worked clubs, emceed talent shows, and had record store-sponsored shows. A few, like Washington's Tex Gathings and Al Jefferson, even produced some records, while others promoted particular vocal groups, either as a business venture or simply to do some kids a favor.

The radio personalities of the 1940s and 1950s were very much a part of the community. That was the way they felt; that was the way people felt about them. They put themselves out there. Disc jockeys also had a different view on things, different certainly from vocalists, business, or record people. They immersed themselves in the public sphere, the cities, and its neighborhoods, and often met local talent, harmony groups among them. Their narratives add another dimension to the story of group harmony and help us understand how radio was a kind of middle ground for the music industry, especially for this postwar period. Radio stations at that time breathed with their surroundings. They established a format to which people reacted, but at the same time stations absorbed much from the surrounding community. In those days nearly all of what a station became was the result of disc jockeys and their individual tastes and styles.

Tex Gathings

Tex Gathings staked out a wide territory over the years in the radio, television, music, and entertainment industry. He was a ubiquitous public personality in Washington for over forty years and seemed to know everyone in town. He was born on May 24, 1928, at Freedman's Hospital in Washington. His family moved to Texas, where his father was a physician. They returned to Washington in 1936. Gathings's first radio job was with WOOK.

WOOK was white owned, but it was not a white station, and apparently it was some of the white-owned businesses in black neighborhoods—they are familiar names to Washingtonians of that period—that encouraged WOOK to move into a "black" format.

"When he [Richard Eaton] put the station on the air he tried every format under the sun—country, middle of the road, whatever that meant in the 1940s. Max Silverman at Quality Music; the Feld Brothers, Irv and Israel, who had just started the Super Music chain of stores, and Nate and Norman Bernstein, who ran NB Records in about the 600 block of Seventh Street, Northwest. The only, quote unquote, I'll use this term, as it was known in those days—race programming—was maybe an hour on WWDC. Maybe thirty minutes or an hour on WOL, that was the extent of it. They urged Eaton to go into the race music format."

We can only guess as to what their motivation was, but it was most likely economic. In a sense, these small businesses also had a "race" format, in that they focused on black customers. I suspect that they wanted to get WOOK into the neighborhood, so to speak, to have a venue with which to collaborate and advertise. But on that point, Gathings rightly observes the intra-fragmentation of the black population in Washington at the time. Segregation forced blacks to shop in certain places, but as for the notion of one unified black audience for "race" music, "It was meaningless. This community per se was considerably segmented, along its own very special—it was a stratification based on income, education, and color of skin."

This did not, however, prevent the radio industry in that town from pursuing—actually constructing, to a certain degree, given the complexities of the black population in Washington—one basic "race" market.

When Gathings joined the station, WOOK aired during the day only and Jon Massey was the first black DJ on the station. "Harold Jackson was second, when Harold and Eaton had their falling out, Eaton put an ad in the paper and that advertisement was answered by a man named Cliff Holland. Cliff is my very dearest friend, but Cliff was the, Cliff was the morning, early afternoon man at WOOK from about '47 through about 1980."

Gathings, like the other DJs, worked all aspects of radio broadcast and even made the transition from radio to television broadcasting. Television broadcasts adapted what had already been successful on radio—talent shows, for instance. The approach, from the station owner's perspective toward the surrounding communities or "markets," was the same.

"I did talent shows too. In fact, Harold Jackson and I probably did the biggest of all, which was called the Marvin's Howard Theater Amateur Program. It was the first television show ever produced from the stage of the Howard Theater, on channel five, Dumont Television. I was the primary producer." He laughs at that thought. "Let me try to pin this down. We're looking at about '46, '47. Some of the elite of the Washington music industry, John Malachi, Dee Dee Clark, oh hell, another dear friend who's dead now, the left-hand drummer, Al Dunn. Rick Henderson. All of the elite of the Washington professional musicians served as the music coordinators, et cetera, for that program. And, interestingly enough, the way we lost it, Harold, Jackson that is, gave a segment to a then-current girlfriend who was a dress designer. And the client, Marvin's Magic Credit, objected because, after all, a good part of their business was the sale of clothes on credit, so they canned him. That's when the client brought in Jon Massey to do the show. And Massey stayed with it until it was canceled late '48.

Then the next big talent show was Bob McKuhn's talent show, which also
appeared on local television.[7]

"You're talking about the beginning of the Clovers. You're talking
about the beginning of—the Orioles were very much, the biggest thing out
here was the Orioles because Sonny and them were right, you know, across
the pike there in Balt—as they say, Bal'more. Nobody said Baltimore in
those days."

Local talent shows—first on radio, then on television— were immensely
popular with and important for young people. Singers had an opportunity
to practice and competitively copy.

"Anybody who could emulate the Orioles or the, well the Clovers were
just hitting. The Ravens, yeah, Jimmy Ricks, the Ravens.

"There were kids, adults, there was the usual gamut of aspiring stars,
doing everything from—this was television—everything from dancing to
impersonations to poetry reading. You name it; we had it. And interestingly
enough we used to have the screenings at any place we could find. I think
we taped on Saturday morning and aired Saturday afternoon. No, we didn't

Howard Theater with the Orioles headlining, March 17, 1951. Courtesy of the Afro-
American Newspapers.

tape. We rehearsed and aired live Saturday afternoons direct from the Howard. In fact, one of the first uses of some sort of a microwave link, because the microwave went on top of Miss Mattie's Restaurant right there on T Street, three doors from the Howard. And to broadcast directly from the Howard, Saturday afternoons, it was called Marvin's Amateur Hour, sponsored by Marvin's Credit Store."

Inevitably, as Gathings explains and as Al Jefferson indicates below, broadcasters encountered all manner of musician. "It's a natural side-bar to the quote unquote, disc jockey slash air personality of those days. People were always bringing you material or asking to audition. And don't forget that the local radio station, if it were so equipped, which we were, was the only place where you could literally cut a record in those days. You know I still have a couple of the old recording lathes, where we actually cut onto acetate discs. We would actually help them cut, literally cut, little demos. Which when I say 'cut' I mean literally cut into sixteen-inch acetate platters."

Al Jefferson

Al "Big Boy" Jefferson was originally from Baltimore, but eventually settled in Washington, D.C. At one point in his career, he worked in Quality Music's "goldfish bowl" studio on the sidewalk, via station WOOK, where he was a disc jockey. Jefferson's involvement with vocal harmony consisted of one single affair with a group from Washington, D.C., which he managed for a while, the Four Bel-Aires.[8] The group had one record in 1958, "Tell Me Why" b/w "Where Are You," on the X-Tra label.

As he was growing up, Jefferson used to sing. It was singing as something to do, and the amateur shows and talent contests around town helped him. "It gave a lot of poor kids an avenue of escape if they had something."

As it happened, the Philip Morris Company came through town one day in the mid-1940s. It was an indication of one way that big businesses in the U.S. began to look specifically at black consumers and, not surprisingly, the vehicle was to be music. "They decided that they wanted to create some impact in the black market for their product—cigarettes. They felt that the best way to do it would be through music, so the Philip Morris Quartet was formed, and it was in Baltimore that a baritone and first tenor were sought."

Jefferson auditioned for the part, got it, and went out on the road. The job was to give out sample cigarettes in nightclubs and give impromptu shows by performing three or four numbers. The pay was sixty dollars a week—very good money for singing in those days. Jefferson was the baritone. According to Jefferson, one of the people with the group was Neddie

Washington, granddaughter of Booker T. Washington. Phillip Morris made some engaging connections. "They were sort of tying history and entertainment together, you know. And at that time the Booker T. Washington half-dollar had been minted."

After that tour, Jefferson made his way into radio, first in Atlantic City, and then to WOOK in Washington. The WOOK program director at that time was the black DJ Cliff Holland. "When I first came to Washington we used to do split shifts. I would come on in the morning from ten until twelve, play, you know, rhythm and blues."

Although "rhythm & blues" meant "black," occasionally Jefferson would slip in a white artist—Frankie Lane comes to mind because he sounded black, according to Jefferson. "And there'd be a two hour period for the gospel lady. Cliff Holland would come on at two and stay 'til six. I'd come back at six and stay until the station closed down. Because then they only had a license to go up until two in the morning, then they had to shut down."

The WOOK studio was at Eighth and I, Northwest. The building is still there. Jefferson makes an interesting comment on the DJ, Tex Gathings. "When Tex was on the air, Tex did not play, nor did he have any inclination to play, any of that what he called 'garbage,' which was [vocal] groups, you know. Tex was a jazz man. He was strictly jazz, and he used to do a jazz show from eleven at night to say two in the morning when the station shut down."

When Tex Gathings left Washington, Al Jefferson took his radio slot, including the famous Quality Music "goldfish bowl." "Tex I think had it up to here with the goldfish bowl, so when I came in they put me into the bowl to replace Tex. I would go on the air at seven o'clock from the goldfish bowl and I would stay on until eleven at night. Store would close and I would jump in my car and drive back down to the station and get on the air to finish up the broadcast day until two. So that's how we worked it."

The goldfish bowl was just what it sounds like, a space behind glass in which people on the sidewalk watch you work. It was a very popular venue. At one point Jefferson did a one-hour, noon to one p.m. show called "Cool Noon Tunes. "I think a lot of my reputation in Washington came from the goldfish bowl. A lot of people see me, 'Oh yeah, I remember you, you used to be in the goldfish bowl."

In those days commercial radio disc jockeys had theme songs, which sometimes led to nicknames. "My theme, and all jocks had a theme in those days, my theme was "Big Boy," by Bill Doggett. He had a thing called "Big Boy." And so a lot of people used to call me Al "Big Boy" Jefferson.

Tex Gathings sits in the Quality Music Goldfish Bowl with three of the Four Bars. Courtesy of Al Feemster.

It was at WOOK that Jefferson met young performers like the vocal group Bel-Aires. He refers to them as "these kids." "One of the shows I used to do on WOOK was a Saturday show called *Teen-o-Rama*. On *Teen-o-Rama* from say, seven until nine at night, I let the kids take over completely. They would do all the announcing. They would come in and talk about social events, where the next hop's gonna be and stuff like that. It was my idea, and I would just be there to make sure that everything went well and nobody went crazy, you know. And in the big A studio, the kids would be dancing in the big A studio and in the small studio my staff would be making the announcements and putting on the records.

"So, any way, these kids [the Bel-Aires] were a part of that group that used to come down. They used to sing together.

"They had a pretty good blend. You know I used to listen to them. And they had one guy named Robinson, fat dude all out of shape, but he had a beautiful first tenor. He used to do all the lead work. So I said, well maybe something can be done with these guys. So I got involved with them."

Like a great number of others, Jefferson had no experience managing or producing music groups, but something about this group struck him. "I got them a shot on stage at the Royal. And it all depended on how it went, you know. I bought them suits. They had blue suits and tie. It didn't go too well because you can't, these kids just weren't ready for that pressure, you know, that audience out there and everything. They died, they died out there, you know. But they did make a record, but I've forgotten now, it's been so long ago, how that came about. But they did make a record, but nothing ever came of that."

Disc jockeys in those days, they huffed and they puffed, and they blew doors down. "I was pretty strong in the business at the time and if Al Jefferson said to certain parties, 'Hey man I got a group and I would like to record them,' they would make arrangements. But it was a disaster, their first public appearance was a disaster and I think it all went down hill from there. But they came from good homes and their parents really didn't want them doing that, you know. Well that's how they got together, they came out of that Teen-o-Rama group."

Jackson Lowe

The Mayor of Connecticut Avenue
"Take it Jackson…Take it Jackson… (Vaughn Monroe, "Take It Jackson")

The Washington talent show that was arguably the best known came first from station WWDC. Its host was Jack Lowe.

Jackson Lowe was born Jack Lowe Endler in Brooklyn, New York, on December 1, 1915. He attended New York City public schools and then entered New York University. After his second year, he left to pursue a radio career. He eventually ended up in Washington to take a job with WINX. They promised him $22 a week. As it happened, he got into Washington a day early and went over to WWDC, where they offered him $27.50 a week. He accepted and, indeed, remembers the day—Friday, December 5, 1941. Two days later, he was on the air during the Pearl Harbor attack.

At the time WWDC had been on the air about six months. As we have heard, the disc jockeys played pretty much what they wanted at the time, conforming to the general drift of the station and responding to popular taste and the record industry. Promotion men and record salesmen who wanted to sell in the area would bring records for the stations. According to Lowe, one of his earliest sponsors brought to his attention a great deal of music—Max Silverman, from Quality Music. Lowe used to hang around the music store and met Ahmet Ertegun there, when he was still a teenager. He also went out to the black clubs to take in the neighborhood up on Seventh Street. Black music of the period, he says, "just, you know, became a part of me."

The record people who came in to the stations to sell records were pure businessmen. They pushed anything that they felt would sell. The basic instinct of the developing record industry during the 1940s, especially among the independent labels, was to market, push, sell, and get customers to purchase. The independent record companies like Atlantic, Chess, and King (there were dozens of others) centered their recording efforts on material the major labels—Mercury or RCA, for instance—avoided. What did the major labels avoid? They failed to notice the palpable changes in black popular music during the 1940s, the so-called "race," or "sepia" records. Part of the reason was a gross insensitivity to those changes; and part of the reason was a reluctance to alienate their core constituency, which was white. It was no different from a white department store at the time not welcoming black customers for fear of alienating the white ones.

The "indies" seized on an opportunity to fill an emerging market— black rhythm & blues and gospel—partly because there may have been some casual interest in the sounds, but also because there was indeed interest in the entrepreneurial possibilities. Record people, at least some, would try to sell whatever they could or whatever they had to move, to whomever.

Lowe considered for a moment the issue of race and record salesmen. "I don't think there was any racial overtones either way. Whatever they had. For instance, King Records had an awful lot of black artists so they were naturally pushing a lot of black artists. But then, we mentioned Lou Krefetz [the manager of the Clovers], well Lou Krefetz used to work for Mercury. Actually, he worked for a distributor in Baltimore who handled, who distributed Mercury before Schwartz Brothers came into being — Henry Nathanson, general distributing. And he used to push a lot of 'off' labels, but he also brought me Patti Page and Vic Damone who were on Mercury. So it was just what they were pushing at the time.

"I used to have a half-hour I set aside once a week, I guess it was on Monday night from seven to seven-thirty or seven-thirty to eight, I can't remember which, where I played the best of the new releases for that week or that month, depending on how many came out. And they used to be a pretty good mix of black and white."

Lowe also had a theme song and a nickname. Because the station was up on Connecticut Avenue, Lowe became the "Mayor of Connecticut Avenue." His theme song came about this way. "We had a music director who used to buy records and catalogue them in the music library. I guess he was a music librarian more than anything else. He was also a radio announcer. He was also a musician who played music at night, and he was also my roommate when I first went to work at the station, named Willy Goff. And Willy was in the music library and I was in the studio on the air in the afternoon; I started as an afternoon show. And I had some high school kids in the studio and they used to dance to records in the big studio, and I'd talk to them once in a while on the air. And this one kid kept saying, 'Yeah Jackson. Solid Jackson. Way to go Jackson.' You know, I like that talk. And he kept calling me Jackson, and I was Jack Lowe at that time. And Willy in the music library just happened to have "Take It Jackson" by Vaughn Monroe in his hand and later he said this is your new theme song and your new name is Jackson Lowe. So that's the way that came about."

Over the years, Lowe worked Washington as an entertainer, and he spent a considerable amount of time outside the studio, as did most DJs of that era. He did a lot of remote broadcasts out of various black clubs in Washington, including the Club Bali, the Stardust at Virginia Avenue, Southeast, and other local clubs with various artists that ranged from Billy Eckstine to blues artists. "Dwight 'Gatemouth' Moore, before he started singing gospel, I used to have to make him write the lyrics down to make sure they were clean enough to go on the air."

Lowe's first show on WWDC—the 1450 Club—was first on in the afternoon from one-thirty until five-thirty. At three-thirty he programmed for high school kids. The one-thirty to three-thirty music was "nondescript . . . like big band music."

Lowe had kept a 16-inch radio transcription of his 1450 Club program in his basement for forty years. The disc label, from 5/10/49, indicated "9–9:30." The show time had moved by 1949, to the evening slot. From his introduction, we know that particular segment of the show was "requests

Jackson Lowe, the Mayor of Connecticut Avenue, circa 1948. Courtesy of Jackson Lowe.

by postcard, letter, or telegram." Lowe's introduction was short. Following his theme song, Vaughn Monroe's "Take it Jackson" (with the band repeating "Take it Jackson, take it Jackson," over and over), Lowe responds with a voiceover—"And I got it." He then moves right into his introduction, with a snappy, on-air style. The first song is a request, Frankie Ross's "Lemon Drop." The thirty-minute recorded segment alternated between jump band dance material—Lionel Hampton's "Central Avenue Breakdown"—to easy pop ballads, like Vic Damone singing "Again" and Perry Como interpreting "Bali Hi," from the musical *South Pacific*. One highlight was Lowe reading an advertisement for Senate beer, from Washington's only brewery. The spot ended with a short vocal harmony rendition of the product song—"Get together with Senate; the beer so refreshing it's tops." The set concluded before the news with Mel Torme singing a tepid version of "Blue Moon." The content of the show, Jackson's monologues, and the tenor of the requests and dedications indicate a racially mixed listening audience.

For the high school kids he played everything, including "race music" and later rhythm & blues. How did he know what the kids wanted to listen to? Once again, we see that DJs back then worked the streets and learned what their audience wanted to hear. They were very public about it.

"They came up and told me. They came up and told me. And I used to find out through Waxie Maxie in his store, through being on the street and talking to people. This was a friendly town; this was a real friendly Southern city when I came here originally. And you know, if you went somewhere and they say, 'Yeah, I heard you on the radio the other day, why don't you play such and such, it's a great record.' And of course the war, in the forties, World War II, I used to play Clara Ward. Clara Ward, yeah, gospel, because people would write and ask for things like that to play for so-and-so who was overseas, you know, and so forth."

Washington may have known Lowe best for his talent show, for which African Americans in the city and vocal groups had a particular affinity. "Now the best recollection I have of groups, O.K., black-oriented groups, is the amateur show which went on WWDC every Sunday, twelve-thirty noon until one-thirty for eight years straight. I guess I started it about late 1941 or early 1942, and it went through 1950. I don't remember if the show was on before [1941] or not. I think possibly the program director, Norman Reed, might have thought it up, and one of my sponsors, Morton's, a clothing store. They used to have one downtown at Seventh and D, and they had another one somewhere else, around Irving Street. The show was called WWDC Amateurs, and then it was named Jackson

Lowe's Amateurs after it got popular, after about a year or so, sponsored by Morton's. And we used to have a Morton's theme song that the program director recorded as a parrot, the Morton's parrot. It was Polly—how did it go? I know it ended up with [sings]—'Mor-tons Mor-tons Mor-tons,'—as a parrot singing it, you know. He wrote it and performed it for the show."

It was arguably the definitive venue for amateur black talent in Washington during the 1940s. The Morton amateur show aired weekly, in thirteen-week cycles. The twelve weekly winners came back on the thirteenth week to compete for the grand prize. Toward the end of the show's run, the stations had a deal with the Howard Theater, the only theater left in town offering vaudeville-type live acts on stage. The deal was that the final prizewinner would get a week's engagement at the Howard for a salary of $125. District Theaters and Mort Gerber owned the Howard then. Bill Hoyle was the publicity man for District Theaters. Shep Alan was the stage manager then, as he was for many years.

While the radio station did not pointedly aim the talent show at black Washington, Lowe said, "they just responded so, so well to it." He reasoned, as did Al Jefferson and others, that there were few other venues. "Well they had no other outlet for their talent. No other way to show their talent."

While Lowe fondly recalls Washington of the World War II era and later as being "real friendly," he was white. For blacks, Washington was a virulently racialized and segregated city and it would be difficult to ignore the social limitations. This made the nondiscriminatory radio talent shows especially valuable, as Lowe realized. With this in mind, he theorizes on the success of his show. He tries to choose his words carefully. You sense that his interpretation of the popularity of the show among Washington's African American audiences—and we have no demographic data to help us understand—is just barely within reach for Lowe. "Well they had no other outlet for their talent. No other way to show their talent. And I think the blacks as a race are more—how shall I say it? I don't want to say aggressive, but they are more prone—"

Lowe pauses. "If they have talent, to perform—less inhibited. And they used to come up and audition and I auditioned everybody for the show. I used to audition right before the show and ninety percent, ninety-nine percent of those who auditioned got on. Now I had a philosophy on this—the show was a terrible show because the talent was just fair. Every once in a while you would get a fairly good one, but I had a philosophy on the show, and I felt that everybody who listened to the show had a little ham in him.

Everybody at one time or another had said to himself, 'Gee, I want to be in show business. I can do that.' So I made sure to put on one real stinker on the show. I mean a real clunker, and I never gave them the gong or anything else. I let them finish so that all these potential hams listening in could say, 'Gee, even I could do better than that.' And that's what brought them back every week, not the good talent."

The paucity of city-wide venues for African American talent contributed to the show's popularity for blacks. Also, no one interviewed ever intimated that Lowe's show limited black participation or black winners (as some other shows around the nation may have done). However, other factors may have included the notion of musically competitive attitudes fostered historically in black culture. Many of those interviewed mentioned the competitive attitude in the black public school. Lowe wanted to avoid the term "aggressive" because he knew intuitively that something else was at work, and probably because he was sensitive to pernicious stereotyping. Music, dance, and verbal duel had long been a part of African American culture and fit in well with the competitive nature of local talent shows. They were also public venues where African Americans could perform on an equal footing with whites and often outperform them, although there are no data on how many black winners actually won the first prize.

Record labels also used the talent shows as a way to publicize, generate, and recruit talent, as *Billboard* reported. In the case described below, the company owner organized his own show and thus remained fully in charge of who would win. Note also that this particular tour culminates in Baltimore and Washington, attesting to those cities' importance in the rhythm and blues market.

> Eddie Mesner of Aladdin Records is going to sponsor a talent contest thru a belt of Southern theaters. The contest will begin in October. Mesner will tour the theaters with one of his several Aladdin recording bands and will conduct contests in 50 or so houses in the District Theaters chain, the group which operates the Howard Theater, Washington, and the Royale, [sic] Baltimore. From the talent gathered on the tour, Mesner will select a sufficient number to make up three packages which will be brought into the Washington and Baltimore houses for a final run-off. Nightly winners will be awarded a cash prize and the winners of the contest tour will be signed to Aladdin recording contracts. (*Billboard*, September 1951, in Gart 1986: 448)

Jackson Lowe's talent show went on live in front of a studio audience that the competitors brought in, and many vocal groups from Washington responded to the show. Indeed, they demonstrated great skill in getting on the show and returning as often as they could.

"Well the Armstrong Four and Jimmy McPhail came out of it. Yes, I remember the Dunbar Five, and I remember 98,000 groups that came on and they used to come on every week under a different name because they wanted to get on more often, you know? Every time I had an opening they'd be there and they'd say, 'Well, we're the Joe Shmos this week, you know, and last week we were the Shmo Joes, you know."

He laughed. "I needed to fill the time and I knew they were adequate performers and they needed a showcase. And I used to have guests on the show. Sometimes they'd be groups like the Orioles, or Bullmoose Jackson came on. I had Coleman Hawkins one time. This show covered the whole conglomerate of people. The amateur show did produce an awful lot of groups. I think what it did was it gave people an opportunity to perform, O.K.? To be heard, to be seen. And I think that the groups evolved from the fact that a lot of them didn't have the confidence to perform by themselves, so they banded together and formed a group, and that's when they came up to me. Or any other place where they could get exposure and be heard."

Around this time, in the late 1940s, the Clovers—before they actually became the Clovers—participated in Lowe's radio program. This was where Harold Winley had first heard the group. Jack Lowe remembered Harold Lucas as the "pushy one" who asked every Sunday, "Have you got room for us today?"

"I knew them all. The Clovers were on my show maybe seven times out of a year period, under seven different names. They were there every week, and if I had an opening they would fill in."

Jack Lowe referred to Lucas as "the pushy one" because he was always trying to get on the program. This, once again, points to an active posture on the part of these youngsters who made as much use of the radio stations as the stations permitted. There seems to have been a push and pull pattern of mutuality between radio and the groups.

Lowe went on to say that most of the individual vocalists were black teens. He did not recall any white vocal groups. "Well no no no, I had plenty of white kids on the show, but not the groups. And I didn't have that many groups on in one week. I would have maybe one or two in a week. So out of twelve performers, you see, you had maybe two groups."

"I had singers. I had people doing recitations, supposedly dramatic readings. I had instrumentalists. I had tap dancers. Anything that could be done on the radio, and some of the things that you didn't think could be done on the radio, were done on that amateur show."[9]

WWDC was the first station in Washington to play rhythm & blues on a regular basis, according to Lowe. He returns to the subject of his fondness for the city:

"I tell you, this was a great town in those days. Great, great to be living here, great to be working here, and just so enjoyable because you had everything available to you. And there wasn't the highly competitiveness and cutthroat attitude that you find in New York."

Nevertheless, the subject of race and Washington's segregation must always bear down on the romance of the 1940s and 1950s. The different white and black perceptions and perspectives about those years can be alternately subtle and flagrant. As close to the African American community as DJs like Jackson Lowe were, and as important as he was to black Washington's entertainment sphere in those years, he did not sense those unvoiced sentiments, the ones below the surface.

"I really never found any animosity or beef or enmity from black people because of the segregation at the time. I guess they were resigned to it, either that or—I really don't know. Now organizations came along, like Pride Incorporated, which Mayor Barry was part of at that time; other equal rights types of organizations, but I never found any blacks in the music business or in business, retail business—some of whom were my sponsors on the air—who had anything either way to say about it, negative or positive. They just didn't discuss it. They didn't bring it up. I think that prosperity was so rampant in the war days, World War II days, from like 1942 right up to 1950 that nobody had any complaints."

African Americans at that time no doubt exercised the right to complain judiciously. It was a time when all but a few black citizens would not openly state grievances, unless couched in the typically polite discourse of assimilationist groups such as the Institute on Race Relations.

Maurice Hulbert

Maurice Hulbert, a well-known radio personality in Baltimore during and after the 1950s, well illustrates the black entrepreneurial spirit of postwar radio. He was born in Helena, Arkansas, in 1916. His mother took him to Memphis, Tennessee, as a "baby in arms." His father was a dance instructor in Memphis and on Beale Street. The senior Mr. Hulbert, an entrepreneur was "unofficial mayor of Beale Street" because he owned restaurants, dance studios, dance halls, a printing business, and homes on different parts of Beale Street.

Maurice Hulbert left Memphis as a band director in the 1940s, but wanted to pursue a career in radio at a time when there was not yet a black

radio disc jockey in Memphis. By the time he returned, he found that Nat
D. Williams, a former high school teacher, had already started as the city's
first black on-air person. One day Williams invited him on as a guest disc
jockey. This was something Hulbert had never done before. They "threw"
him in there for fifteen minutes, and Hulbert thought he had done well.
Later the general manager asked him if he'd be interested in going on radio
and Hulbert found himself a job at WDIA—thirty-five minutes a day and
twenty-five dollars per week. Bert Ferguson, the manager, gave him the
name "Hot Rod."

Hulbert says that WDIA in Memphis was having financial problems at
the time they hired Nat Williams, and were looking for the "black dollar,"
as he phrased it. Tex Gathings said the same thing about WOOK.

Buddy Deane, a white entertainer, had a music television show in
Memphis before heading to Baltimore. He told Hulbert that Baltimore was
looking for a black disc jockey. Hulbert had high ratings in Memphis, and
because of that reputation, WITH in Baltimore hired him in 1951. "So
that's how I came to Baltimore."

Hulbert gives credit to the managers at WITH for allowing him to
develop and create his on-air personalities for his three daily shows: *Hot
Rod*, *Maurice the Mood Man*, and *Maurice Hulbert*. He was a prolific professional, for while he was working in Baltimore, he also sent a taped show
daily for the Philadelphia area, aired on three stations there. After that, he
had a weekend taped show in New York, occasionally doing a live show. In
the early 1960s, he left Baltimore for Philadelphia, when he also did an
evening broadcast in New York on station WWRL.

"In the '50s at WITH I had a mixture. I played, when I got here, I
played a mixture. I played Stan Kenton, you know. I played Ruth Brown,
Lionel Hampton, Count Basie, you know. I played Ink Spots."

The station was looking to a black market. "That was their purpose for
bringing me in, to get a strong black audience. But my program, it went
over so well, my white audience was as strong as my black audience."

When Hot Rod arrived in 1951, Baltimore, he said, "radio-wise, it was
sad." Some of the other stations in Baltimore at that time were WSID, with
Bill Franklin and Mary Osborn (who managed the Marylanders). Paul
"Fat Daddy" also worked at WSID, along with Paul Johnson, Billy Fox,
Kelson Fisher, and Douglas Henderson. At that time, WSID was *the* black
station in town. WITH, on the other hand, had only one black disc jockey
and that was Hulbert. WEBB later came along as another "black" station.

Hulbert also booked acts into the Royal Theater, as what he termed
a "side way of earning money." He booked groups like the Flamingos,

Coasters, Swallows, and Orioles. Despite these connections, Hulbert had a very eclectic play-list. "At WITH I played music. I played Eydie Gorme. I played her husband, Steve Lawrence, before they were married. I went from my taste, my gut feeling, about the way in which I felt about a song or a tune."

He also used to broadcast from a dressing room in the Royal Theater, where he produced and emceed shows. He did three shows a day and four on Friday and Saturday. His show was in the evening on WITH, so when he had a show at the Royal, he broadcast right from there. He also broadcast from the window of the Club Casino, on Pennsylvania Avenue. Another club in Baltimore during those days was the Comedy Club (Dinah Washington sang there) and the Tijuana Club (between North Avenue and Fulton), where Billie Holiday appeared for the last time in Baltimore.

Hulbert named his up-beat format radio program *Hot Rod's Rocket Ship Show*. His other on-air persona, the *Mood Man*, was for low-key programming. He said that when he got to Baltimore there were no "disc jockeys" per se, but just "announcers" who were "very staid." What black DJs brought to radio was action, in the form of personality and style—as well as links to black listeners and musicians.

Hulbert, like so many other disc jockeys of his generation, hosted numerous shows outside the studio. That was how he came into contact with groups and singers, like George Jackson. George said, "Well we all come from the neighborhood. Yeah, Lexington and Schroeder and Poplar Street. West Side, yeah. We formed a group and we went to the Royal Theater with Hot Rod. He put us on the Royal Stage. That was our first break."

This was before the Plants actually formed. Hot Rod Hulbert had put some other singers—friends of George—on a show he hosted at the Royal Theater. "Vernon Hawkins, who was singing with a group, he had them on the show, so Vernon said, 'I want you to meet Hot Rod. You know he might put you all on the show, too.' So I say, 'Oh, he ain't gonna put us on the show.' He said, 'Come on let's go up there.' It was his show at the Royal Theater. Well during that time, he was on WITH. He met us and he heard us, he said, 'O.K. you all on the show.' Bam, just like that, and put us on the show. That's how I met him. We auditioned for him, so he heard us, he said, 'O.K., good. I like you. You're on the show.' We worked Christmas to New Years. It had to be about '56. It had to be about '55, '56, before I recorded, you know. And from there he did a couple jobs for us, out at Carr's Beach and other places and all that. He was a helping hand."

Hulbert, helping hand and all, recalled the same incident, only he remembered the group as the Plants. Well, it wasn't the Plants quite yet, but that's not the point. Hulbert brings up the other side of trying to manage vocal groups and another side to all of the romantic notions about positive group energy.

"I tried to work with them, and I thought they had potential. But I'll tell you what drove me away. I had a girl—Jean Hill was a girl I managed once. And two things, well, I don't need this, you know what I mean. I was doing all right in other things. I was doing shows, promoting shows, and coming out of seaplanes and helicopters and all that kind of stuff. The Plants had great potential, but when you have three, four, five guys, you have three or four, five different minds to deal with. You know. You have three or four, five different mentalities. You know. And then you have egos that get involved in it. And when this happens, they bicker among themselves, they won't make rehearsals, some will be there and others won't be there. And, you know, it just became a nightmare, you know. So I said, O.K., no more groups."

Hulbert, like so many of the other disc jockeys, could be a tireless promoter and self-promoter—note the reference to the seaplane and the helicopter. Nevertheless, Hulbert seemed always there for local talent. "Sometimes the material wasn't too good, but you could win a few friends. You know if it was a dog—when I say a dog, I mean the record's a dog—at least you played it some, you know. And sometimes it might sound pretty good, you give it a little more play, you understand. One time, I can remember, there were some guys that were around where you could go back and pick up that record every once in a while to help them in their personal appearances around town, you know, just for that purpose."

Hulbert, like his contemporaries Al Jefferson, Tex Gathings, and Jack Lowe, never really articulated a very clear reason why he became a DJ. It seems that each, in his own way, slipped, stepped, or stumbled into the position and then took control, established their own individual sense of professional public purpose. Their contact with vocal groups was inevitable because group harmony was beginning to dominate black popular music—rhythm & blues—by 1951, as *Billboard* noted that year.

> Vocal groups have taken command in the r&b field. Never before in the history of the specialty field have so many groups developed and taken so deep a root both on wax and in personal appearances. The development of the vocal group in the field dates back a couple of years to the successes originally achieved by the Ravens and then the Orioles. With these two groups still potent box office in the r&b market, almost a dozen others have sprung up, most of them in the past six months.
>
> The Dominoes, the Swallows, the Clovers, and Five Keys, the Four Buddies, the Cardinals, the Four Tunes, the Blenders, etc, are some of the

groups in the business doing well at this point. These vocal groups have taken the play in the r&b field away from the small instrumental groups and intimate solo blues singers which held sway for some time. (*Billboard*, September 1951, in Gart 1986: 448)

Managers, Agents, Arrangers

Disc jockeys, as the previous narratives tell us, were never full-time, hands-on managers or booking agents. They helped if they could, when they could. Other managers were most often just businessmen or -women from around town, friends, even schoolteachers. A few were also involved in small local record companies. These managers were a ubiquitous group who seemed involved in many different but related things at one time. Music on some level was either just one part of their lives, or something new, to capitalize on the popularity of rhythm & blues groups. The managers knew the cities and the business of business, but not always music. Even the record shop owners were probably more like peddlers than music connoisseurs. Many of these business people, and other kinds, like teachers and friends, were new to music managing specifically.

As is so often the case when it comes to understanding "truth," the truth about managers and how they treated their charges is a matter of perspective. In our case, it is a case of perspective stretched over thirty to forty years. There was a range of relationships that ran from good to worse and back again. Managers came in all flavors and attitudes. Some had a smile; others guile and wile. Their reasons for getting involved with group singing ranged also, from benevolence, doing some kids a favor, to making an investment in the group vocal thing and hoping to profit from it. They were intermediaries, go-betweens, who probably spent a lot of time trying to shove their prodigies and product out into the market. Sometimes group managers functioned strictly as career organizers, sometimes they also acted as agent and booked jobs, and sometimes they even helped with coaching and material. "Managing" often meant a combination of organizing, booking, coaching, schmoozing, producing, investing, and collaborating with their charges. Most groups wanted to cooperate with managers on strategies to succeed. That was the whole point, eventual success. The groups may have been, as Maurice Hulbert indicated above, difficult to work with, but the groups usually were not passive. Often they were just young.

When Andy Magruder was a young teenager and sang harmony, he used to go up to Circle Recording, near Washington Circle at 2138 Pennsylvania Avenue. At Circle—"Now Using High Fidelity Ampex"[10]—you could make a transcription, as Andy and his friends did. Eventually they found a Washingtonian, a brother named Boscoe Boyd, as a manager. "He used to wear a French tam and smoke cigars."

Andy said that Boscoe used to drag the group around from one record company to another trying to get a contract. One day, with the families' permission, he took them out of school and drove them to Chicago, where in 1954 they recorded four sides as the Five Blue Notes for the Sabre label. Andy maintains only a fleeting but poetic memory from that trip. "Yeah, in his Lincoln. Oh man, we used to have our heads hanging out the window, and fog on through the mountains and whatnot."

Alfonso Feemster of the Four Bars of Rhythm recalled their manager, a mid-level city government worker. That's all we know about him, other than that he knew someone who knew someone and that was how things— and groups—worked in those days. "Ah, Perry, Perry Sprigs. He was our first manager. He used to work for the old recorder of deeds in D.C. Now, I think him and Eddie Daye had a connection. I don't know how they really met. And then, of course, Eddie brought him into us and say, 'Hey, this is going to be our manager. He got some connections and can get us some work, and what have you, and we gonna'—we always had this big dream about making a recording. That was our primary goal and that's what we wanted to do. If we had to walk the streets of New York all month, we were gonna do it, and he was gonna help us, you know. So anyway, he worked with us for a while and he was a pretty sharp guy. He knew, he had some contacts, but not as many as you would like."

Alfred Buddy Slaughter had little good to say about managers. He, you will recall, sang with the Buddies and the Cap-Tans. They often played a popular downtown Washington club, the Blue Mirror, where a local agent found them. "We tried and we sang a few songs and things, old Ink Spots songs, and it sounded pretty good, you know. So we went over and talked to Les [Lester Fountain], see if he could play behind us."

Fountain was a Washington songwriter and guitarist. "He gave us some other tunes to work on and we worked and worked and everybody got interested in this thing we were building up, right. We had a repertoire of about seventy-five songs before we even started working. And the first place we worked was the Blue Mirror, at Fourteenth and I Northwest. That was a very nice club. They had a rotary stage that would move while you were up there, you know. It was strictly a white club. The owner was from Russia and he nicknamed himself Davis for some reason, I don't know why, but any time that the Mills Brothers, or Rocco, a piano player in those days, any time those guys couldn't make it he would call us. But we knew a lot of songs. And we would go there and we would make there, too."

That was where Lillian Claiborne met the group, known as the Buddies then. "We picked up our manager through the Blue Mirror. Lillian Claiborne. I don't think she did us too fair. I know not, because that record, 'I'm so Crazy for Love,' was a hit."

Miss Claiborne—which is what many who worked with her called her—arranged for the Cap-Tans to make that record with Dot, in 1953. "She handled a lot of groups in Washington. Nobody ever went too far, that she handled. She lived in Washington. I think [Harmon] Bethea knew her, she had something to do with that spiritual group."

Harmon's first group was the Progressive Four, a gospel group; he then formed the Cap-Tans. "So that's how she came about. Anyway, we went to MCA, the Music Corporation of America; an audition. And these people wanted us, and she wouldn't turn us loose. These people are LTD, London, France, you know. That was our break, but we couldn't go, she wouldn't let us go."

Slaughter is contending here that Claiborne somehow prevented the group from going farther than they did and that, in general, managers were inhibitors to success. That view, however, by no means obtained with others. In most cases, singers viewed managers as hopeful facilitators. For instance, when in high school in Baltimore, Melvin Coles sang in a group called the Rialtos. A white grocery storeowner tried to manage them. "So this guy, he was a very nice guy, and he, well he did a lot of things for us, you know. He tried to set us up the best he knew, he didn't know anything much about the business, you know, but he was telling us, he said, 'Well you guys got to, I like your sound, you got a pretty nice sound.' "

Managers also maintained over the years a range of memories about the groups with whom they once worked, as did "Papa" Lou Krefetz, the Clovers manager and a Baltimore record store owner. He was very sure of his own abilities, at least when he looked back from 1972. From his perspective, the singers were supposed to be passive. Krefetz was the man.

"You see, I used to be the leader; I called the shots. When they started calling their own shots, that's when they broke up."[11]

Buddy Bailey, the Clovers lead singer, remembers Lou Krefetz this way. "Well, when he got us he was, I would think, around forty. What happened with Lou Krefetz was, he said, 'If you don't make over a thousand dollars a week, I'll only take ten percent, but if you make over a thousand, I'll want fifteen percent.' Graduated, you know, so our first gig was like—"

Buddy laughs here. "I think we [the whole group] made about nine hundred dollars for that night. It was some kind of dance."

"Which was nothing, but see, what happened was he had us in an air-tight contract where we had to have expenses to come out of the money from the top. You understand what I mean? Plus giving him his manager's fee. Oh man. But we never really got with an agent now. We were with an old agent, an agent that booked only the rhythm and blues acts of the fifties I would say. Shaw Attractions out of New York.

"Shaw would only book us in mediocre places. This was as soon as we signed, when we had the first record. All right, we got the first hit, then we signed with a booking agent. O.K. A fellow named Billy Shaw. He's dead, too. But he had Ruth Brown, he had the Cardinals, he had Earl Bostic, he had everybody. All soul attractions, you know. But what happened was the guy wasn't booking us in these good places, you know, Copa Cabana and places where you could really do it."

The Swallows' manager, Irv Goldstick, was the one that heard them out on the street and made the group learn a hundred songs. He ran an electronics shop in Baltimore and also stocked records. Herman thought that Goldstick was a good manager.

"When he first became our manager there were some contractual problems. But it wasn't because he wanted to cheat us; it's that he's ignorant of some facts too. I was about, what, between eighteen and nineteen then. When we started singing, we had our own instruments, which he bought for us. And then we paid him back as we worked. You know what I mean? But he was very good. Very good to us. Very good to us."

Irv found the Swallows a place to rehearse. "Yes. Above the record shop there was like an apartment that was empty. We used to go up there and rehearse. We used to rehearse up there.

"He had a friend that knew about groups and what have you. And I think he told him that this was the going thing, this is what's going on. You know? And these guys are going to be something one day. This was like '50, '51." Evidently, this particular relationship between group and manager was a good one.

There seems to have been a wide spectrum of benevolence and malevolence (and the intervening years may have either softened or hardened people's memories). The manager "was ignorant of some facts" that caused some problems with a contract. Goldstick was not a professional manager and most likely interested in making money through the success of the group rather than through deception. The manager, after all, bought instruments for the group (though they had to pay him back). He had a friend who "knew about groups" and said, "this was the going thing." This suggests that Goldstick's involvement was not particularly calculating, but casual and a bit amateurish at first. He was a small, local businessman and most likely became involved with the Swallows in the hopes that they would be successful, which they were for a short while. He may or may not have really liked the music, but music was the product that he was used to dealing with as a shop owner. He does not have to like every record he sells out of his store. He knew that vocal harmony was beginning to hit big, as *Billboard* reported. It would have been a logical step to take, to work with a group because, as Denby said, it was what was going on.

Goldstick had the group learn as many songs as possible, even some country material, as we heard, but did not necessarily make suggestions about performance style. Had he known more about music performance perhaps he would have. In the case of the Swallows, it was the artist and repertoire representative from King Records, Henry Glover, one of only a handful of African Americans working on that level in the early 1950s, who suggested changes in performance style. Another field representative of King had already heard the Swallows and pronounced them "too much like the Orioles." He suggested they change their sound. Goldstick, however, was the person responsible for getting Glover back down to listen to the group again, and that led to a recording contract. The Swallows, of course, made changes that Glover recommended. This suggests not passivity, but simply doing what was necessary, learning to learn to succeed in what was, for the singers, a new business and a tough one.

Sometimes a group's first manager was like a first love, at first sight when young it was one thing, but now, recalled long after the flame had gone out, another. Ernest Warren remembered with little enthusiasm his first manager with the Cardinals.

"But one fellow that was singing with us was working for Super Music Stores, and he was located at 570 North Gay Street. We used to go up to meet him to get off from work and we went in there one afternoon and sang a couple songs. Right away, he decided he wanted to be the manager. His name was Sam Azreal. He was the owner of Super Music. Yeah, he got interested. And he was the first one to get a piece of us. But Sam Azreal, he was no good. He was just like all them other sorry-ass managers, you know, he, he just wasn't no good. You know he was after that almighty Jewish dollar. And then he sold us to a guy named—"

Someone interrupted Ernest here and he lost his thought, but the name he was about to utter was that of Lou Karpouzie (which Ernest pronounces as "Lewkapoozie"). Karpouzie was the Cardinals' second manager. Ernest's comments, that the first manager "sold us" to the second, refer to contractual agreements, but they surely are an instructive choice of words. He continues with the story of Sam Azreal, who owned a record store where Donald "Jack" Johnson worked. Jack was one of the original Cardinals and Ernest and some guys would hang out there at the store, the record shop that Azreal owned. Because Ernest worked across the street at Epstein's, he was over there all of the time, just hanging out, as he phrased it.

Even hanging out, creatively and with purpose, can lead to something. "And he had a guy worked for him called Goody. He knew how to put things together so he could record you, and we did a couple of recordings. Yeah, we hung around there for a long time." Ernest is talking about the recording machine in the store that can cut demo discs. Sam, the store-owner, must have heard these guys hanging around all of the time. Then he heard the demo recording that Goody put together and he became more interested in hearing the group.

That seemed to be how things came together informally for many singers—through loose affiliations.

On the other hand, record people in those days would cruise into a town and nose around for talent. They would also go into record stores, check up on their discs, and see what was happening. The independent labels especially had a feel that was closer to the ground than the major labels. All of the contacts and connections were local, word of mouth—somebody always knew somebody else. That and their good work was how the Cardinals came to record for Atlantic.

According to Ernest, "Well, Ahmet Ertegun had a partner named Abramson. They were hunting talent and they were going from New York down South. And I don't know how they got word to Sam Azreal. Well see, Super Music was a big store in Maryland. And they found out which music stores was the biggest and they came through here and we just happened to be there. And we auditioned, and the following week they had a man named Jesse Stone down here to groom us for recording. He was the best, except for Quincy Jones, and he taught Quincy all he knew. Quincy Jones arranged two or three songs for us when Jesse wasn't available. But this was, I'm talking—nobody knew anything about Quincy then, you know. He was young. He was younger than we were. And Bill Harris arranged a few songs for us. See, that was the Clovers' guitar player. We had the best of everything. When we had the right song, we had a girl come down from California to play harp for one of our sessions. We had the best musicians in the world. We had Sam "The Man" Taylor on every session that we done."

The Cardinals recorded and released six sides for Atlantic Records in 1951 and 1952 (Ferlingere 1976), before Ernest Warren left the group. At the same time Ernest was speaking, Stone was living comfortably in Florida and still quite active in music. "Is that right? I wish I'd knew where he was. I'd like to see him myself, man, to thank him for a lot of things that he said to us, a lot of things, and as we were growing up we found them to be true, you know."

Back in the 1950s, Jesse Stone and some other musicians—older and more experienced than the kids singing as the Cardinals—took it upon themselves to mentor them. This was very much in the tradition of older black males, especially musicians looking after younger ones.

Ernest said, "The first time we recorded, and we were a little excited up there on what, Times Square? Yeah, there was so much light and people. He said, 'Go home, you be back before you know it.' I guess about three or four weeks we were back."

Stone kept them out of trouble by simply telling them what to do.

"Yeah, and where to go when we were there and where to go eat an—he was just like a dad, man, you know? But young people just don't understand that. Well, a whole lot of them didn't understand it too much then when they was away from home, but you learn. You live and you learn, man. And right today that man, and a few others, deserve medals, man, for trying to take care of them young guys was out there then. And you will get that from a lot of artists that paid attention to the people they work with."

Jesse Stone

A little old lady from Baltimore
A little old lady from Baltimore
A little old lady from Baltimore
Let's see what you can do

I can do the Suzy-Cue
I can do the Suzy-Cue
I can do the Suzy-Cue
And I'll show you what I can do (Jesse Stone)

You might debate the contribution of managers or agents, but not of a good arranger or producer. The rhythm & blues sound came about in part because they put the sound together, and helped most vocal groups develop and perfect their sound. Jesse Stone's story is important in several ways and apart from the local aspect of group harmony he is clearly one of the great figures in American popular music. I think one of the more intriguing aspects to rhythm & blues is its constructed sound. Stone was one of the first to develop that approach to the music and he certainly became good at it. He created and built a distinctive sound through writing and arranging—particular chords and song structures, bass patterns, rhythmic figures, horn and voice combinations. He worked for Atlantic Records, and what he produced is inseparable from the record company, the technology and equipment they used, the sidemen they employed, and the sound engineer who helped make the recorded sound, not to mention the groups doing the recording.

Jesse Stone learned the mechanics of making a group's sound *recordable*. Also, he tells us a lot about how the tangential parties worked with the singers and musicians and with each other, illustrating once again how rhythm & blues group harmony was not made in isolation, but interrelated with other entities. In addition, his involvement with Atlantic Records gets us back, eventually, to Baltimore and Washington. Recall that the Erteguns were from D.C., and before they started Atlantic they used to buy records from Max Silverman. Ahmet in particular used to meet people there, and through that connection the Clovers' manager met him and won a contract from Atlantic. Later, Atlantic sent Stone down to Baltimore and Washington to rehearse and prepare groups like the Cardinals and the Clovers for recording.

As he recalls all of this, he makes an important point about arrangers and rhythm & blues/rock 'n' roll. He reminds us that in the beginning, no one arranged rhythm and blues. It was put together mostly by ear, from "head charts." Atlantic Records, Jesse Stone's talent and knowledge, good New York studio musicians, and Ahmet Ertegun's inner musical vision, began to construct a particular sound in black music, the Atlantic sound. They took the talent they had and built around what the performers had to offer. This is production, and the importance of "production" in American popular music has one of its beginnings here. Production, recording, and arranging became as important as the song and the talent performing it. That, coupled with the performative strength of African American music making, began to change the sound of popular music. In his narrative, Stone's opinions reveal his resourcefulness and entrepreneurial skills, born of necessity, insight, and ability.

"Well, in the beginning, there wasn't many arrangers in rock 'n' roll, rhythm and blues. Most of it had been done by ear, you know, head, and there wasn't many musicians that were available in New York that could even play that type of stuff because they were all into big band, you know. Most of the musicians that could make any money was in big band work. And of course by me fooling around with the Apollo Theater, I came in contact with everybody in the business."

Stone explains how he coached singers. He makes it sound as if he were teaching the kids how to harmonize all over again. "Well the guys didn't know how to read and they didn't know the good harmony and then I would get on the piano and plunk one note and say you make this and hit another note and say you make that one, and they would sing it, you know. I'd rehearse them over and over and over until they would get [it], and that's what I called coaching at that time."

He makes an important point about Atlantic Records, which seemed early in its history to have stuck a balance between letting the musicians be themselves, but changing the sound at the same time to either improve it or make it more marketable. "Atlantic gave each individual group more attention than the other people. They would just, whatever they sang they'd bring them in there and let them sing like that. But we made certain that the harmonies were better and they were rehearsed, and we put arrangements of a band behind them and everything and so it sounded better, you know."

Polish it up a little bit.

"Yeah, uh huh. So we avoided the neglect that National gave all the talent over there where we did just the opposite, we gave everybody consideration, examine their material and improved on it and whatnot. Try to make it better."

Did he have a specific sound ideal in mind when he coached and recorded vocal groups?

"What kind of question is that? Well, everybody don't seem to be able to conceive that you can come up with an idea without that idea coming from somebody else, you know. My ideas began with me; it didn't start by me listening to somebody or somebody telling them what to do or what not to do.

"One of the reasons Atlantic made it [is] because we didn't do things like the other records were doing, you know. If you go back and look at those early Atlantic records, you'll hear the difference between what they were doing and what the other records [were doing]."

"I came to Baltimore to rehearse the Cardinals. I rehearsed the Cardinals and I rehearsed the Clovers down there. I can't remember the names of those groups because a lot of them, they didn't stay together."

He acknowledged that the Clovers, for instance, performed standards when Atlantic first heard them. "Yeah, they continued to do standards [and] even though we did a lot of original things, we also stuck to those standards."

Some might find it interesting to know why.

"Well, it was just what they sounded good doing—and you ask reasons, why does there always got to be a reason for something?" Jesse Stone did not think "why" questions were particularly good questions.

"People were experimenting back then in those days. Nobody knew what was best, what wasn't best. You did things and if it sounded good you kept it; if it didn't, you stopped doing it. That's all it was to that. There was no way to know what was good and what wasn't."

Did the specific song choice make any difference?

"No it didn't really."

He returns to talking about the coaching trips. "Well at first I came [to Baltimore] by myself. He [Abramson] sent me down there and I contacted the kids at where they were working and everything. Then I would stay in a little cheap hotel or something, eat in out of the way restaurants and all that sort of thing. That's the way it was. I figured that the company didn't have a whole lot of money. They weren't paying me all that much so my expenses I kept down to a minimum.

"I listened to the voices involved and whoever had the best possibility to do the lead. Sometimes we had two lead singers. And if we had a bass that could lead you or give us a little extra variety to it, you know, and stick him in there for a part or something. Always trying things, that's what that was."

Ernest Warren recalled the very same thing. "Believe it or not, they could tell by your voice what was good for you and what wasn't good for you, and if it was close to what they thought you could do they'd call Jesse in and Jesse would make it like that."

Ernest put his two fingers together to indicate closeness. He continued. "He'd build the harmony around it, and it would sound just like they wanted it to sound like and they would record it. Yeah, they knew what, like Clyde McPhatter, they knew what was good for him. Ahmet Ertegun's good, man. Herb Abramson, that's his name. Herb Abramson. Him and Herb Abramson was good. Then later came Jerry Wexler. And they had an engineer that was tops. Tommy."

Ernest is thinking of Tom Dowd, Atlantic's longtime recording engineer who would, among other things, place the singers around the microphones. "Yeah. He was good. And he would listen. All he want you to do is stand where he tell you to stand, and he make it come out, man."

In addition to coaching sessions on the road, Stone would also accompany Ertegun and Abramson on trips to find new talent. Record company people from the North, especially New York, had been making road trips down into the south regularly since at least the 1920s, when they went in

search of male blues singers. In that regard, things had not changed significantly by the early 1950s. Here, Stone alludes to the strong southern roots
of rock 'n' roll.

"We would make trips going down South. In fact, that's how rock 'n'
roll really got started. We would get in—Ahmet, myself, and Herb—we get
in the car and drive down South. When we get past Baltimore they would
have to hide in the bottom of the car because it was against the law or something for black and white to be riding around together or something like
that. In certain areas I would hide in the bottom of the car and then in other
areas I would drive and they would hide in the bottom of the car. When we
went in the black neighborhoods, they would get down in the back seat so
they couldn't be seen and I'd do the driving. And we'd go around to certain
joints and sometimes I'd stop at a hot dog place or something and ask questions and they'd tell me about somebody entertaining in a joint in an alley
somewhere, you know. We go around there and see them, you know. And
then I'd go in there and I'd tell them that I got guys who represented
records and they would be interested in getting on records, you know, and
is it all right for them to come inside. And that's the way we'd go in and listen. Sometimes we'd listen to them there and sometimes we'd have to have
a place somewhere else to listen to them because the people were too rowdy
and whatnot in the place. They'd interfere with what we were trying to do."

Stone makes clear how Atlantic took the "raw" talent and sound of a
group or musician and preserved it while they formalized and produced it
at the same time. It was what really established that Atlantic sound in the
1950s and made it so convincing. Here is the importance of careful production in determining and defining what we hear in recorded music. If performers spend enough time in the studio, that experience can begin to
define their performances outside of the studio. They begin to try to duplicate the "studio" sound. Atlantic seemed to develop a collective vision for
the sound they wanted, but they based it on what they were finding, not
necessarily what they were looking for.

"We weren't hunting for anything. We listened to whatever they did,
and that's what we accepted because we decided that this is what we gonna
do or this is not what we gonna do. But we didn't try to set down rules and
laws and all that sort of stuff for them to conform to. We just listened to
them they way they did it. If they had a style of singing we tried to keep
that style [of the] group, you know. Only just clean it up though.

"They'd sing out of tune because a lot of those kids didn't even know
when they was out of tune. And sometimes they would be making the
wrong note in the chord, well I switch that particular note, clean the chord

up so it sounded good and then help them rhythmically, you know, and sometimes do a little format of sorts; how many choruses to sing or where the band would come in and make a solo or something. But we didn't try to interfere with them much or re-mold them or anything. It was basically what they were already doing, but just cleaned up and put together a little more professionally. But we tried not to change their sound or anything like that, you know. Because if you did too much of that then it ought to take a whole lot of time. They didn't understand, you know, the music basics and you couldn't really speak a language that would help them to improve quickly, you know."

Stone wrote out arrangements, if needed, for the studio musicians who worked behind the groups, but the majority of singers could not read music and thus did not need "charts." "No. No. They didn't know one note from another. I taught practically all of them to read finally, because I used to have little games I would play with them, you know."

The way Stone describes it, the singers learned by rote. Brother Stone preached to the youngsters the musical might of the note by rote. "I bought those little books they call 'catechisms' and they had, the way they wrote them out, they'd ask a musical question and underneath that they'd give the answer, you know. And so those books only cost about thirty cents then back in those days and I would get four of those books and give it to the guys and tell them that the one that could answer the most questions without making a mistake will get five dollars at the end of the week. And so everybody would be working hard to try to learn all the questions on the first two pages, something like that, you know. And then they began, later on, they began betting among themselves, you know. 'I bet I could do ten pages without making a mistake.' And so that's how they ended up learning about music, you know, because I made a game and they got a kick out of doing that because that was something they could do while they were traveling or waiting between shows or something."

Perhaps the lesson here, in addition to Stone's pedagogy, is that he reminds us that the singers worked "hard to try to learn." Ernest Warren, again, recalls Jesse coming down to Baltimore for the Cardinals: "Well, Atlantic saw the potentials, and we were here, and rather than to pay for our expenses in New York, in a hotel and the studio, he just sent Jesse down here. And they rented a hall over here on Read Street I think it was, on top of a drug store. And it had a piano in there and that's where he worked with us until he got us ready and he went back to New York, so we could stay home every night. But Jesse preferred staying in a hotel, so, every day we would go down to that studio with him."

Atlantic paid the group to record, but not to rehearse. Ernest explained those coaching sessions. From his perspective, the harmony was right, but the music was not. "Well, see a lot of guys, like you say, how did we learn harmony and how to sing? Our way of doing it was right, but musically, musically some things wasn't right. Because ain't no such thing as between keys; it's either on key or off key, you know. And he came down and put the voices more closer together, gave us more than we had."

The Cardinals were a quintet. Sam Aydelotte sang second tenor and played the guitar. "We had a guitar and his voice was also in there. But Jesse made it, he always arranged a simple song for us, but that was simple to him and to us after we learned it. But other people think it's hard. You know you very seldom hear a group copy behind us, when we were singing. They thought it was—Jesse Stone knew what he was doing, then Quincy Jones when he did it. They really thought it was complicated."

By "they," Ernest means people who heard the Cardinals. What he means is that the harmonies were relatively simple, but a good arranger could still do an awful lot with five voices and five good singers could do a lot with what an arranger showed them. The Cardinals had their own style.

"Real simple. Very simple, but you have to know it, see. But, everybody had their own way of harmonizing. The Orioles had their way. The Four Buddies was from here [Baltimore]. We had the Four Buddies and the Four Buds (and you heard one, you heard the other). And the Swallows had their own harmony. And Johnny Page had his own harmony. And coming out of D.C. you had the Cap-Tans, you had the Rainbows, and you had the Clovers. All these guys had their own way of singing harmony, but they still had to have a musician to put it right before a band could play behind it. See, because if you singing one thing and the band playing something else, they ain't look at no band they look at the singers, see. So Jesse Stone just, and he showed us as we went along, because if we couldn't sing a note he'd make us play it and sing it, too, see. And that sound would get in your ear and it would never leave."

He explained that the guys in the band all had "good ears." "Oh man, you had to at that particular time."

They were not reading music. "No. Later one or two of us—Meredith and Leon—they learned to read because they had some knowledge of playing, see. Meredith Brothers' father taught him how to play ukulele. Treetop, he just liked the piano and he thought he was Jimmy Ricks. He used to play the piano and sound like Jimmy Ricks. That was another group had their own way of singing, but they sang right because they had, you know, their piano player Howard Biggs, remember him? Piano player.

Well, he arranged all their stuff and he was extra good, man. But the two guitar players we had, they just played from here."

Ernest points to his head. "They had to straighten that out. That was the only thing that wasn't right, but everything else we did was right, from hearing, you know."

According to Jesse, the Cardinals and other groups at the time had little contact with company heads. "Well, at that time they were far removed from the people of the industry. When we rehearsed we rehearsed away from the offices. The only time they came in contact with the executives of the companies and other people that worked for the company is when they came in to record, and they didn't record in the offices, they recorded in the recording studio. So now and then, maybe, some representative would come to the studio during a session. That's the only way they saw them. I wouldn't say there was no real close relationship between them."

The singers would sometimes come in with their own material. "Some of the kids had tunes that they'd written, you know. Not written, but that they sang, they made up themselves. For instance, like 'Sh-Boom' was a tune that these kids — they'd been singing that tune for a couple of years before we got hold of it. And of course there wasn't much to do with it other than routine it a little better and take out some of the bad notes that they were making. And that tune proved to be a unique tune, it wasn't like any other tune.

"It didn't follow the format of what most other people were thinking, you know. Even the 'sha-la-la-la-la,' that little thing they did, nobody else was doing those kinds of sounds, you know. And even the word 'sh-boom,' that wasn't like anything else. That was their own thing. And the only reason they came up with things like that because they were rehearsing in a place where they didn't hear anybody else and nobody else heard them, you know. And so what they were doing didn't get around and then they didn't copy from anybody else because they heard nobody else."

Obviously Jesse Stone likes to stress the importance of originality, his own and that of others as well. In truth, the sounds were out there for everyone to hear and use, and they did, but Atlantic was unique in their approach to handling musicians and producing records. The sound and feel was new, unmistakable, and very upbeat. It was perfect for young people and, looking back, it must have been the perfect bright foil to the grey hues of the Eisenhower era and the 1950s. The Chords recorded "Sh-Boom" for Atlantic in 1954. It was the group's only hit, but it was an exultant performance that transfixed white teenagers and helped galvanize the emergence of black rhythm & blues-inspired rock 'n' roll. Popular music history books since the 1970s generally acknowledge the song, in part because of its crossover appeal, as the beginning of the rock 'n' roll era, that is, white teenagers buying into black music (Shaw 1978: xxvi, 135, 393).

"See most of those historians, they were far removed from black people. And they didn't know what black people were doing. They heard it on the radio or on a record. But we were molding rock 'n' roll before the word rock 'n' roll was created by a white disc jockey after he heard what we had been doing for a long time. Because our music was barred, they wouldn't play it on the radio, the white radio stations refused to play black music. And of course we were way down the road by the time they finally came up with the description for what we were doing."

Jesse Stone worked at Atlantic in its important formative years, from 1947 through the mid-1950s. He was unsure of the specific date he left.

"Oh, I don't know. As they [Atlantic] got better, you know, they began to come up with ideas themselves, they didn't need me so and besides, I got involved in things that were much more lucrative than making arrangements for them. And I start coming up with my own groups, I had another group called the Cues which they were musicians, singers, and they could read music. Yeah, it was a black group. They did a lot of background for other big singers, you probably heard a lot of records that they worked on. They ended up in Las Vegas, they did things out there on their own and they recorded for Capitol Records. I had several female groups. I had one called the Cookies, I had one called the Yams, I had another one called the Rhythm Debs, and they all did pretty good. They were much easier to work with than boys. You know, boys back in those days had so many ways of hanging out, going in bars and getting juiced, you know. Girls didn't do that back then in those days. They, more or less, would make rehearsals and go home, and a lot of them were still trying to go to school and all that sort of stuff. They seemed to be more ambitious than the boys."

Jerry Wexler, the peerless producer for Atlantic, wrote of Stone:

> Jesse's musical mind had as much to do as anyone's with the transformation of traditional blues to pop blues—or rhythm and blues, or cat music, or rock 'n' roll, or whatever the hell you want to call it. Jesse was a master, and an integral part of the sound we were developing. He had the unique gift of maintaining a hang-loose boogie-shuffle feel in the context of the formal chart. Jesse was a record producer's dream come true. . . . Jesse seemed to know everything. . . . (Wexler and Ritz 1993: 86–87)

No question, Jesse Stone helped define Atlantic Records in the 1950s. Stone was a true musical entrepreneur, but the only African American among those who started the company. Back in those days, even with Atlantic, "race" was an unspoken determiner. For all his work from the very beginning, Jesse remained labor to Ahmet Ertegun's management. Ertegun had even made Jerry Wexler a partner eventually. It is difficult to draw firm conclusions from this. Yet, in a published profile by Nick Tosches, Stone's comments are revealing.

> Ahmet was good to me. He'd say, "You're not charging enough," and he'd write out a figure and say, "This is what you should get. If you don't get it, the government will." But I was after a piece of the company, and I could never pin them down to give it to me. They kept offering me a lifetime job, but I didn't want that, I wanted a piece. (Tosches 1984: 16)

A piece—isn't that what everyone wants? Isn't that what distinguishes one segment of American society from another, given the absence of a formal ruling class? Jesse Stone's goal, ultimately, was simply to own a part of the company, as well it should have been, for he already owned a piece of the company's sound during those early years. This one aspect of the relationship between Jesse Stone and Atlantic records became his arrival point and his point of departure. It speaks to us, I believe, about the real nature of relationships between whites and blacks.

Henry Glover

Another African American in the business was Henry Glover. He was a producer, later artist and repertoire director, for King Records during the 1950s. Unlike Stone, who was self-taught, Glover was a college graduate. A former retailer in Cincinnati named Syd Nathan founded King in 1945. King became, alongside Atlantic, Chess, National, Savoy, Specialty, and a handful of other postwar independent labels, a player in black popular music recording that changed the sound of America by the end of the 1950s. Nathan, whom Arnold Shaw termed "one of the Henry Fords of the record industry" (Shaw 1978: 279), recorded, among many others, James Brown, who stayed with the label, more or less, through the 1960s. Nathan was a character, a retailer, and he certainly relied on people and producers around him to first tell him what "good" music was and then to find talent and get them ready to make records.

Henry Glover was one of those individuals that Nathan relied on. Like Jesse Stone, and as Jesse Stone said, if you worked at a small label in those days you had to do a little bit of everything. Glover played by the rules, more or less, of industry insiders like Nathan, but also knew the politics of race and music.

> Henry Glover was a multiple talent—arranger, songwriter, record producer. As a songwriter he ranks with the leading creators of R&B material, though he little likes the R&B handle. He feels that it was a "tongue and cheek, trade name given to Negro music to keep from saying 'race,'" and that "soul was an expression of black resentment toward that designation." (Shaw 1978: 279)

The black establishment—given voice through publications like the *Baltimore Afro-American*—touted Glover as a successful role model in business. They ran a short paragraph on him in 1957, after he had left briefly and then returned to King Records. With the article is a photograph of a smiling Glover holding up a catch line of 10 fish.

> ON VACATION—Henry Glover, artist and reportoire [sic] of King Records, who recently was elevated to special assistant to King Records' president Sid [sic] Nathan, is taking a brief vacation at Hot Springs, Ark., at Lake Ouchita, where the music man displays his catch of fish (crappie and bass). Glover is the man who produced Bill Doggett's hits of "Honky Tonk" and "Ram-Bink-Shush." Also, he is the writer of "I'm Waiting Just For You," which is a hot "hit" by Pat Boone.[12]

Glover, as noted above, worked with Herman Denby and the Swallows. Herman's story picks up just after a King representative heard the group and told them they sounded too much like the Orioles. They had to find a new style. "And we had some work to do. We weren't going to give up on this. So a few months went by and then Irv called him again, and he came down and he heard us. And he had a music director from King with him named Henry Glover. And he heard us also."

Herman said that they kept the same songs, but changed the way they harmonized. Glover listened to the reinvented group. "We gave him a variety of what we could do, you know, and he set up a recording date, which we didn't believe. We didn't believe it."

The Swallows traveled to Cincinnati. "Well, they sent us tickets, train tickets, and we went up to Cincinnati. It was all new to us, you know what I mean."

It was the first time these guys had been away from home. Irv Goldstick, their manager, did not travel with them. "We didn't know what to expect, you know. And when we got in the studio and everybody was so nice and made us comfortable, you know what I mean, so we just sing. And then, you know, in a few minutes only, we got to the point where, well, we just sing. That's it, you know."

Henry Glover, whom Herman refers to as "the music director," selected the material that the group would record, chosen from their repertoire. The group had a one-year contract. "Well I think the first one was for a year, with a year option, I think , if I can remember correctly. That's what it was. It specified so many recordings within that twelve-month period. I remember that. It was so many recordings we had to make."

The original Swallows were Eddie Rich, lead tenor; Herman "Junior" Denby, lead and second tenor, string bass; Earl Hurley, tenor; Fred (Francis) "Money" Johnson, baritone and guitar; Norris Mack, bass vocal. Herman also wrote "Beside You." Ferlingere (1976) lists twenty-two recordings made by the original group and released by King between June 1951 and early 1953.

Herman Denby tells the story of how Henry changed his vocal style. "See, Eddie [Rich] used to do 'Beside You.' And he [Glover] said, 'No no

The Swallows at the Club Troca Vera, Columbus, Ohio, circa 1951. Courtesy of the Afro-American Newspapers.

no, that tune don't do nothing for me at all.' So Earl [Hurley] said, 'Why don't you try Herman?' He said, 'He imitates everybody. He can change his voice to be like a whole lot of people.' And I went through some people, and when he got to, Henry Glover got to Charles Brown, he say, 'Can you imitate Charles Brown?' I said, 'Yeah.' So I did it for him once, and he said, 'No.' He said, 'I don't want you to be too much. Take a little off of it. I don't want you to be too much.' Now, at my young age we understood all this stuff. 'I don't want you to be too much like Charles Brown, but just give me a flavor of it.' You know. And when we did it, it was the biggest thing the Swallows ever did."

That's what good producers were for.

The experiences of one generation of singer and group resonate to the next: the Ink Spots in the late 1930s and early 1940s; the Ravens after the war; Orioles after 1948; Clovers 1950; Cardinals and Swallows 1951. The postwar radio personalities, managers, and producers—the mediators and intermediaries—changed reciprocally with the entertainment industry after the war. The rise of the independent record labels—and the characters that defined them—altered the American popular entertainment industry. The focus began a shift to arrangement, production, and recording, although it by no means moved completely away from performance. The growth and popularity of that medium—of record stores, the use of jukeboxes—surely would have made it more of a thing that young kids wanted to do. The rewards of some of the talent contests were record contracts, and that became the focus of the young singers. What also changed, eventually, by the 1960s, was the involvement in music by professionals. Fewer and fewer everyday people managed groups, whether they knew what they were doing or not, and the groups became more professionalized. Despite Jesse Stone's assertion that nobody really knew what worked or what was good and what was not, he and others like him learned, and thus emerged the rhythm & blues music professionals. They included managers and agents, producers, recording engineers, artist and repertoire representatives, salesmen, and radio people. They experimented and began to draw on their years in the business. They were just the beginning.

Just as individual singers and vocal groups based what they did on previous generations, American popular music as a whole defined the new from the old—common thread, different cloth.

5

Patterns

"The past is a remarkably copious source of information about the present."

—Cater and Jones (1989: 107)

"I mean, the only thing that has changed now—there are no chains around my ankles, as a people, but they're around my brain now. You know, you are made to believe that these things are better, but they're not. They're not. They're not."

—Herman Denby

The Black Vocal Imagination

A pattern is a form or model, design, prescribed route, system, interrelationship of parts, or something that occurs over again. A pattern also is or has an observable characteristic. A pattern need not necessarily be fixed and unchangeable. Indeed, within the context of black music, patterns are flexible and do change, but they show the way back nonetheless.

Black group harmony was a musical pattern, a historical model for music and, in some instances, for social behavior. Postwar group harmony, from the Ravens through the 1950s, established guidelines to vocal performance based on earlier models, became indelibly linked to a historical period, and continued to resonate into the 1960s, 1970s, and beyond. Performance patterns defined the style of both the entire genre and individual vocalists and groups. Style was the vocal imagination in voice arrangement, use of the bass and falsetto range, backgrounding, and blend. These left an indelible mark on singing and on popular music after the rhythm & blues period. These are the larger issues that reach beyond the mechanics of harmonizing.

On the one hand, the crucible of popular music tended to homogenize group harmony after a period. Because there were a finite number of successful models on which to base a successful sound, many groups would sound generally alike. On the other hand, as Ernest Warren said in the previous chapter, "Everybody had their own way of harmonizing."

Lawrence Berry explained what he thinks the difference was, for instance, between New York and Washington vocal groups. He suggested that in Washington there was more of a "Southern style of singing, and coming from the Southern churches." The groups sang a lot of "bottom." In New York, they sang a lot of "highs," that is, first and second tenor combinations as opposed to bass and baritone combinations. "So therefore we are bottom-heavy; they're top-heavy."

He goes on to say that this "bottom" and "growling type sounds, with that bass/baritone combination" came from the churches. "In church, everybody had a spot to be, you had that five harmony combinations: baritone, bass, second tenor, first tenor, and lead, so, you stayed right there. And it's distinctive. You can hear it."

He maintains that Washington groups sang all five parts, but elsewhere you would have three or four voices trying to "cover" the five parts. In Los Angeles, you would hear a completely different sound.

The above analysis notwithstanding, distinguishing a specific Washington or Baltimore style is problematic. Some groups from New York maintained a distinctive sound, as Berry says, and there is an argument for differences between New York and Washington and Baltimore groups. It is, however, difficult to determine precise factors without overgeneralizing, and you have to factor out the influence of record companies, producers, and arrangers who modified the sound of a group.

The Harlem-based group the Crows recorded a song called "Gee" for the Rama label in 1953. The quintet sings a wide-open style, with a youthful, slightly nasal sound typical of some New York groups in the 1950s. They have a real edge to their voices and much exuberance, with an insistent, irresistible background riff typical for the time and style:

> doot—doo d' doot—doo d' doot—doo d' duh-doo-duh—doot—doo d'
> doot—doo d' doot—doo d' duh-doo-duh—doot—doo d' doot—doo d'
> doot—doo d' duh-doo-duh—doot—love that girl.

Vocal harmony groups were popular in New York, which some maintain was the "center of the vocal group universe" during the 1950s simply because of the sheer number of singers, groups, and record labels there

(Hinckley 1976: 3). Arguably, there was also a quality, an edge to the vocal sound in some of the groups originating in New York during the 1950s, and thus you get that New York "sound" or performance style. Devotees of group harmony, especially dedicated record collectors, are good at locating a vocal group with its place (and time) by identifying its style. But distinctions are subjective. One factor is that style intersects with the production values of particular record companies, which tended to alter the sound of group. This was less of a problem with local groups on local record labels. However, there were still common characteristics and patterns that helped define the genre of group harmony, as whole.

Vocal Arrangement

The voicing of group harmony followed any number of variations on the standard four-part, bottom-up pattern. Depending on the group, four or five singers cover the parts of bass, baritone, second tenor, first tenor, and lead. This is the basic SATB arrangement of European music and church music, as well as jazz and popular music. In much rhythm & blues era group harmony, based on gospel and pop traditions, a strong lead voice and a strong bottom frame the harmony, while the inner voices, the first and second tenors, further structure it. Johnny Page called the second tenor part "silver tenor," a term he apparently got from singing in the church. "Because in spirituals I was a second tenor. That's a silver tenor."

He explained voice parts. "I was singing a second tenor, which is silver tenor. The second tenor is, like I said, a gut voice. And he can, he balance the harmony with the baritone, in between the bass. And the tenor, it doesn't make no difference whether he go way out there in left field. There's those three voices are coinciding together, he can take any kind of liberties he want, as long as the pattern is together."

Page is saying that certain voice parts need to anchor others—a basic tenet of tonal music. In most styles, the inner voices really qualify the harmony, but can be difficult to perform. Anyone who sings second tenor, or plays second chair in a band, knows this. Singers who took the two inner voices did so because they were good at "hearing" them and had the appropriate voices. Howard Davis and Mel Lipscomb were two such singers. They had the ability to sing those inside parts and to change and substitute parts in performance with ease. They really prided themselves on singing with each other. Here, as in their description of singing the national anthem in the opening chapter, there is a social tangent to the musical frame which is very much in evidence when Howard and Mel are talking with one another.

"But see Curly couldn't do with me or Melvin what Melvin and I could do with each other."

"That's right."

"Without fanfare."

"Right."

"Curly was a soloist. Rich baritone voice."

"Uh huh."

"And so he would try to do the bass and hope to be the bass, but we would hear Curly singing what we were doing if he had the baritone line."

"Exactly. Exactly."

"You see? And so he just couldn't find that other place up there."

"He didn't have that fifth, whatever."

"That fifth place, even though he was a baritone, that other place. You know, lead, first tenor, second tenor, baritone, bass. He never got in there and so it didn't work, and it wasn't anybody's fault or nobody fell out about it. We just went with what's easy—the flow."

Here, Howard and Melvin again mention "flow," this time in passing. The specific issue is the need for a fifth voice. They are explaining why the Hi Fis worked well as a quartet, but had trouble when they tried to be a quintet. They could not easily fit in a fifth vocal part. "It was unwieldy. It was unwieldy because you had two guys who could do anything with anybody who lived."

Howard means that he and Melvin both could cover the parts between the lead and the bass. "And this other voice that didn't quite, wasn't, you know, it didn't work."

Curly's stay in the band was short-lived.

Buddy Slaughter said that sometimes it didn't matter which part a singer assumed because they could always cover the parts as needed. He could sing either first or second tenor. "Second tenor mostly, or either first. Bennett and I would switch sometime."

The first tenor sang just below the lead. "It was the lead, first tenor, second tenor, and baritone. You know, we would switch harmony, sometime the bass would be a baritone instead of a bass."

Slaughter says the same thing about switching voice parts with Floyd Bennett as Howard and Melvin. These were not isolated cases. "We'd switch harmony around a lot. And nobody taught us this, we just worked on it so much, you know, that it just come to like I got so that Bennett could look at me and almost know what we going to sing next, you know. That's how close we got."

Alphonso Feemster was also capable of switching parts, to do both lead and second tenor in the Four Bars of Rhythm. He describes the harmony

voices under the lead as "background," and points out that without instru-
mentation, you need to rely more on the voice—the joy and challenge of a
cappella.

"A lead singer of course is singing the primary, whatever the song is
about. He's out there presenting it. The harmony is background. Back in
those days, we didn't have all the instruments like they got today and all the
trickery that they use to make you sound, the synthesizers and all that stuff
they got now, so you use your voice for that, you know, for all those type of
things. And of course tenor, first tenor, was way up high, and then second
tenor was just below it, then baritone was a little lower, and then bass.

"I liked harmonizing lead tenor vocal, because I knew I had a voice to
lead. But harmony just fascinated me because I couldn't understand how
four voices could get together and make that kind of music. One night we
were rehearsing with the Four Bars and we were in my mother's kitchen,
because we would rehearse in each other's house every week. It wouldn't
be the same house every week. So we was rehearsing on a song, and so we
hit this harmony note and my mother had some china on the shelf and it
shattered. And it amazed me. I said, 'we must of been right on.' "

He laughs. "But she didn't mind, you know, 'cause she knew what we
were doing. We just sang, and harmony began to take hold of me. 'Cause it
was so beautiful; you're really singing it right, you know."

Harold Winley said that in order for the Clovers to sing in the way that
they wanted—this was before they got to Atlantic Records—they found a
guitar player to work with them. "Here in Washington, after Lou [Krefetz]
got us to cut at Eddie Heller's Rainbow Records, to cut this record on us,
Renee Hall was the guitarist, unamplified guitar and piano. That was all."

This was the first record for the Clovers, "Yes Sir, That's My Baby"
b/w "When You Come Back To Me," in 1950. "Bill Harris wasn't with us
then. Bill Harris was working across the street at the Offbeat. Seventh and
T had the, at that time Club Harlem was upstairs, it was a jazz club.
Offbeat was mostly, you know, jazz. Groups worked in those two clubs.
And Buddy had gone over there and heard Bill. Said, 'Man there's a guitar
player across the street.' You know, and we went to meet him. He and I
went to meet Bill, and Bill just sat there and looked at us and says, 'O.K.'
At the time Bill was living in Georgetown. He says, 'You all come over to
my house at such and such a time.'

"So, we sat down in Bill's house and sang every song that we knew as
a group. Every now and then he might say, 'yeah man,' until we sang
'Black Magic.' That's the song that got him. And when he heard us do that,
then he said, 'O.K., we'll work together,' you know. 'I see you all sing a lot
of wrong changes.' Well, we had Buddy, you know, and Buddy would tell

you in a minute, say, 'Well I can't make them changes.' I don't know, you know. So that was the reason. We knew we had to have a guitar player to do the things we wanted to do."

The Clovers had songs that they knew as individuals and brought to the group. The one who knew the song would teach it to the others and sometimes determine the parts and assign the harmonies. With the guitarist Bill Harris, they began to work again on their sound, mostly pop standards that the lead Buddy Bailey knew. They got everyone making the same chord changes, the correct ones according to Harris (guitar players are usually good for that). Harold says that Buddy Bailey, the lead, knew many songs. Of course, one sign of any outstanding musician, in any genre, is the size of his or her repertoire.

"But the songs, Buddy, man, his repertoire is extensive. Is extensive, you know. So I would listen to him. I'd learn a lot from him and from Harold Lucas. With Lucas singing harmony, because Lucas is one of the best baritone singers I ever heard. You know. And if you hear any of our old records you can hear that, you know. He sang his part and he sang his notes. And he being the next voice to me, often times, early in the group and sometimes in sessions, he would hit notes with me that I couldn't hear at that time. He would, you know, show me the note. You know what I'm saying? Yeah. And, so, Buddy always listening—loved Dinah Washington. But he also loved Doris Day. You understand what I'm saying? So you draw your material, like I said, "Blue Velvet" come from Tony Bennett, Arthur Prysock, then we got it. But we listen, you know, be listening to these things. You know. Eddie Fisher."

Of course, a lot of that changed when the Clovers signed with Atlantic and they began to perform what the record company promoted, that is, a "blacker" sound. The point is, though, if the group had not already come up to that point on their own, they would not have been as attractive to the record company. Their repertoire and basic sound was already set, and set to change. Although they sprinkled their Atlantic repertoire with standards, that was not really the prevailing Atlantic sound.

Bass and Falsetto

Group harmony had two distinguishing characteristics that constituted perhaps the most endearing and enduring influences on popular music—the bass and falsetto voices.

The individual voice of group harmony, when featured in the lead parts, establishes and defines the group sound. Vocalists like Sonny Til, Buddy Bailey, Ernest Warren, and Rudy West (from the Five Keys), all had distinctive, memorable, and quality tenor voices. Some, like Bailey and West, could sing well in the tradition of pop crooners. Other lead singers from the early 1950s—Clyde McPhatter of the Dominoes was among the best—drew from gospel in emotionalism and grittier vocal qualities. Not all groups featured a lead at all times. However, when they did, it essentially defined the group's personality, which is what the "front" singer is supposed to do. The inner or background voices were essential in another way, by defining the overall harmonic configuration of a group.

The bass lead in group harmony was much less common than a tenor lead, but bass "padding" or backgrounding became very common. The origins of the bass lead are obscure, but one of the earliest gospel groups, the Dixie Hummingbirds (formed in 1928) used a bass lead with William Bobo. The Golden Gate Quartet (formed in the mid-1930s) would switch lead voices in songs and used a strong low voice, probably more of a baritone than bass. Another gospel quartet, the Soul Stirrers (formed in 1935) used a bass/baritone (James Medlock) alternately with the lead singer, R. H. Harris. The African American scholar, singer, and actor Paul Robeson, who recorded in the 1930s, had a rich, expressive bass voice. The Ink Spots' Orville Hoppy Jones sang bass/baritone. The Delta Rhythm Boys (1946) occasionally used a bass lead (Lee Gaines) as well. There was a clear black male tradition of singing bass lead. Young singers probably knew some recordings well enough—like Paul Robeson's "Old Man River," from 1938—to have learned or gotten something from them.

Paul Robeson recorded "Old Man River" because of his role in the Jerome Kern musical, *Show Boat*, in the 1932 stage revival and then the 1936 film. He brought as much dignity to his performance as he could, but he sang it in character and conformed to white expectations of the period. When the Ravens covered it in 1947, they changed the climate of the song from a sorrowful lament sung in dialect, to an unapologetic jump tune, bright and bristling with youthful confidence. The Ravens influenced younger groups, who would instill in their group harmony a similar sound. Afterward, groups would always look for a true bass, or at least a low baritone (difficult for the very young, but they would try). No group, however, developed the bass lead as well as the Ravens' Jimmy Ricks—his voice was unmatchable, unworldly, especially on ballads. Jimmy Ricks was a true bass, and sang with much authority.

Despite the high standard set by Ricks, or maybe because of it, the bass part endured in black music. After the Ravens, groups from the Clovers to the Four Bars (Eddie Daye was the bass singer) used a bass voice on certain arrangements. In the 1950s, the Cadillacs, Dominoes, Flamingos,

Spaniels, Swallows, and Marcels all used bass, and then the Temptations in the 1960s used a bass voice, usually as a featured "hook" or background figure. Most of those same groups balanced the bass voice with a falsetto part, although not always as a full, dual lead, as the Ravens did. The Ravens not only had a great bass lead, but a terrific falsetto lead, as well.

Portia Maultsby credits the Orioles with pioneering the rhythm & blues use of counter melodies—"obbligato tenor" parts (Maultsby 1986: 16), but Maithe Marshall and the Ravens were doing it earlier. The use of high falsetto to ornament a lead melody, sometimes called the "floating tenor," had a much earlier history in gospel quartets, although it was Marshall who set a precedent for the kind of falsetto background and especially the lead vocal in secular pop music since the late 1940s. If Jimmy Ricks' voice was unworldly, Marshall's was unreal. When some youngsters today hear those two voices, someone inevitably will ask what they did in the studio to get them to sound that way. Bernice Johnson Reagon suggested "the angelic floating tenor was a transitional development within the jubilee quartet that along with changes in the bass, baritone, and leads, led to the development of the gospel quartet."[1]

Some lead singers, like Rudy West or Jackie Wilson, had a very high, natural tenor range. They would border on falsetto, or even go up into it for a few notes and make a smooth, little-noticed transition between the two registers. Rhythm & blues leads who performed entirely in the falsetto range were less common before the 1960s. At any time, good falsetto singing is difficult to pull off convincingly.

Falsetto nevertheless constitutes a defining moment in the history of American popular music. The African American tradition, the black attitude of falsetto singing, is unsurpassed. Falsetto has a history that covers a wide part of the globe and extends back hundreds of years, if not more. It is the male alto range, also called counter-tenor, and occurs when voice production shifts from resonating in the chest to the throat. Peter Giles (1994) places the possible origins of falsetto in utterances, shouts, cries, or calls by early man, and stresses that we can find males who use their falsetto range in a musical way in many different cultures. He suggests, however, that the early European use of falsetto lies in Moorish influences, dating back to early medieval times (4).

Fascinating, though speculative, is the connection Giles maintains falsetto has to the Morris tradition English folk dance and pre-Christian rites of magic. He describes them as seminal "blackface" traditions and gives one possible interpretation:

> The Blackface Traditions, originally country-wide, are the oldest form of
> Mooris dancing. All others derive from them. "Mooris" is thought by

some to have evolved from "Moorish." Because falsetto singing and nasal resonation entered modern European tradition through the Moorish invasion of Spain and parts of France, Moorish, Mooris and falsetto-use appear to be linked. In original ancient practice, however, the "black face" was made with ash and soot from the magic fire, rubbed on to imbue the dancer with the potency of both sun and fire. This resulted, certainly by Shakespeare's time, in "Moorish" being applied loosely to the existing Blackface male folk-dancing tradition. (1994: 386)[2]

Giles places later use of falsetto voice on British ships, especially among those Africans hired out on voyages during the eighteenth and nineteenth centuries (389). Falsetto, he writes, was "an instinctive predisposition of Negroes and probably common practice among European seamen."

Giles's unfortunate use of racialist terminology ("instinctive predisposition") does not take away from his suggestive historical connections between Africa, Britain, and falsetto. In the New World, especially in the United States, male falsetto continued through an admixture of Anglo- and African-derived traditions—theatrical productions, minstrelsy, folk songs, yodeling, field hollers and arhoolies, blues, gospel, country music, and finally rhythm & blues and pop. Giles makes other challenging assertions:

> It might be suggested, other than as a manifestation of one aspect of vocal instinct, modern "pop" use of falsettists on the Afro-American pattern is merely another example of outside creative influence on European music and thus a healthy cross-fertilization. It could be argued that Moorish falsetto techniques were exactly this, especially in the tenth and eleventh centuries and later. Yet, when it is not a genuine inheritance from jazz and blues (which were originally both black art forms and a cultural catharsis: a freeing from perceived restriction), the adoption of falsetto by the "pop" industry often seems contrived and, like the industry itself, crudely commercial in aim. (1994: 4)

Giles crudely misunderstands pop falsetto, not to mention the notion of "commercial." Yet, the idea that African American falsetto has a political component, this "catharsis" (which, incidentally, is what blues performance was to begin with) and "freeing from perceived restriction" (although there was nothing "perceptual" about chains), is worth consideration. The masculinity of bass and the femininity of falsetto can take on new meaning, perhaps, if placed in the context of old, minstrel-based stereotypes of the "black buck" and the black "dandy." Despite gender ambivalence (Giles treats the history of this), male falsetto can be the most masculine of performances as it persuades (women, as the case may be) in a subtle, disarming manner. Falsetto in black popular music takes tremendous strength and stamina and, in a less strident manner, is parallel to any instrumentalist (trumpet, saxophone, guitar, for instance) playing in the extended, upper range, or off the neck (in the case of guitar). Indeed, the male falsetto voice in black popular music, including gospel, is arguably one of the most emotional and evocative of male vocal performances.

The framing of much group harmony with a floating falsetto on top and a bass voice on the bottom is part of the lasting influence those voices have had on popular music. After the era of group harmony, the falsetto lead of individual vocalists like Russell Thompkins (Stylistics), Philip Bailey (Earth, Wind & Fire), Marvin Gaye, Curtis Mayfield, and occasionally Jackie Wilson, among countless others, began to define a certain soul/funk/disco black male aesthetic (found also in gospel backgrounding, as with Robert Blair's Fantastic Violinaires). In the context of these singers, falsetto exuded masculinity. In addition, Marvin Gaye and Curtis Mayfield captivated with their voices and sang lyrics about society and its problems, especially in the "What's Going On" and "Superfly" recordings (the Temptations did the same in some of their later recordings). Falsetto that defined a group sound — Earth, Wind & Fire, Ohio Players, Spinners, Stylistics, the Temptations, among others — similarly could sugar a political message in the music, although the Ohio Players and Stylistics stayed on their purely apolitical, entertainment ground.

The models established by the earlier falsetto vocalists were important, especially in Maithe Marshall of the Ravens. The communicative quality of the male falsetto voice resides in its ability to cut through (in a strong voice, anyway) the normally thick textures of group harmony. There is the quality of the voice, beyond its cutting ability. In a good falsettist, say, Marvin Gaye, Curtis Mayfield, or Philip Bailey, the best characteristic is the softness and the strength, the roundness of tone, the rich overtones, and the convincing nature of the expression — the emotion. As with blues, you cannot pull off a performance without great skill, vocal strength, and an understanding of the poetics and emotional power of the sound, not to mention the ability to work an audience (even on record). The black vocal imagination in this regard is an elegant, effective performative gesture, and one that many white singers continually try to capture and emulate, if not always entirely successfuly.[3]

Structure and Basing

Buddy Bailey of the Clovers told of a basic vocal arrangement and structure — background (chorus) and foreground (lead).

"We were singing some of the tunes of some of our idols, but some-times we'd put a record on of a singer and we would background him. You know what I'm saying? I was slated to be a background singer, not lead. I accepted it. So one day, Shelton was hoarse, I believe. Billy [Mitchell] said, 'Buddy, why don't you try one?' And I said, 'O.K., I think I will.' But Shelton never liked harmony. You know, strictly a lead singer and he—so I fell back—went back to the first tenor part. And we made, we felt alright, I mean, we did O.K. I didn't particularly want to do the lead work. And of course that came later when Shelton decided he had had enough of the singing. That's what it was. And they more or less pushed me up into the lead."

Buddy's description is typical of the process by which singers figured out their performance roles. The typical structure of group harmony estab-lishes a foreground voice and background voice, when a chorus answers the lead—old-fashioned call and response. When the leader and chorus sing concerted harmony, they elide the distinction between foreground and background. Mel Lipscomb and Howard Davis well understood these approaches. They told of how they worked parts out in rehearsal and could play it any way.

Mel said, "We could do the whole thing. For example, 'Moonlight in Vermont' is something that comes to mind very quickly. We would all sing the whole thing—"

Howard cut in: "We thought we ought to do that whole thing."

"—Right together."

"Because that's a pretty song."

"All in harmony, the whole entire thing. And there are some times when you—now, O.K. now, so the later groups are going 'doo-wop, doo-wop'."

By the mid-1950s many vocal group concepts became standardized, copied, and clichéd on records. One typical bass pattern, for instance, cen-ters on the root-notes of the chords; the singer would vocalize the root notes of I-vi-ii-V^7-I. This pattern and its many variants are at the heart of what some call "doo-wop." By "doo-wop," Mel refers to these characteris-tic background vocals of mid-1950s vocal harmony. A contemporary mean-ing of the term is simply of genre—people will use "doo-wop" to designate any form of rhythm & blues era vocal harmony (in the same sense as oldies-but-goodies). At one time, among singers, doo-wop meant something more specific. It referred to a typical, repetitive background vocal part. Sometimes the line appears in the low voice, baritone or bass. It functioned to support the lead with repeating melodic/rhythmic phrases—riffs.

It also provided a pulse in a cappella singing—and happened to be a very happy sound. A singer simply could not "doo-wop" in a dirge. "Doo-wopping" or any similar sound appeared in song arrangements around 1955 and "added drive and danceability" to songs (Shaw 1978: 232). Rhythmic vocal bass-lines, however, appeared much earlier. These lines are similar to "walking bass" patterns and occurred in gospel quartet groups of the 1930s (Maultsby 1986: 17). The Mills Brothers often imitated instruments with their voices, and one part would function as the bass, with repetitive bass figures. In an earlier era, black slaves used their voices to imitate drums and other instruments, and so the whole aesthetic probably draws to some degree from the vocal accompaniment to juba (slave body music).

The Ravens were probably the first pop/rhythm & blues group to use a distinct, prominent bass introduction on a vocal arrangement. They did this on a recording of the song "Count Every Star," for the National label in 1950 (Sbarbori 1985). In that recording Jimmie Ricks, the bass singer, voices that I-vi-ii-V^7-I pattern, using "doo" syllables. By 1955, such background figures had become a signature rhythm & blues sound. The vocal bass pattern kept the pulse and made the changes.

Mel Lipscomb and his group, the Hi Fis, did not buy into that style of performance. What he preferred, rather than a single repetitive bass figure ("doo-wop"), was full voice accompaniment behind the lead.

"We weren't the greatest doo-woppers; we could do it, but that's not music to me. That don't make me right when I say it, but there are times when we sang a lot of a cappella, that's what helped you so, when you had a group behind you. You could go off and do a little more experimenting, couldn't you? We had that bass behind you, and that guitar and the piano, you could do more, but when you've got a cappella and just your voices, then it's important to keep those voids filled with harmony."

Group harmony fills the space between foreground and background, so to speak. From the lead vocalist's perspective, it is important to have voices "behind" you, to back you up. This is a structural aesthetic with very deep roots in early African American group song. Singers referred to backgrounding in an earlier time as "basing." It was not necessarily limited to just a bass voice, but a fundamental background accompaniment. The idea reaches back to early black vocal music and remains one of the most singular of continuities in African American music. It is at the root of so-called doo-wop style and the sensibility of guys "backing" each other.

In 1867 William Francis Allen, Charles Pickard Ware and Lucy McKim Garrison published their *Slave Songs of the United States*, . . . The authors confirmed the absence of part-singing but added, "yet no two appear to be singing the same thing." The leader, who would frequently improvise, was generally supported by a "baser" who provided a vocal background and interpolations. (Oliver et al. 1986: 5)

Although those authors in 1867 did not analyze slave song in terms of voice parts, there is evidence of a distinction between a lead and background, which intimates part-singing. Southern wrote of that period, "those who constituted the chorus called themselves 'basers'; when they came in on the refrains, they were 'basing' the leader" (Southern 1997: 197).

The rhythm & blues bass voice functions as did the nineteenth-century baser. Basing the lead is what Buddy Bailey referred to as backgrounding: that is, harmonizing with the lead. Basing grounds a song and establishes a two-part organization in which antiphonal and polyphonic relationships predominate. In older performances, the song structure was usually "open-ended" and organized only around repetitive call and response patterns between the lead and the basers. Contemporary and some historical Western song structures have always been "closed" in that they exist as a fixed set of pulses, measures, and song sections of an established length. Open-ended structures are performance based, their parameters established as the song unfolds in performance. This type of performative aesthetic is very much a part of African and African American preferences. Postwar harmony groups often organized songs both ways in performance by imbedding one kind of musical structure into another. A Tin Pan Alley, 32-bar, AABA written structure would also include a more open-ended performance-based structure of call and response. Thus, as Howard and Melvin stated, during a song the group had the flexibility to switch from concerted harmony to a call and response "basing" section.

This sensibility and the importance of having somebody "back you up" points to other kinds of sociomusical relationships. You can hear backgrounding in more than musical arrangements. You hear it in the church, or in everyday conversation. Backgrounding strategies, of which there are many, are forms of call and response that extend beyond musical strategies and constitute important, ongoing social imperatives (to wit the conversations in this book between Herman Denby and Ernest Warren, Howard Davis and Mel Lipscomb, and Melvin Coles and George Jackson).

Style and Blending

Gene Hawkins, the bass singer with the Magic Tones, said something worth recalling about harmonizing, something that other singers of his time also said. He compared harmonizing to "blending." Like Buddy Bailey, whom he did not know, Hawkins used a baseball metaphor with which to describe vocal harmony. He said the blending was just like being on a "baseball team." Sport analogies are common, but it was a revelation to hear that blending metaphor more than once. For Buddy, blending seemed to mean more than just a merging of voices.

"Well the first tenor is the top voice. O.K.? Then your baritone, and of course your lead, and your bass. The blending—if you don't blend well, you're not going to get much anyway, you know. And we sort of prized ourselves on blending, we concentrated on, like, cohesiveness, you know?"

Buddy gestured as if rehearsing a song." 'Buddy, you hold that note— Lucas . . .' and so on. 'Tommy, you O.K.?' It was like that, you know, just parts."

What did he mean by "blending"?

"We had to be satisfied that it sounded good, you know. We had to please ourselves. You know what I'm saying? It's like a baseball pitcher, you know, and this guy's going to keep throwing, and he says, 'Oh man, my arm feels good today.' You know. Very much like sports, or what have you. We sing merely—we were harmonizing because we just like a good sound, you know. We wanted to sound good."

Singers from Washington and Baltimore described a musical need to blend in harmony. This comes as no surprise, since blend is a desirable consequence of singing well together, but the manner in which these vocalists seem to have internalized and socialized "blend"—and then talk about it years later—was distinctive. There was no standard for blending. It was not simply singing in tune (which, according to Jesse Stone, they did not always do on their own). The singers themselves spoke of something that to them sounded or felt good, or right. Blend was something emotional as much as musical. When singers spoke of blend, they as much meant getting along, falling in with each other, participating and anticipating, as they did a purely musical blend. Clearly, this was a process, and not something you could measure.

James McPhail told about what he found so attractive in harmonizing. "Well, I think the blending of the voices. The thing was that each one of the guys had different voices, especially our group. We had tenor, bass, baritone, and a guy who would sing falsetto."

Other singers talked of blending, too, like Al Feemster of the Four Bars: "The blend. That got me. How you can tenor, bass—of course I knew that in Glee Club, anyway. But just to hear four guys do it instead of a whole chorus, you know, it was amazing. And it fascinated me and I really liked it."

Blending for the singers seems to have been as much a social ideal as a musical one. Blend meant that something had to feel socially and sound musically subjectively "correct." Many of these feelings relate directly to group affinities in black neighborhoods at a time when most had to position themselves, geographically as well as emotionally, vis-à-vis the dominant society. These qualities are reminiscent of "flow," as indicated in the first chapter, and certainly consistent with the "spontaneity, [the] sense of almost instantaneous community" that Levine describes in nineteenth-century African American singing (Levine 1977: 25). Placed in the context of postwar black communities and the history of black harmony groups, blend was a social as well as musical process, a sonic model for behavior. An ideal that extended past the last song afforded youngsters, beyond the music, a measure of emotional and social control over their lives. Music in this sense becomes a utopian ideal, both the Land of Nowhere[4] and the place of somewhere, the far end of revolution. It is not difficult to sense that with group harmony, there was for these youngsters a rich potential in musical, social, and economic possibilities, at least in their own minds.

Alfred Buddy Slaughter said, "And nobody taught us this, we just worked on it so much, you know, that it just come to like I got so that Bennett could look at me and almost know what we going to sing next, you know. That's how close we got. I just love harmony so much. I just like the sound of it, you know, the feel of it. Yeah, it's beautiful."

Other singers spoke in remarkably similar ways about harmonizing.

Harold Winley: "They were hearing things, and some of the guys had individual talent. You understand what I mean? But, when you, alright, when you bring them together as a group, then something else has to happen. You can't stand up there and yell your brains out because you singing harmony now so you have to, you know, blend. So it takes time to learn that, learn each other, you know—evidently one of the things that made the Clovers so proficient."

Melvin Lipscomb and Howard Davis: "And it was difficult to explain. Like Howard and I would sing, we'd learn the song in five minutes. And sometimes if I had the higher note and he was beneath me, in terms of music structure and sound, it didn't matter. Because whoever was there the other would automatically fall beneath it. Or you would flip-flop, whichever was—

"Yeah, you want up? I'll take it."

"And we could never understand, we'd look at each other in awe."

Al Feemster: "Pure harmony is when everything is on, man. I mean when it's *on*. When it's on, I mean, you know, God. We did a thing, we would do it every rehearsal, called 'Down by the Riverside.' That old song. And Eddie would be basing, without the guitar, I mean, you know, then you could hear it."

These patterns were very much a part of the social and cultural patterns of young black males in the postwar period: the cities, neighborhoods, communities, schools, businesses, and personal networks. It seems that the process of getting together to make music, secular music, according to those that sang back then, occurred with friendliness, ease, and social grace. It happened sometimes around the home, but more often in the street, social club, or around school. Youngsters in school, no matter what particular song, established something that "was created or constantly re-created through a communal process" (Levine 1977: 30). "Getting together" was a cultural imperative from and an antidote to exclusion and it provided a sense of belonging. By singing, harmonizing, youngsters were able to control exclusion and inclusion on their own terms, both musically and socially. And while the popular music industry chose to categorize and segregate some of these styles as so-called "rhythm & blues," the vocalists who made the music operated on another intellectual plane. They felt what they did was beyond categorization. Herman Denby echoes the sentiments of many singers from that era.

"The musicians used to get together and say, 'Hey boy, let's do something.' And everybody knew what he meant, you know. It never had a name. You know. 'Let's do something.' What do you want to name it?"

Buddy Bailey told of how he met his vocal group at a party. They eventually went on to become the Clovers. It was a situation that took place out of school, but the social dynamics were the same as within the school, and very similar to experiences of others from that era.

"It was a party one night—a lot of birthday parties, they used to give them. So Lucas and I met, you know, and Tommy, and we just latched on to each other. It was a friendly thing. 'Let's hit one, let's sing one,' you know, it's like, 'you know, guys.' "

The way these guys describe the ease with which they fell together to sing, it was like, hey, what's up, let's do something. This, again, was "flow." Here, it was not so much that music socialized these singers. They socialized the music and made it more than simply something to do. They made it a way to do something. The manner in which these kids expressed themselves as young black males of their time was their style, as individuals and as a group. Before any recordings, before production and arrangements, before professional performances, the singers brought to singing their style. Style is the result of choices we make to identify and distinguish what we

do and who we are. Black "style" in performance and in everyday life is perhaps the most elusive of cultural forms to comment on without falling into
the chasm of cultural essentialism. Yet, black style—as a concept, perspective, qualifier, identifier, and manner of expression—remains the strongest
of frames through which we understand how the African Diaspora continues to resonate. African American "style" remains a tool to inform and com-
municate, as well as identify. That style has had a profound influence on the
total cultural fabric of this nation.

The vocal imagination and musical patterns of one generation carried
over into the next, and in the case of rhythm & blues group harmony,
established a type of template for groups to emulate if not outright copy. At
one time everyone wanted to sound like the Ink Spots, and then the Orioles
came along.

The Orioles

You could ask anyone who grew up and sang in certain neighborhoods of
Baltimore and Washington about the Orioles and they would look at you
and say, "The Orioles? Are you kidding?" After they hit big in 1948, everybody was getting into the Orioles.

Harold Winley describes how the Orioles replaced the Ink Spots as
performance models. "All right, their format was Sonny Til, I mean everybody—not everybody, but just about everybody—went to the Ink Spots for
a format of some kind. See, the Ink Spots were hot, hot, hot, but 1945, that
was their swan song, for many reasons. The group broke up and everything
else happened in there. The Orioles, Sonny would do a lead, and then
George Nelson. Did you ever see them work? O.K. Sonny was like so, on
a mic by himself. Alex Sharp, George Nelson, and Tommy Gaither over
here. George is in here; this is George in the middle. When Sonny changed,
sang his part, George would spin around, man, from here, and go over
there and tear the house down. Just that. He had a raspy, whisky sounding
voice. He had just the right chemistry to keep, I mean Sonny had taken
them to one high, but George even shot it a little higher. And Alex Sharp
lying there with that obbligato tenor. Which Gregory Carroll sings to this
day—in every song that he sings.[5] But, you know that was the uniqueness
of that group. Each has, you know—the Cardinals, they even were built
like the Orioles to an extent, except nobody was as large as Alex Sharp.
Their demeanor, alright, so they were from Baltimore and their demeanor,
their early stuff on stage, was just like them [Ink Spots]. But they were different, you know, their sound's different, man."

The Orioles took what they learned from the Ink Spots and changed it—the harmony, the look, the feel, and the dynamics. This was the new generation. The Orioles were the same, but they were different. One of the things that differentiated the rhythm & blues era was dance and movement on the part of the performers. In the big band swing era, the musicians sat locked into their seats; eyes fixed on the music. Singers of that era barely moved, and even the Ink Spots were very poised and controlled. The Orioles began to change that in 1948.

"The Orioles, their thing was a little more active than the groups that you had seen before. A little more active, you understand what I'm saying? Because I'm saying now this man is pleading now, he's down on his knees, he's begging, he's sweating profusely. Sonny, you know. And he's beggin', you know. And this is different, different type of thing."

The Orioles had one lead, Sonny Til, but he worked very closely with George Nelson, who had a contrasting, lower voice, so the two would trade leads—contrast and work off of each other. In addition, Til was a dynamic lead. He was much more assertive on stage than previous singers and the group as a whole used dance steps and choreography to distinguish themselves. On record, their sound was distinctive, and they worked on their visual presentation as well, to match the changes in sound.

George "Icky" Tillman, the singer from the Georgetown section of Washington, like so many others, modeled his singing after the Orioles lead, Sonny Til. The success of the Orioles clearly inspired other groups to form, especially in the Baltimore and Washington areas. It seemed as if everybody wanted to sing.

"My voice was very similar to his and I sang just about every song they recorded. And I met these other guys in school and we formed this little quartet."

The Orioles moved in ways that the earlier pop groups did not—as Winley said, they were "more active." Deborah Chessler, the group's manager, points out some of their subtleties on stage, including the way Til switched leads with George Nelson. She also stresses that even though their stage movements of course did not come across on record, their vocal changes did.

"I believe that they influenced a lot. They were a big influence. I tell you they had their own style, Sonny had his style. And the group had a style because they had a baritone who used to switch and take second lead. Now when they switched the microphones, because they used to work on two mics, and when they would switch from Sonny to George, George had a little way of twisting from one mic to the other. The audience used to go crazy; they'd scream. It was real cute. And then on the records of course you couldn't see the twist, but it was such a good change from Sonny's voice to George, to the second lead."

Like the Ink Spots of a generation earlier, the Orioles had the look, they had the sound, they achieved success, but they were different in their performance approach—the steps, a dynamic emotional appeal—and those were the lasting influences on younger, emerging groups.

Harold Winley said of Sonny Til, "Doing a blues ballad getting on his knees and sweating and pleading. When they said they [girls] threw underwear and stuff at him, they weren't lying, whether it was planted or not, I've seen this done."

Like groups before them, the Orioles had the integrity to pursue their musical goals, and they worked hard. One step in that process was that they found an astute manager who also happened to write some very good songs for them—their first hit, in fact. From one perspective, the group perhaps found, in the manner of a much older African American necessity, a "white sponsor."[6] This was something noted by the *Baltimore Afro-American*, in a manner common for the period:

> Led by [George] Nelson, the unit appeared in a downtown talent show on Friday night, April 10, and won first prize. Earlier they had recorded a tune, "Too Soon to Know," [sic] which they sang over WBAL, attracting the attention of Miss Deborah Chessler, white, of 2420 Eutaw Pl., who took them under her management. (*Baltimore Afro-American*, May 8, 1948, 1)

The paper mistakenly lists Nelson as the lead, and also implies that the song, "It's Too Soon to Know," was the reason Chessler became interested in the group. In fact, Chessler knew them already and wrote the song. The Orioles and their manager met in a manner that suggests social and business acumen from both parties, and some elegant serendipity. All involved were in the right place at the right time. Chessler managed the Orioles from 1947 until 1954 and helped with the group's initial success, and it seems to have been a remarkable and productive relationship. She grew up in Baltimore, Maryland, and wrote a few songs before she finally tried to sell some in 1947. She did not know why she wrote songs.

"People just do it," she said.

Chessler was a young working girl in Baltimore—she neither played piano nor read music. She must have been compelled to write songs, and I think many of the best popular songwriters—from Chessler to Woody Guthrie, Johnny Mercer, Jim Webb—are like that. They seem to have been born to write, with little choice in the matter. Chessler's strategy was to write lyrics and create melodies by ear, and then pay someone to write a lead sheet. She said that as she got started, she sang a number of her songs to people in the music business and always got a good response. A disc jockey in Baltimore suggested she try to sell her songs. She then went around to music publishers, but quickly realized that the publishers "don't do anything unless there's a record." So she next went to record companies in New York and got Savanah Churchill to record "Tell Me So" for Manor Records in 1947. Then, Dinah Washington covered the song after Chessler sang it for her one night backstage at the Royal Theater in Baltimore. Disc jockeys in Baltimore started to give Chessler's songs airplay. Although she said she knew very little about black music as such at that particular time, she always listened to records. Obviously, she had ears. After the Orioles had a hit with it, Chessler's "It's Too Soon to Know" was recorded about 30 times by different artists, including Ella Fitzgerald, Dinah Washington, the Ravens, and Pat Boone. And obviously singers like Churchill, Washington, and other black performers did not necessarily look for "black" material to record—they simply wanted what they thought would be good songs—appealing songs, as Harold Winley had put it. "It's Too Soon to Know" was a simple song of young love and hope. With recognizable, step-wise ascending melody, most anyone could remember it. It was as good a pop formula as any standard and in the hands of the Orioles, it quickly became a new kind of standard.

At the same time that Chessler was perfecting her songwriting craft, in another part of Baltimore five singers called themselves the Vibra-Naires. They looked for appealing material and rehearsed whenever they weren't working their day jobs. The time was 1947. The place was an area of West Baltimore, south of and near where Pennsylvania and North Avenues meet. The group members were Lloyd "Tommy" Gaither, who lived at 1813 Edmondson Avenue; Earlington "Sonny" Tilghman, 1318 Whatcoat Street; George Nelson, 435 Druid Hill Avenue; Alexander Sharp, 452 Watty Court; and Richard Williams, 2035 McCulloh Street. Tilghman, who used the name Sonny Til, sang tenor lead and switched on some songs with George Nelson, a baritone. Gaither sang accompaniment and played the guitar, Sharp was a first tenor and Williams (replaced by Jimmy Reed sometime after 1949) sang bass. As Chessler recalled the story, the group was singing in a small place somewhere around town when they heard of a man named Abe who had a home recording machine. "He fooled around with things like that. He liked anything mechanical."

She did not wish to give his last name: "He passed away and I don't know whether his wife would want me to."

Some stories about the origins of that group have it that Chessler "discovered" them, but that was not the case. The guys "got to" Abe, as Chessler put it. He liked what he heard and agreed to make some demo

The Vibra-Naires. Top row from the left: Sonny Til, George Nelson, Alex Sharp, Richard Williams; sitting with the guitar, Lloyd Gaither. *Philadelphia Afro-American*, May 11, 1948. Courtesy of the Afro-American Newspapers.

recordings for them. He produced a number of home recordings and handled the group as a sort of manager. After Chessler had a couple of her records on the air, Abe, who was a brother-in-law to one of Chessler's friends, telephoned after hearing her name.

"They're here. Would you take a minute to listen?"

She said sure. So, the first time Deborah Chessler heard the Orioles (still the Vibra-Naires) was over the telephone. She liked what she heard immediately and later listened to the demos—the group was singing standard songs like "I Cover the Waterfront." She liked them even better after she heard the recordings. "I thought they were great."

She agreed to work with the five singers. Both Chessler and Abe—both amateurs—managed the Vibra-Naires for a while until Abe admitted he was not up to the job. "He didn't really know anything about show business."

Chessler took over the group and booked them on Arthur Godfrey's radio talent show for Monday evening, May 4, 1948, in New York. This is an often-told tale of how the Vibra-Naires broke into the public sphere beyond Baltimore. The story has several versions, spun from various sources over the years. The different versions say a great deal about power and politics in retelling cultural history (on this more in the epilogue), but as Chessler herself pointed out, "There's only one story that's true."

Godfrey's show was, as Chessler phrased it, a "talent scout night," and was popular in its time. Because she was the group's manager, she could not introduce them before their performance. Her cousin, Shirley Green, acted as the "talent scout" and introduced the Vibra-Naires on the air. The group at that time maintained a repertoire of popular songs of the day. Chessler thought they sang "Two Loves Have I," a hit song then. The group lost the first prize to a then-unknown pianist named George Shearing. The audience decided the second prize, which went to what Chessler called a "soprano suite."

The Vibra-Naires went home losers, but four nights later Chessler received a wire that requested they return to do the Friday morning *Chesterfield Show*. She and the group soon discovered that the home radio audience had responded to the station with about 7,000 telephone calls, letters, and wires between Godfrey's Monday and Wednesday shows. Apparently a good number of talent scouts listened to the show looking for new acts, and they responded as well, discrediting the original decision; many requested more information about the vocal group. The consensus was that the Vibra-Naires should have won. Unable to locate the group, Godfrey broadcast an appeal on his Thursday morning program seeking the whereabouts of the Vibra-Naires. He found Chessler and the group and brought them back for the morning show on Friday. The *Baltimore Afro-American* covered the Vibra-Naires in its Friday, May 8, news story, and in the prescient lead line to the story anticipated the group's imminent success:

> From singing for peanuts to being the nation's outstanding vocal quintet may be the destiny of the Vibra-Naires.
>
> Little known, except for stints around some of the local night spots, the group "crashed" the charmed circle on Monday of this week when it appeared on the Arthur Godfrey talent show in New York City. (1)

Just to wrap some context around this story, seven years after this incident, in 1955, a vocal quartet from Washington also appeared on the Arthur Godfrey show. The group was the Hi-Fis, who had attended Dunbar High School in the mid-1940s. By 1955 the group members were all in their late twenties, and had jobs outside music, but they continued to sing as a group. They did almost nothing but standard, mainstream material a cappella. For Howard Davis and Mel Lipscomb, the two middle voices, harmonizing was almost a compulsion. Mel Lipscomb, the second tenor, tells the story as he sits next to the other tenor, Howard Davis. The story might explain what had happened to the Vibra-Naires.

"We got there and we were a little surprised that Godfrey wasn't doing the thing [he was ill at the time] and we went through our thing, and they thanked us. We knew that we were very much prepared for that day. And our sound was good and we did it good. We did it upbeat, we hit the ending right, we felt very, very comfortable completing that set. And we stayed around a while to see who the other—well, we weren't first on to begin with, so we heard them. Then we stayed around a while to see who the others were. And it was a little young group, teenagers, teens, right. That were little drum and bugle, you know, tossing the baton and all that kind of stuff. They won it.

"They were a white group. But the guy told us that, this guy behind the scenes—"

They knew someone from Dunbar High School who worked at the network. "—[He] told us that, and as you may or may not know, during those days the sponsors of that program were Lipton Tea and Campbell Soup. And prior to our arrival, I wasn't that aware of, that several groups before—whenever a black group was given the opportunity they won. They won. And what he said, they were saying this has got to stop, the sponsors. Because this show is being piped through or beamed back, whatever, to North Carolina and the South and all that kind of stuff. And hey, we can't deal with this thing. So when we came, this good group, these good voices, man, we think we had that thing locked up but it didn't work. Don't mess up where the bread come from, so we just, that was the end of that experience."

Although this story is anecdotal, there is no reason to doubt its veracity and in concert with the Vibra-Naires', it is more than suggestive about what was going on with these national talent shows. The broader lesson perhaps is the curious position in which black entertainers found themselves—critically superior, socially inferior, and if it made good business sense, as in "black sells," then whites would go with it. However, if a black presence was thought to interfere with commerce, then the doors were quickly closed. The whole picture is contradictory, if not absurd.

After the Godfrey show, the Hi-Fis returned to Washington and to their respective careers outside music. That was not the case for the Vibra-Naires. Chessler and the group returned to Baltimore. "I was a working girl, a working girl," she said.

Chessler returned to her day job for a while and then returned to New York with the demos the group had recorded earlier. A friend in New York suggested Natural Records, which became Jubilee in November 1948. The owner and president was Jerry Blaine, a former bandleader, and he wanted the group as soon as he heard the demos. "He knew about records. He was a good person to get with for one reason, he was out to make a success. In other words, he didn't have a big backlog of other people, so when he took someone, he really wanted to work on them. The group went up to New York and they all signed."

Two of Chessler's songs became the group's first releases in 1948: "It's Too Soon to Know" and "Barbara Lee." The only thing Blaine did not like about the group was the "Vibra-Naires" name, according to Chessler. "The word 'Orioles' came out and we all agreed. We all said O.K. because it represented Baltimore and they were from Baltimore."

They obviously drew from a tradition of earlier vocal groups, both sacred and secular, that had bird names: the Dixie Humingbirds, Ravens, Swan Silvertones.

The Orioles made their first recordings in July 1948 ("It's Too Soon to Know" b/w "Barbara Lee"), just a couple of months after the Arthur Godfrey show appearance. Through the end of 1950, the group made about 32 recordings (Ferlingere 1976). They produced seven "hits" in 1949 alone and won an award from New York disc jockeys—"in recognition of their tremendous popularity" (*Baltimore Afro-American*, January 21, 1950)—delivered in the form of a trophy at the Apollo Theater. Chessler described the Orioles as "very anxious to succeed," and as hard workers.

"They had long rehearsals, you know, because most of them didn't read music. So they had to learn it from the guitar player, or in the case of my songs, I would sing my songs and they would learn the background and then pick up the lead sheet and read it. Yeah, and sing it at the same time because they already knew the music, the melody.

"They were a good bunch of guys. No drugs, no problems. You know what I mean? In those days, they were clean. I think the biggest thing they ever did was some whiskey, you know. But they were a clean group and a good group. And they were good for me to manage because they didn't give me those problems. The problem was to get them started, and then after getting them started, to make sure they kept going with other hit records and good bookings."

Deborah Chessler's narrative suggests the way to understand the success of the Orioles: they had as much to do with their own success as she or the record company. How did the group choose material?

"It's the easiest thing because if they didn't feel the tune was good, you just forget it, and go for something else. They had to like it. They had to be

The Orioles in 1949. Courtesy of the Afro-American Newspapers.

able to fall into it right away. If they didn't like it—like one of the first songs I sang to them was 'Tell Me So,' and they liked that. And I sang 'It's Too Soon To Know,' and I sang a few others. In fact, 'Barbara Lee' was written on the day of a rehearsal because we were short of one tune. I just wrote up 'Barbara Lee' real fast. But the thing is, the main thing is they had to like it. And if they liked it, it usually came out good. There was no sense in giving them something they don't like.

"The record company always, always gave us, always gave us material. Always. There was never a record session that we hadn't looked over at least twenty, twenty-five songs. And most of the times I didn't have anything on it, you know what I mean? I just had them on the sessions where I had written something and the boys liked it. But they were with Jubilee for a good many years, and maybe I had six or eight songs in that whole time.[7] But the thing is that the record company always—because people send in material, like I ran to Manor that time for the Savanah record. People always send in to the record companies. And the record companies look them over, pick what they like, and then they submit them to the groups or to the singer. And even then, if the groups or singer didn't like it,

The Orioles on stage at the Apollo Theater in 1950 receiving an award. Deborah Chessler is on the right, Jerry Blaine of Jubilee Records on the far right; note Dizzy Gillespie on far left. Courtesy of the Afro-American Newspapers.

oh, well, they could say yes, we want you to do that one, but most of the time they would let them pick from what they sent. Although, like they were at the Apollo once in New York, the Orioles, and the record company sent over a demo record, a record, of a guy singing a song called "Crying in the Chapel."[8] And he was the writer of it and he was like a hillbilly sound. We heard it and the Orioles said they liked it, and they rehearsed it the next day and before they left the Apollo they went down and recorded it. And it was a big hit. It was a real big hit."

Til's version of "Crying in the Chapel" (1953) was an emotional, spiritual anthem that belied its origins—and also revealed the close relationship between African American music and some white southern, rural music. As Andy Magruder stated above, vocalists would "make your music mine." A country song? The singers of the 1940s could and would sing everything, as we have heard throughout.

For the Orioles there was no problem getting into the feel of a country or "hillbilly" song. When the Orioles came across "Crying in the Chapel," according to Chessler, "They liked the feel of it and the words. And the melody came real easy. As soon as we put it on the record player everybody looked up, they liked it."

They made it their own.

After its initial success, the group suffered a setback in November 1950 when guitarist Tommy Gaither died and vocalists George Nelson and Johnny Reed were injured in an automobile accident. Ralph Williams replaced Gaither and Reed left the group, replaced by a pianist, Charlie Harris. The group quickly performed again at the Earle Theater in Philadelphia in December and went on to another personnel change in late 1954 and then again around 1962. After the group's early hits, they went on to have only a few significant recordings. They could never duplicate their initial impact on popular music and youngsters, especially back home in Baltimore, but they didn't have to. That initial impression was enough to help establish the character of early rhythm & blues.

Singers tried to copy the Orioles after their first successful recordings. The group especially made a big impact back in their neighborhood, on local kids, who first sang like the Orioles and then moved on to establish their own sound. Herman Denby of the Swallows lived in the same neighborhood as some of the Orioles. "We sang everything that they sang."

Put another way, the groups coming up just behind the Orioles "covered" their material. Cover bands in the more recent sense, from the 1970s through today, generally want to sound as much like the original as possible, and this was also true for the Swallows, who at first copied the Orioles and then established their own sound. The younger groups just behind the Orioles used them as conceptual models and performed their songs, as a combined aesthetic, imitative, and pragmatic gesture to capitalize on their success, for which no one could blame them. For one thing, fans did not have the original group around all the time, so they settled for the next best thing in local derivatives and covers. This phenomenon continues today and seems to be a vital aspect to pop culture.

Ernest and Herman and their respective groups, however, went on to develop their own distinctive sounds and artistic trajectories, this despite the formulaic aspect of group harmony. But the Orioles were an inspiration for them and other groups as well, just as the Ink Spots and Ravens were for the Orioles. The Orioles served as a direct link between the past, present, and future. The Orioles, who went national in 1948, served as local impetus for others—if they could do it, then others would try. The story of the Orioles illustrates some points made in the preface—the circumstances out of which groups emerged, who controlled the groups, and the difficult issue of race as it intersects with music style and stylistic category. Their story was a unique one, but others would repeat its general framework many times over the following decade.

The Orioles in 1950, with new members Ralph Williams and pianist Charles Harris on the left. Courtesy of the Afro-American Newspapers.

The Orioles came out of their Baltimore neighborhood with the help of an exceptional manager and songwriter. However, they clearly did their work and had the wherewithal to develop their talents, find Abe, listen to advice, choose material, shape it, and change their performance practice enough to create something new and popular. Nobody did that for them. Although we do not have personal accounts by group members, we did learn enough from Deborah Chessler and others to know that the group maintained a considerable degree of control over what they did. This was not the case with all groups, especially very young singers, but the general sense emerges that youngsters developed a strategy to *use* group harmony. It became a resource to advance their goals. Narratives by other vocalists in the other chapters show a similar picture. Group harmony, which was a resource for the singers themselves, became a commodity for agents, managers, record companies marketers of nostalgia later on, and eventually record collectors. There was enough entrepreneurial resource and recourse to fuel group harmony successfully through the 1950s and beyond, in one guise or another.

Sonny Til and the Orioles had a number of subsequent hits and personnel changes in the 1950s and continued as a group through the early 1960s. By then, the time and place of group harmony had changed. It is the narrative of these early years, however, that tells us about the transition of group harmony from a local sphere to a national one. The Orioles, with the help of Deborah Chessler and others, managed to engage with their circumstances and control, after a fashion, the trajectory of their careers — good luck, bad circumstances, race issues, and serendipity notwithstanding. The Orioles established a new time and place for group harmony. In the 1970s and until he passed away in 1981, Sonny Til performed mostly as a solo act, with different singers accompanying him as the "Orioles."

The Clovers

The Clovers were a slightly different, slightly later style of group harmony. They emulated the Orioles at first, and then became much more of a mediated and produced enterprise in partnership with Atlantic Records. The Clovers originated in Washington sometime around 1948 or 1949. Beginning in 1951, in the hands of Atlantic Records, they moved in a musical direction clearly rooted in dance, blues, and male teenage anxieties. Their songs had great crossover appeal and would tell a good story: "One Mint Julep," "Comin' On," "Hey Miss Fannie," "Lovey Dovey," "Love Potion Number Nine." The story of the early Clovers, like the Orioles, again illustrates the web of intrigue out of which postwar group harmony emerged.

John "Buddy" Bailey was lead singer of the Clovers from their beginning through 1961 (except when in the army in 1953–54). When John Bailey was five years old in 1936 (he died in 1994), he lived with his grandmother Mary in Gladys, Virgina, near Lynchburg. Buddy called himself a "grandmamma's boy." She and her friends put a little guitar in his hands when he was about five. This gesture was his first experience with music, sustained later by strong religious song. As long as he could play and sing "Just a Closer Walk with Thee," Buddy's grandmother, who taught school, did not mind that he played music. Those years, he said, were great fun. "I didn't want for nothing that I can recall."

He cherished listening to Art Linkletter, Dr. I. Q., Amos 'n' Andy, and Jack Benny on the radio. When he was eight years old, his grandmother moved them to Washington so they could be near relatives and good schools. "She wanted me to get a good education in Washington," he said.

Buddy attended Cleveland Elementary School at Eighth and S Streets NW. He lived on Second and V Streets NW in the Le Droit Park section of town behind Griffith Stadium, home of the Washington Senators. Buddy said his life was comfortable there with his grandmother, his mom's sister Isabella, and her husband in a "four bedroom house with full basement" owned by Aunt Isabella. In Washington, music became more of a focus in Buddy's life.

"I was still playing the guitar. I liked to play on the streets. This was during the summer. I had a guy playing the old kazoo like it was a plastic sax, as a toy sax. And we had another guy that was playing the homemade drums, which was a bucket, the homemade bass fiddle—a string hooked up to a bucket and a stick like, you know. And we made a pretty good sound. We were around twelve, maybe, thirteen. People would throw us change, and stuff, you know."

These youngsters had their own "territory" in which they would move. "Always in the Northwest area, we'd go along U Street a lot—pretty safe in those years. We had the Lincoln Theater, the Booker T, and the Republic. And we'd go up along that strip and we'd come back sometimes with maybe twenty dollars."

By the time Buddy got into Dunbar High School he was hanging out with friends and making music at parties and talent shows. It was around this time that he met Harold Lucas, Billy Shelton, and Tommy Woods. They formed a group called the Melody Four.

Someone—Buddy thought it was Harold Lucas—suggested they change the name of the group to the Clovers. This was around 1949 or

1950. After Shelton and Woods left the group, Matthew McQuater and bass vocalist Harold Winley joined, and then guitarist Bill Harris.

Buddy said that Harold Winley "just walked up to us on Florida Avenue, right in back of the old ball park." Harold Winley remembered it slightly differently. He said he first heard the group that was to become the Clovers on *Morton's Amateur Hour*, the show hosted by WWDC's Jackson Lowe. Winley recalled hearing the group performing "Yes Sir, That's My Baby" (the first song they would later record) on the radio show. That inspired him to send in a card and compete as a solo act. He sang "Lucky Old Sun," won, and got to go back for a final competition with other weekly winners. It was there he met the Clovers and, as he recalled, invited himself to a rehearsal with the group as they roamed around their northwest area of the city.

Working within the constraints of a segregated city, the Clovers used whatever public space was available to them to sing. The period stereotype of "street corner" harmony was not all that off the mark in some cases, and the voice is the most portable of instruments. The Clovers hung around and sang all the time. "Anywhere," Winley said. "Anywhere you saw us singing, that's rehearsal."

Winley moved easily from acquaintance to regular group member, and part of the ease with which he made that transition had to do with the social dynamics of group singing.

Winley was born in Washington in 1933, after his parents had migrated from North Carolina in the late 1920s. He attended Moore Elementary on R Street NW, between Fifth and New Jersey Avenue. He and his family of six sisters and four brothers lived at 1611 Sixth Street NW, in a white clapboard house.

When Winley's parents passed away in the 1940s, he moved back to North Carolina to live with an uncle. He said a desire to sing made him return to Washington when he was about fifteen years old: "By 1948 I was what they might call today frustrated or whatever, and I walked up to my uncle one day and told him that I wanted to go back to Washington. He said, 'what do you mean? You're in the second semester, what are you talking about, go back to Washington for what?' And I said I wanted to leave."

Winley recalled hearing music from a neighbor's window in Washington —Fats Waller, Annie Churchill, Bing Crosby, and most of what was around at the time.

"I got quite a musical education there. There was one gentleman that lived in the house [next door] that used to have weekly gatherings, and he used to play his music. He was upstairs on the second floor and our bedroom was right, you know, like adjoining the house and you just open the window, especially in the summertime, and you get it all."

Like many other Washington youngsters, Harold Winley's very first musical experiences came from around the home and in school or church. His teacher Miss Smith taught him songs for school assemblies. His mother, though, "did all the singing in the house. My mother had a beautiful soprano and she sang all the time. She was a magnificent cook and she would sing these songs and she would be telling us about this because she belonged to the Episcopal Church. And the anthems, you know, she could run them."

Winley fell in with a group of boys in elementary school and "there were a lot of cats in there singing." He did not remember any of the girls doing a whole lot of singing, and he reasoned it was because of the popular male vocalists like Billy Eckstine and Bill Kenny. When Harold was about eight he got together with his friend Leonard to sing an Ink Spots-type version of "We Three." This was at a neighbor's party. "I wanted to sing like Kenny. You know my voice was up there at that time, I'm eight years old, you know. We all go to the party and so I told the girl's mother that I was going to sing a song, you know. I get up. 'Come on Leonard.' Leonard wouldn't move. So I sang Bill Kenny's part, and then I did Hoppy Jones's part. You know the gig had to go on. So that was my introduction."

Like the Orioles before them, the early material of the Clovers consisted primarily of standards performed in the tradition of groups like the Ink Spots and Ravens. Winley's thing, after his voice changed, was to sing bass. By the time he began with the Clovers, he sang solidly in the style of the Ravens' Jimmy Ricks. One result of a strong bass voice is that it redefines the group sound. "Real quick, in 1946 my voice changed from that tenor that I used to sing when I was eight years old to bass. And that's when I heard 'Ol' Man River,' by the Ravens. I started singing it then; I still sing it."

To young kids, to anybody with ears, Rick's voice was a wonder. "Because his voice, man, was frightening. I ask him, I said, 'Man, what do they do to you, what do they do to your voice when you go in?' Ignorant question, not knowing. 'Say, what do they do to your voice when they go in the studio?' He say, 'Huh?' [laughs] He say, 'They don't do nothing to it.' In other words, 'you don't sound human to me.' That's a natural thing with them, and then when you hear them on the stage—whew. Class."

After Winley joined the Clovers, they found their manager, Lou Krefetz. Krefetz used to play cards with Max Silverman and others at Silverman's store in Washington. The Clovers by this time were singing just a few blocks away at the Old Rose Social Club and hanging around. The details vary, but all the lines came together in 1950 for the group when Krefetz became manager.

"Quality Music. And it was a gentleman that used to play, what is it? Gin. Yeah, Earl and a bunch of guys. Not a bunch of guys, but a few guys would go around with Max Silverman and they'd play gin. But Earl was a hustler. You know. And he was a very nice guy. Low key. And he just moved about, he was a gambler. And then, these were the type of people that would be around those places, people that had the money, you know. He said I really like you. I got a guy that want to hear you all. So he set up a meeting with us and Waxie Maxie in the back of his store with Lou Krefetz. Lou Krefetz as I told you was a record salesman."

Buddy Bailey had said he worked informally for Silverman, selling records sometime in the late 1940s and that Silverman knew Krefetz. "Well, we gathered in the store. I used to go in there and help sell records. He [Silverman] used to let me sell records. He'd give me a few bucks, I forget what it was, just to hang around. But he said, 'I got a friend named Lou Krefetz, from Baltimore, he's a record salesman. He's a wholesaler. You know. Mercury Records. He'd like to meet you guys.' So, he arranged for Lou to meet us back in his office. My grandmother, she said, 'I don't know whether I want you to sign up.' By then Lou was wanting to sign us. I said, 'Aw, come on Mama, let us—sign for me.' "

Buddy's reference to his grandmother is endearing and points to the convergence of relationships that got the Clovers off the ground: the vocalists, a swirl of family members, Jack Lowe and WWDC, characters around Max's record shop. There were so many levels of social exchanges, integrated, overlapping spheres, all within the confines of a segregated city. And then, as we have already seen, there were the specific dynamics between young black male singers and the white businessmen, many of whom were Jewish, plying their wares in black neighborhoods—pharmacies, clothing, furniture and appliances, and record stores.

—WAXIE MAXIE'S—
QUALITY
MUSIC CO.
1836 – 7th ST. N.W.
OPEN 'TIL 11PM
One Block Below Griffith Stadium
ALL THE LABELS
17th YEAR OF SATISFACTION (1955 D.C. telephone book)

Quality Music was the same record shop that Ahmet Ertegun visited during the 1940s when he was young and his project was to collect black music. Ertegun began to hang out at the Quality Music Shop, at 7th and

T Streets, which was run by a man called Waxie Maxie Silverman and was by then the most successful record store in the black district of Washington. Ahmet had known Waxie Maxie from the days when he and Nesuhi [Ahmet's older brother] were forming their collection, because Waxie Maxie (who had begun his business as a radio-repair shop) sold secondhand records, but by 1944 Waxie Maxie had begun to sell new releases by black artists, and in Maxie's shop Ahmet began to get a feel for contemporary black popular music. (Trow 1978: 176)

It was Ahmet to whom Krefetz brought the Clovers when their first recording (the Sammy Kahn song "Yes Sir, That's My Baby" b/w "When You Come Back to Me") on Eddie Heller's Rainbow label, failed to inspire purchasers, and for good reason. It was not particularly good, by Buddy's own admission. "It was almost a cappella; very bad record. I heard it not long ago and I almost broke out laughing at the thing."

The performances had promise; the recording quality was poor. After that, Krefetz arranged the Atlantic contract and afterward the style of the group changed dramatically, to what record people later might describe as a "ghetto sound" compared to the Ink Spots. By today's standards, it sounds like good clean pop. It was new (for some), smart, bluesy, very danceable, and appealing. The group fell under the production influence of Ahmet Ertegun and the direction of writer/arranger Jesse Stone.

The Clovers were singing "Skylark." And there's nothing wrong with the urban black man getting into the general taste of the world, you know, except that taste is never as good as what he had to begin with. (Ahmet Ertegun, quoted in Trow 1978: 179).

According to Trow, "In the case of the Clovers, Ahmet had taken five obscure young men (who had come to his notice through his friend Waxie Maxie Silverman) and coached them in a style that made use of one or two musical modes in which he had an interest" (1978: 190). This is a curious turn of phrase." We can only assume that Trow means some blues themes and a particularly rhythmic bass pattern sometimes referred to as the Atlantic bass line. Atlantic writer/arranger Jesse Stone said it was his creation.

I designed a bass-pattern, and it sort of became identified with rock 'n' roll—doo, da-doo, dum; doo, da doo, dum—that thing. I'm the guilty person that started that. (quoted in Tosches 1984: 15)

Although Ertegun fancied that he had a conceptual frame for 1950s black music, in 1947 he simply had the interest and the money to start Atlantic Records with his brother and then Herb Abramson. They hired Jesse Stone, who did considerable work translating the ideas of Ertegun and the talent of groups to help create the Atlantic sound of the early 1950s—the bass line was one formulaic aspect of that sound. Atlantic was arguably the very first label to develop its own distinctive sound—through consistent production, engineering, writing and arranging—that cut across numerous artists under contract.

We can first look at the development of the Clovers' style from the perspective of Ahmet Ertegun. He seems to have had a particular stylistic model in mind when he, through Jesse Stone's arrangements, began altering the Clovers. After he signed them, he had them learn his blues-based material. 'Don't You Know I Love You' was the first, which they recorded in 1951. Harold Winley remembers how that episode evolved.

"So Lou presented us next, he said I got somebody else I want you to meet and he presented us with Ahmet Ertegun and Herb Abramson. Same place, in back of Waxie Maxie's. And we're singing now, we don't know, we're singing 'How High the Moon.' Buddy is scattin' all over the place. And then 'What Is This Thing Called Love,' 'Pennies from Heaven.' All these type of things, you know.

"That's what we were singing when they met us. 'Ahmet,' he said, 'now Ahmet,' he said, 'this guy's got a song he wants you all to hear. He wrote it on the plane from New York to Washington.'

"He wrote a song? You imagine the expression on our faces. Now here's a guy, a Turk singing the blues. You know. Now he tried his best to give us that song, 'Don't You Know I Love You.' You know, and he was showing us how to do the, 'you know you gonna'—we're looking at—we laughed our asses off. And Lou said, 'Don't laugh you fools.' So now, so what is this shit, man? Muddy Waters, Lightnin' Hopkins? What is this? I mean I heard some blues, because Lionel Hampton had, what was his name? Sonny Parker. And Jimmy Rushing, you know. And a few other people, you know. Wynonie Harris. And Larry Darnell was out there with Paul Williams, you know, and so forth and so on. What is this he's singing though? He gave the introduction and everything. He had it all in his head. And it worked, after we got over the initial shock. And we still weren't ready for it, even down to recording—then when we recording it? O.K."

How did the group feel about recording somebody else's material?

"Oh, I didn't have no, I had no feelings for nothing, not like that. That was recording, and we were going to New York to record again. You know? And not knowing that Atlantic was bigger than Rainbow. Well, Atlantic was also heading down the tubes because Atlantic had been involved in jazz, and stuff like that, in their infancy. Bebop and all that stuff was on the way out. And then the man is standing there scatting, singing, 'How High the Moon.' "

Winley laughs, "You know. So, well yeah, you know we were quite excited about singing it. And we did the back of it, back of it was 'Skylark.' "

Jesse Stone corroborates what Winley says about Atlantic Records and jazz. "When Atlantic Records first started, at the end of 1947, we were trying to do jazz. The jazz didn't sell. . . . The kids were looking for something to dance to" (Tosches 1984: 15).

The patented Atlantic sound was born of necessity and fueled by new, younger sensibilities — driven by kids themselves — Ahmet's sound creative vision notwithstanding. Abramson, Ertegun, and Stone were listening to the market — the kids who wanted to dance. In the Clovers they had gifted and talented performers, and the group had the wherewithal to listen to their producers, the men paying them. This was already a different era from a few years earlier, when the Orioles chose their material. The Clovers had the good common sense to sing anything the man asked them to because Atlantic was taking a more participatory approach to their groups than earlier record companies. Together the entire alliance forged a new sound. And a profitable sound it was, at least in theory. In 1952, when the Clovers released "One Mint Julep," they hit big. And besides, what did they have to lose?

In retrospect, the Clovers and Atlantic Records easily brokered a deal. The Clovers had success that helped *make* Atlantic Records in the early 1950s. The group recorded around 44 sides for Atlantic between April 1951 and September 1958 (Ferlingere 1976). They never totally abandoned their love of standard material and the mainstream, but for the most part they gestured toward soulful, danceable pop rhythm & blues. The Clovers' sound made the era — and rhythm & blues — more crossover. Ironically, with a New York makeover, Atlantic Records brought the Clovers over the tracks to a blues-based sound — which, as things were, was also a gesture toward the mainstream. It was a good backdoor move to a place and sound the Clovers had never really been. There was nothing raw or amateurish about that sound, either. In fact, the production techniques of Atlantic were quite good for the period. It still is a great sound. The sound owed as much to the songs and arrangements of Jesse Stone and the studio musicians, as to the sound engineer and sound concept of Ertegun. The Clovers came off as a professional, smooth-sounding group. Instead of singing standards, they performed "produced" blues-based or jump numbers, designed to somehow convey Ertegun's visions of what "the black man had to begin with." In many ways it was constructed "race" music, but the confidence and ability of the singers made it authoritative, professional, and appealing. Atlantic gave the Clovers a very bright production sound, and the group had that "we could do anything" attitude, at least on record. Along with some other Atlantic artists, especially Ruth Brown, the Clovers gave Atlantic success for the decade.

In the end, the Clovers got what they wanted as much as Atlantic Records did, at least in the short run. In this, there is one more perspective from which we can view the Clovers' story. It points to the issue of control. The Clovers did not even come close to the wealth of Ertegun, but despite a couple of personnel changes during the 1950s (when Bailey went into the Army and then returned), they did well for themselves and sustained for over a decade. From the beginning, the way Harold Winley tells it, the group knew Ertegun's trick bag, but they were going to New York so they sang the material he presented to them, not as a sellout, but as a selling point. They were buying in. The Clovers were talented, savvy, and worked hard to become one of the few Washington vocal groups to go national and make some good noise professionally for more than just one hit. The Clovers helped define a decade. Not only that, they got out from the streets and neighborhoods of postwar Washington. For some members, it was only for a while, but to achieve even that was no easy task.

Beyond that, stories about the Orioles and Clovers expose, among other things, relationships between young black males, adults, and institutions that they had to encounter as they grew up. For Buddy Bailey and Harold Winley those relationships ranged from close family members to extended family members, from neighbors to teachers, from a local white DJ like Jackson Lowe to a black music arranger like Jesse Stone. The relationships included white businessmen like Lou Krefetz and Max Silverman, who had maintained longtime dealings in black communities, and a young white female like Deborah Chessler who, by her own admission, had no idea what black music was until she met the Orioles (although Krefetz and Silverman probably had no *real* idea what black music was either).

Peter Guralnick had an angle on similar kinds of relationships, what he termed the "racial mix" of Southern soul music in the 1960s. Guralnick looked for positive ways to characterize the relationship between white record industrialists and black artists. He called it, optimistically, a "partnership with a difference: the principals brought to it . . . divergent outlooks and experiences" and with that, "the promise of integration" (Guralnick

1986: 10). The truth as always, is somewhere in the middle. On one level, young groups used whatever resources were available to resist the segregation of Washington. On another, they were ready to buy into the same system that created that segregation in the first place—perhaps with the dream of the kind of partnership that Guralnick envisioned.

On the one hand music informed the young black male's range of experience and perspective, which really was a celebration. On the other hand, the repressive aspect of a white dominant social structure shaped and constrained their range of experience and perspective. Coupled with (and contradictory to) this was the allure of assimilation and possible "success." If any resistance to repression took place, then assimilation was often the desired goal.

Hi Fis

The Hi Fis, who first called themselves the Dunbar Four and the Rhythmneers, were one such group that eschewed turning completely professional, but not before trying out the idea of a record contract. They performed in and around the Washington area from the mid-1940s, when still in high school, through about 1956, when the group drifted apart. The Hi Fis story is like that of the Orioles and Clovers, but it is also a unique story. The group by their own design was not a "rhythm & blues" vocal group stylistically. They did make, however, an effort during that period to sing for money and popularity, to see where they could go with it all. They made a few tentative entrepreneurial gestures, but very much in their own manner. Like so many other black musicians over the years, they never really had a name for what they did—they simply sang, harmonized, and resisted category. You would hear the same refrain repeatedly: "We were just singing."[9]

The Hi Fis were also different because they sang together for over ten years, which is far longer than a lot of other groups, professional or otherwise. And they had their feelings about rhythm & blues. They insisted that they had rejected it as a genre and as a style. Howard Davis said, "We were never influenced by that stuff." Mel Lipscomb not surprisingly expressed the same sentiments. "We were never influenced by them."

One likely reason Howard and Melvin were so insistent about rhythm & blues is because the Hi Fis came of age musically a little before the looser emotions of the rhythm & blues period. (Actually, so did other artists of that generation, but they managed and wanted to make the transition.) The Hi Fis had a certain musical conservatism that many of their contemporaries, like the Clovers, were able to transform. The Hi Fis never made that stylistic leap to rhythm & blues, partly because of the musical changes the commercial aspect of it would have involved. They found they did not want to make those changes, although they flirted once with the possibility. In 1955, they had a meeting with someone at Atlantic Records for whom they played a demo recording. He said the group was "too good." Mel Lipscomb quotes the man. "You guys are too good."

So we could all be sure, Melvin looks over at Howard to ask, "Is this the truth?"

"That's exactly what he said."

Mel continues. "Now this is a *quote*. I can remember it like it was a moment ago. 'You guys are too good. You sound too much like the Charioteers or the Mills Brothers.' And we were not trying to sound like anyone, we were just singing."

In 1955 the sound of the Charioteers and Mills Brothers was definitely yesterday's news, so obviously the Hi Fis evoked an earlier era, and we have already seen how Atlantic changed the Clovers' approach four years earlier in that regard.

Perhaps too, the Hi Fis sensed the elemental contradiction with the whole rhythm & blues business, that it was marginal music by virtue of its "black" category, yet at the same time it was popular and commercial music, and increasingly so by 1955. Its purpose was to sell, which in the language of American popular music meant it eventually would become a component of the mainstream market.

Howard would say later, "We weren't market."

The Hi Fis chose not to go market and instead remained very close to their musical beginnings. They performed a cappella renditions of standards in clean, tight, bottom up, four-part harmony that was beautifully informed with a cool gospel emotion—"Confessions," "Moonlight in Vermont," "Pennies from Heaven," "Sunny Side of the Street." The group's sound you hear from the few noncommercial recordings is pretty. It was solid, though slightly square at the same time—Fairfield Four-ish. It must have sounded curiously guileless in the offices of Atlantic Records in New York in 1955.

There is yet another element in the Hi Fis' attitude about rhythm & blues. This involves what Amiri Baraka argued as the distinctly non-middle-class sphere of rhythm & blues as a musical expression in the late 1940s.

> Rhythm & blues was still an exclusive music. It was performed almost
> exclusively for, and had to satisfy, a Negro audience. . . . It, too, was a

music that was hated by the middle-class Negro and not even understood by the white man. (Baraka 1976: 169)

This last point especially is ironic, considering that a white man gave the music its trade name. Aside from that, Baraka writes only one half of the formula here. Eventually rhythm & blues moved beyond exclusivity — and there is good reason, as I have argued all along, that black performers never wanted that "exclusivity" (read marginality), but that it was something totally imposed.

All this leads us to the high school the group attended, and to deeply rooted class differences in black Washington that intersected with music making and musical affiliations. The Hi Fis began as the Dunbar group, and surely reflected to a degree the elite attitude of the school in shunning rhythm & blues. There are, as usual, other open issues upon which we can reflect: Buddy Bailey of the Clovers made an engaging comment about a desire to have played something other than rhythm & blues, to a different clientele and at different venues. This was an odd sentiment, one would think, coming from the lead singer of a very successful rhythm & blues, dance-oriented vocal group. But on a deeper level it was not so odd, for Buddy seems to have been revealing common, negative rhythm & blues associations. Buddy laid blame on the group's booking agent at the time, Billy Shaw.

"But what happened was the guy wasn't booking us in these good places, you know, Copa Cabana and places where you could really do it. I always had a desire to [play those clubs]. I liked them because, simply because the money, I felt, was there, among other things. I thought we should be seen by people who are real night-clubbers, you know. Not these out of the way joints, you know. There used to be a place called Capitol Arena, up on W Street and Fourteenth. Before that, it was Turner's, a guy named Turner owned it. Turner's Arena. And they'd book us in these one-nighters and nothing but, just juke joints. You know you dance and you stomping on the floor all night. I look for people who — I want them to sit down. You can't enjoy a show dancing, I don't think. I never did believe it. You got to be half drunk, the people, the patrons, you know."

Buddy Bailey was in his fifties when he made these remarks, and so reflected back on these issues differently from when he was a young man anticipating them. Because the Clovers were commercial and financially successful, it is unlikely that the issue for Buddy was really the money. The Clovers had originally wished their musical end to be pop, not rhythm & blues, if we can judge at all from the material they enjoyed before they went to Atlantic. Yet, are the two ends all that different? Buddy Slaughter says the exact opposite of Bailey, and suggests that an agent kept his groups (the Buddies and Cap-Tans) out of black clubs.

Slaughter complained that the Buddies, who were contemporaries of the Hi Fis and the Clovers, played too many white clubs in D.C., like the Blue Mirror. The Buddies maintained a wide repertoire with pop appeal. Apparently, according to Slaughter, their agent at the time (Michael Graham, a local African American businessman) wanted to keep it that way. Slaughter suggested that because his group was popular in white clubs, they played few black ones and as a result, although the money was O.K., they were never able to break into a rhythm & blues clientele.

This is a curious twist to the notion that black groups wanted to move beyond playing only black clubs to become more popular and successful. Here Buddy Slaughter implies that because of the Buddies' (and later the Cap-Tans') repertoire and popularity in white clubs, they never made a move to rhythm & blues. Rhythm & blues, of course, was "popular" as well—as this book argues—but during the time Buddy is talking about, the late 1940s, rhythm & blues was still an "exclusive" music, as Baraka has said. Slaughter's analysis is remarkable, especially when you refer back to what Buddy Bailey of the Clovers said.

"This is the reason we weren't too hot with blacks; we did all our work mostly in white clubs. Big, white clubs. Money was good, but popularity was bringing us down because we wasn't being seen out here, you know, by the black crowd. I think the only black club we sang in was Jim Dyke's, that was out in Maryland, out that area, and Club Harlem, the big club in Philadelphia. That's about the only two black clubs I can think of."

Like the Hi Fis, the Buddies were not really a rhythm & blues group, but if we are to believe Slaughter—and there is no reason we should not— then it was something that perhaps they wanted to be. Maybe they just missed the moment.

From the perspective of Buddy Slaughter comes a frustration over the inability to break into popular and seemingly lucrative black rhythm & blues. Another perspective—Buddy Bailey's—reacted to having had to play that music, although it was lucrative.

The Hi Fis, on the other hand, just never had eyes for rhythm & blues, as Howard and Melvin have been saying all along. Howard says that they just could not sing it, not because they lacked the ability, but because they lacked the sensibility. "But just the, just the notion was just, we couldn't— I mean we just couldn't sing it. We were set in our ways. We just couldn't sing it."

Through the decade of the 1950s, in its larger relationship to the music industry and to American society, rhythm & blues became mainstream, assimilationist, and middle class. That was one of the contributions of Atlantic Records and groups like the Clovers. Rhythm & blues headed in the same direction that Buddy Bailey ultimately wanted to go and which Buddy Slaughter supposedly wanted to leave. And about that impulse and the middle-class anathema of rhythm & blues that Baraka describes (and the Hi Fis felt), are they not at cross-purposes? It seems the nearer to rhythm & blues you get, the further away you go—black outlines around a white silhouette. Such were the circumstances in which the Hi Fis found themselves—they were very much a part, unavoidably, of the entrepreneurial flow of rhythm & blues and the period. They were also musical products and constituents, so to speak, of their time and place: homes, neighborhoods, churches, and schools.

In 1990 Howard Davis and Melvin Lipscomb, the middle, inside voices of the Hi Fis, were both sixty-one years old, but you would not know it to look at and listen to them. They were still an exemplary act. Howard was a dentist in Washington and Melvin was retired from the National Institutes of Health. Both were native Washingtonians—Howard Southeast, Melvin Northwest. They met in 1943 and were still close after all those years. Very often kids who sang together when young or even into their twenties would get away from each other after a while and lose touch. This was not the case with Howard and Melvin.

Mel leans in toward Howard, "And I met my best friend, which is sitting right here next to you, when we got to Dunbar High School."

The Hi Fis began sometime after 1943 as the Dunbar Four and became an attraction. For a brief while they were the Dunbar Five, when Curly King sang with them, but arranging the five voices was unwieldy and they returned to being a quartet. Benjamin Johnson, the group's original bass voice, passed away when still young. Ernest Breece replaced him. Howard and Melvin sang first and second tenor. On top was Floyd Robinson, the group's original lead singer. He was replaced by Norwood "Turk" Williams, the only member of the group from Armstrong High School. Initially the group centered on school music activities, at the inimitable Dunbar High. They soon moved beyond the school to perform around town.

After high school, the group became the Rhythmneers and, by the early 1950s, they called themselves the Hi Fis after briefly using "the Four Guys," until they realized other groups already had that name. Over the years the group were together they performed at a variety of venues. They sang in the homes of friends and family, at school events, local talent contests, and radio shows, like Jackson Lowe's, and later, Arthur Godfrey's amateur talent show in New York. They also played clubs around town, like the Gaslight Room at Thirteenth and G. Different people around Washington at one time or another helped the group, encouraged them, got them a job or two, or put them in touch with someone. The extended network of influences ranged from relatives, church choir directors, and public school teachers, to interested parties the group met in clubs.

Someone who had heard the group in Washington helped facilitate the trip the Hi Fis made to New York in 1955, as Mel recalls. "How we got to New York to begin with, to get the audition with the Godfrey show was a lady used to come listen to us when we were booked in at Thirteenth and G . . ."

Mel was about to say "club" when Howard cuts him off to complete the thought. "Yeah, Gaslight Room."

"And she would come every weekend, Friday; come back on Saturday for certain. White woman. She was with a big time colonel in the Air Force. She loved us. So somehow or other she had contact with the owner of that club we were singing at, who [also] owned the Blue Angel in New York. She told him and [he] made the connection for us."

The connection was an audition and chance to perform on the Arthur Godfrey show. The group arranged their trip and decided to try for some other meetings, with Atlantic Records, for one. The woman that Melvin tells us about was not in the music business professionally, but we can say that because of her involvement she was at least an unpaid participant in the business of making music or musical contacts. "She just thought we were good and we should be heard by others and that's what she did. She said, 'This is a great group.' And others had said it. We'd heard that, you know, where we been we had heard that, long before we met her. It was nice for her to do it. So we got there, she set that arrangement up for us in New York."

This is a very typical kind of informal, entrepreneurial encounter, albeit, a biracial one, and with a woman. It was, though, similar to what happened with the Orioles seven years earlier. Mel remembered the date. "55. September 1955, because we were there that week that we were going to audition for the Godfrey show and we made a big huge week out of it. In fact, our sole purpose for going to New York was to audition for the Godfrey program, but since we were in New York, and that was cost to get there and we didn't have no big bucks."

The Arthur Godfrey show was, if you recall, the catalyst that gave the Vibra-Naires (Orioles) some play. The Hi Fis ended up with an audition on the Godfrey show for September 27, 1955. They were also supposed to appear on the Steve Allen show. That never came off, although the group sat out in the studio audience. In addition, with demo record in hand, they found their way up to see someone at Atlantic Records.

Mel says, "He sent us to another guy he was on the phone with and he said he should hear this. We left his office, we went someplace else and everything kept triggering something else. We [also] went up to the Major Bowes thing, when Major Bowes [The Major Bowes Family Amateur Hour radio program] had his thing. And we went over to the Apollo Theater to see a fellow by the name of Roland Baker, who was a year ahead of us in high school."

Apparently, Roland was singing in another kind of vocal group. "They didn't sing no rhythm and blues, it was a—what kind of music would you call it? Classical music, operetta-like style music, but as a group, that kind of thing. And in fact they were singing at the Apollo at that time, and they were on the bill with Duke Ellington. And we happened to know that they were there, so while we were in New York we went to see and they invited us up to their dressing room, Roland did. And that's where we met Duke Ellington, who didn't have much time for us, you know, but it was kind of nice being close to this guy. And everything you see about him is true, big bags, the big white tails."

How Melvin Lispcomb, Howard Davis, and the rest of the Hi Fis got to New York, Atlantic Records, and the Apollo Theater is a story similar to others. Melvin, for instance, like Ernest Warren and Buddy Bailey and others, grew up with, as he puts it, a "strong female influence."

Lipscomb was born in 1928 and spent his younger years on the 2600 block of Georgia Avenue, Northwest. "Around the corner from Howard University Hospital, as a youngster, little guy. And of course I started going to church in those days—you either go to church or not live—and was part of the choirs there. I lived with my mom; my dad died when I was two. I lived with my mom then, and aunt. That strong female influence had me attend church. I went to Mount Carmel Baptist Church, Third and I Streets, Northwest. It was there that I met one of our original group [members], Benjamin Johnson, who was a natural bass. And we sang in the choirs throughout this city. We came up through the church.

"I was part of a group that took part in that kind of a situation. So you just sang. And I didn't know music. It was just something that was instinctive. That's where Benny and I met, and we were at Banneker Junior High at the time. We both went to Banneker, as well as another gentleman who was with this earlier group, by the name of Floyd Robinson."

Melvin learned to sing first in church choir and continued to sing in elementary school, junior, and high school. "I guess as long as I've been coming up from elementary school, junior high, and Dunbar, we had tremendous music teachers who were of some renown on their own."

Howard Davis was also born in 1928. "I was born in Southeast Washington, down by the old Evening Star building, in the old Providence Hospital, which is no longer there. It's a park now, new Providence Hospital's out in Northeast. And I went to Randall Junior High School, which was in Southwest."

Howard also went to church. "Absolutely, I mean if you didn't, you'd be scorched. But, I went to Mount Jesuit Baptist Church. It's in the community, about Fifth and E, Southeast. And they had an extraordinary choir. When you getting ready to go to church, without television, then you got the radio and every Sunday morning the radio's on, listening to 'Wings Over Jordan.' "

In addition to music influences from church, the radio, and public school, Howard and Melvin heard music within the boundaries of black Washington in the 1940s and tell an all too familiar story. "There wasn't any place to go. And all of our social activity was along U Street."

"Absolutely."

"And the Howard Theater, where we heard a hundred and fifty stars. All the stars."

"And listen to this, you're talking about the Charioteers, the Orioles, and all these. We saw them constantly, and were in their company, at least the four of us, many times. I saw Sammy Davis when he first started, with the Will Manson Trio. He was a little tyke."

"I mean we have seen Horace Silver, Coleman Hawkins, the Duke, of course, Billy [Eckstine] with his band, Clifford Brown"

"Lucky Millander."

"The Jazz Messengers, Art Blakey."

As you listen to Howard and Mel recall the music they heard as youngsters and as younger men, the diversity strikes you. And yet, who influenced them?

Howard says, "I can't imagine being influenced except, you know, the music about us, the quartets that were on, on Sunday morning before you went to church. 'Wings Over Jordan,' and you know, the gospel quartets."

Despite their claims, we have to wonder how much they could ignore all of that other music, and their stories reveal that. Still, as the Hi Fis say, they "weren't market."

This was the 1955 market, when the category rhythm & blues, six years old, was already undergoing changes. As rhythm & blues moved beyond the purely separatist distinction of 1949, its stylistic variations began to shift. By 1953 or so, vocal groups like the Clovers maintained an upbeat dance style along with other Atlantic Records artists such as Ruth Brown and Big Joe Turner. The sound was edgier than the late 1940s, although the production techniques developing at Atlantic made it a bit lighter and very definitely "cleaner" at the same time. Many of the paradigmatic bass figures from the period came from boogie-woogie piano lines articulated by the left hand (which, incidentally, date back at least to the late 1920s). Drummers long used to emphasizing off beats began to do so even more stridently with backbeat rim shots on their snare drums.

At the same time, other vocal groups like the Flamingos and the Five Keys continued to produce stunning, sentimental ballads. The style, though, was more intense and emotional than, for instance, the Orioles or Cardinals had been a couple of years earlier. Most vocal groups continued to divide material between jump and ballad, but either way, rhythm & blues moved further away from where it had been and became more integrated and, in an odd way, "blacker" at the same time. Part of this had to do, ironically, with the music's growing popularity and influence, and the backlash against that by reactionaries who perceived it as corrupting the mainstream.

Remember that rock 'n' roll and rhythm & blues were virtually identical when Alan Freed, the Cleveland disc jockey, began to use the term rock 'n' roll in 1952 to avoid the black stigma for white customers listening to his rhythm & blues show. Rhythm & blues became black by demand, so to speak, and you can get a sense of what that was supposed to mean from the attitude of Atlantic Records who told the Hi Fis, in reference to both sound and appearance, "You're too neat." Some record people perceived those groups that did not fall into favor with that particular flavor as "too clean," and this tells you the contradictory nature of rhythm & blues at the time. This was where the Hi Fis must have found themselves in 1955. Yet, they were still a popular group in and around Washington and probably could have been elsewhere. Did they ever consider pursuing music as a career, or doing what was necessary to appeal to Atlantic Records?

Mel says they might have. "If we had gotten to that point we probably would have."

"Yeah, but it never came up." What Howard means is that it never came up as an issue. It was not something they at all considered.

Still, as Mel states, people were interested in the group. "We had a whole lot of people who wanted to be our agents. Tell him that, Davis. A whole lot of people wanted to be our agents and won't go on the road with us, send us out by ourself, and sign these contracts. Who [was] the guy who had the record shop down there on Seventh and U for years? What's it, Max?"

Mel is talking here about Max Silverman, of Quality Music, the same one who put the Clovers in with Ahmet Ertegun.

For the Hi Fis, despite their talent and the interest the group generated, the leap into the music industry was not to be. With the group members well into their twenties, they were not heading into the music as a means to earn a living, and they eventually went their ways. Howard says, "That was a crucial time, you know, that was after some college time. 1955, man, we were twenty-seven years old."

Like so many other vocal groups, the Hi Fis went their separate ways, away from music. Yet, there was something deeply personal that most, if not all of the singers carried away from those earlier experiences. They developed patterns, of sorts, that they took from their past and brought with them to the present.

Past Present

Herman Denby and Ernest Warren sat next to each other one afternoon in Catonsville, Maryland, just outside Baltimore, talking about when Herman moved from Ohio back to Baltimore, in 1984. He had been away for about thirty years. Herman was very emphatic on one point here, as he jabbed his finger across and then down at the table.

"And I want this—I WANT THIS ON TAPE. This is Ernest Warren, of the Cardinals."

He jabs his finger again, over toward Ernest. "When I came back here, this is the first man that approached me and said, 'I want you to sing with me.' "

It seems that as Herman was about to leave Ohio he heard that Sonny Hatchet was staying nearby. Hatchet was from Baltimore also, and knew both Herman and Ernest from years ago. In 1984 he was on tour with one of the several representations of the old Ink Spots. When Herman finally got back to Baltimore, he looked Sonny up. "So when I came here, Sonny told me, said Ernest lives here, and gave me his phone number. We talked over the phone, and I said, 'Good grief man, I didn't know you were around.' "

And then Ernest makes this point about group singing and about the commitments you were supposed to have—and keep. "At that particular time, when we did something back there, we did it to be together for life."

Group harmony was a way of life, and for men like Ernest and Herman that meant *for* life. Maybe when they were young, they thought that a group should sing together for life (some individuals, like Howard and Melvin, actually did). But on another, less literal level, they meant that the values you brought into or learned from group singing, you take with you for life. The same values you learned at home, you take with you into a group, and then back out again. That was what Herman and Ernest were saying.

For the first and second generations, group harmony clearly connected to life experience, and had African American underpinnings within the frame of white society. What was true for slaves, and was true earlier in the twentieth century, was true for group vocalists. Whether they made records or not, making music "gave a sense of power, a sense of control" (Levine 1977: 297) where there was no other. Beyond that, music became a resource—for vocalists, for others—and continued as a wellspring from which numerous factions would draw. Group harmony remained very much a part of its time, yet moved beyond its original time and place and became a part of post-1950s American popular styles and images.

What changed in the 1960s was that neighborhoods changed, schools changed, music taste changed, and group harmony became less and less a way of life. By the end of the decade, it was "doo-wop," the genre, the sound, the look, and eventually a kind of 1950s stereotype. Finally, its *remarketability* emerged. Group harmony became packaged nostalgia, historical and cultural stereotype, a style associated with what became "oldies-but-goodies," and a significant resource for record dealers, collectors, and recording reissues. The resurgence of group harmony appeal also gave some of the original vocalists new opportunities to perform. They did not make new careers, but Ernest Warren, Herman Denby, Andy Magruder, and others regrouped with different personnel and performed occasionally throughout the 1980s and beyond as "oldies" acts to appreciative fans. During the 1980s, Rudy West performed at fraternities in Virginia, just as he had when he was starting out in the late 1940s and early 1950s. This was after he had retired from a day job, which had come after his original career singing with the Five Keys. His voice would take, make, and melt your heart, just as it once did. So too, would the voices of Ernest, Herman, Andy Mack, Howard Davis, Mel Lipscomb, Buddy Bailey, Harold Winley, James McPhail, and the other singers in this book—their voices as singers, their voices as storytellers.

The "oldies" phenomenon, the nostalgia for the 1950s especially, emerged nationally in the late 1960s. The singing group Sha Na Na formed in 1969 and established that elusive (and exclusive, for whites, whose collective sense of remembering is so different from that of many African Americans) link to the past when they performed that summer at, of all venues, Woodstock. The members were white, save one. Angular and dis-junct from both the present they were in and the past they were attempting to recreate, they created a good-natured parody at just the right time and in precisely the right place, New York. It was a feeling people fell for and a feeling you could begin to sense in other media—film and television in particular—to wit the movie *American Graffiti* (1973) and the subsequent television show, *Happy Days*. The entire reproduction of the era—the "oldies-but-goodies" phenomenon—not by coincidence, was a remake by whites for whites, almost exclusively. Generally speaking, the only partici-pation from blacks came from reforming the groups to perform live.

I can't help but think of it as another kind of blaxploitation, where the makers reversed the "for blacks" exclusivity of the spirit of early rhythm & blues. White-produced nostalgia for the era bleached blackness from rhythm & blues/rock 'n' roll. Whites had already created the "rhythm & blues" category, and so why could they not remake it two decades later? Whites had always tapped into the black musical imagination, to one degree or another. Young white teenagers especially in the 1950s found much appeal in rhythm & blues/rock 'n' roll as the music socialized them to black musical sensibilities yet, at the same time, reinforced the differences between "black" (Little Richard's "Tutti Frutti," late 1955) and "white" (Pat Boone's homogenized cover version). And this was a good thing, although at the time not everybody thought so. The frames of reference for white teens, vis-à-vis black music, however, were different from what young black teens felt.

The white sense of propriety, if not ownership, of the whole era, including the black music from the period is strong—at least from a recent perspective. Could we expect anything less? We should remember that group harmony still resonates powerfully for a postwar generation. We should take note of how it resonates, not to mention for whom.

> For those of us who were teenagers in the 1950s and early part of the 1960s, OUR music often equates, at least in part, to doo-wop music. The group sound of doo-wop reminds us of our friends and exploits, the male- and female-bonding activities of our generation: the practical jokes, ball-playing, drag racing, the candy store or malt shop hangout, the cliquish-ness, the insecurities, the pool halls and bowling alleys, the poker games, the school hallways. The innocence of the lyrics of doo-wop songs recall [*sic*] our first feelings of romance and lust. We grew up with doo-wop and now, thirty-odd years later, doo-wop helps us retrace that journey from childhood to adulthood. (Gribin and Schiff 1992: 7, emphasis theirs)

Given this type of sentimentality, much if not all of the packaging of nostalgia related to the rhythm & blues era comes from whites, where there also appears to be a strong tactile urge to collect, deal, and sell—record discs, sheet music covers, photographs. If you ask a vocalist from the group harmony period about records they might have, most inevitably would answer, "They got away from me years ago" (probably to collectors or dealers). The memories are there, but whites mostly still control the products—the constructed nostalgic images, the "plastic," the recordings, reproductions, reissues, films, photographs, the licensing, and the laws.

The post-rhythm & blues era dissemination of group harmony from the period became a commodity. People detached it, like older blues, from its time and place to use it in a variety of ways. Only fragments of the original phenomenon survived. This process was historically very similar to other black popular music as it moved from a more marginal status to overtly change the sound of mainstream music.

Group harmony began to change musically through song selection, vocal style, through racially mixed groups (such as the Dell Vikings, the Crests, the Marcels), and gender mixed groups (Platters, Six Teens). In the mid-1950s, the so-called "girl groups" began to emerge. The process began as early as 1954 with the Cookies (Jesse Stone's group) and continued through 1957 with the Bobbettes. From then into the next decade, female groups became more popular with the Shirelles (1958), Supremes (1961), Shondelles (1962), Martha Reeves and the Vandellas (1963), among many others. Women brought to group singing fresh perspectives, attitudes, and images. In female harmony groups, the male domain of bass and falsetto gave way to female vocal ranges. The love standards sung by the males were not the chosen vehicles for female leads. Women groups, like their Classic Blues counterparts in the 1920s and the female rap artists in the 1980s and 1990s, challenged and changed the sounds and broadened the appeal and audience for the music—male dominance in the industry as a whole notwithstanding.

Male groups like the Four Tops, the Temptations, the Miracles, all began as harmony groups in the 1950s. They made the transition into the 1960s and 1970s, along with harmony derivations such as Earth, Wind & Fire, the O'Jays, Parliament, Spinners, and then into the 1980s with groups such as Take Six. Huey Lewis and the News was a white pop group that imitated a stereotypical a cappella group harmony arrangement in 1987, with its single "Doing It All for My Baby/Naturally."

Countless commercial jingles also drew from the style and some groups were even able to capitalize on that. The Four Tops returned with harmony and dance steps in the late 1990s with a television commercial for Kraft Foods. Musicians and the music industry continually updated group harmony as it entered the mainstream and the consciousness of greater America. In this regard, it was similar to the many other components to American popular music that prevail for a while, move beyond their time and place, fall in, out of, and back in style, get used, reused, reinvented, and recycled.

Yet, in another sense group harmony never moved beyond its original time and place. It's still stuck in time as an embodiment of the 1950s. The re-commodification of group harmony began in the late 1960s as an "oldies" style and the new entrepreneurs that capitalized on it kept it "old" in the spirit of the 1950s. "Oldies" acts today remain abundant.[10] Most groups lack original members, save for one or two, if that many. For many fans, original members do not need to be present, only the memories—the name, image, and voices are enough. Indeed, over the years there have been competing versions of the same group, usually with a copyrighted name, and subsequent lawsuits over who has the rights to the group name. This phenomenon is not limited just to black vocal harmony, but it does remind us of the importance of a group's image and name, something Carroll Williamson and the Imperials realized early on. This recalls the relationship between music and popular theater. It is important to have the original cast, for a while, but a good play lives on in its own memories, title, drama, meaning, plot, text, and subsequent productions. Theater based on a written script and structure communicates beyond its original time and place, as does art or "classical" music. Sometimes the original production resonates so strongly that subsequent ones thrive off of the original, long gone. Perhaps this is a subtext to the story of black music in America. As twentieth-century American popular music fades from the public consciousness and is transformed, inevitably, into twenty-first-century popular music, time will test its enduring qualities. Such is the past present of pop and of group harmony.

Rap

The past present of group harmony has to include rap, but I can offer only the briefest treatment of the subject here. I like to think that one reason we study history is to better understand what has changed and what has not changed. I see in black music (and other aspects of black in America) a continuum of circumstances, and as I have asked rhetorically several times throughout the book, what's changed? The similarities between group harmony and rap are not on the surface, but resonate beneath it.

One thing we can say about many of the singers in these pages from the rhythm & blues era is that they did not particularly care for rap and hip-hop. If they discussed it at all, they had different notions of what it was at the time, and what it was supposed to accomplish beyond entertainment. Every generation has some problem or another with its children's music. Some singers just could not pull on the aesthetic strands of rap to make sense of it. Others paid no mind to it and shrugged it off, and yet others like Herman put rap into historical context—word games he used to play—but with no empathy for it. Instructive is that many of that generation say they have no eyes for rap, but also admit that they did similar kinds of things in their day; the past is the present and there's nothing new under the sun.

"Well we used to do the same thing on, like when we used to sit out on the steps. Like what rapping is now? Oh that's not new. We used to do that."

As Ernest Warren said, he liked everything out there—all kinds of music. "Yeah, anything except rap. I don't like no rap. We was doing that years ago, and, hey, we thought that wasn't nothing. You don't use nothing on rap, man. We was rhyming words, that's all, you know."

Lawrence Berry, a generation younger than Herman and Ernest, did not like rap music either. Rap lacks the lyrical essence of the vocal harmony ballads, he said. The sweetness is gone. "Rap music doesn't do anything but stir you up. It keeps you on a high."

Andy Magruder talks about rap music also, but not getting the message. "But it's no message, it's just the beat."

He suggests that rap is connected to what's going on today. In 1980s terms, that meant black-on-black urban violence. "It's adding to it."

Jesse Stone, who had lived through and participated in nearly every popular music style in the twentieth century, also had something to say about rap. He seemed to take it in stride with all of the other developments in popular music he was a part of and makes what is perhaps the keenest observation about how popular music works. It may have been new music, but the story is old news. "Yeah, and the whites are beginning to rap. But by the time they get into the rap, there are some [black] kids right now that somewhere they're doing something different. They're doing it, same as that break dancing, spinning on the heels and all that sort of stuff. That's gone. They ain't thinking about that no more."

What Jesse is telling us is that young black kids continually generate new styles for popular consumption. And we can add, of course, that the styles they generate emerge out of older styles. Stone is annoyed, as we all should be, by the white categorization of black style.

"Yeah, well there is something, but not like it used to be because it takes too long for it to get through. They got to break through that barrier of categorizing that the white people have put up there. And there just may be some white person of importance might accidentally walk down through the slums somewhere and see these kids doing something and then they'll say, 'Heyyy, I've discovered something great,' you know. I remember the kids used to do a little old dance years ago and they called it 'Little Old Lady from Baltimore,' and they'd make a ring and whatnot. And I know there was a—these kids have been doing this for years, you know, maybe five, six years. And a white lady drove up in a big car and see what they were doing and she stopped there and she must have stayed there an hour watching those kids do that thing. It was a game that they'd been doing for I don't know how long. And I said to myself, now if she's a theatrical producer or something she'll probably take that downtown and put it on Broadway and they'll give her credit for coming up with a real masterminded something."

Jesse Stone's stark assertions are neither paranoid nor apocryphal. They perhaps are closer to being apocalyptic, in a cultural sense, at least if you believe that integration helped kill rhythm & blues (not the white-created category, but the black-generated style). At any rate, it's an old story, one that suggests the mainstream emerges from the marginal (not at all a new concept). This is certainly a consistent dynamic in black and white cultural relations. It has occurred regularly, cyclically, from the nineteenth century through the twentieth and constitutes one of the basics that tie various black musical forms to one another—black use of white music notwithstanding.

On a stylistic level, rap and hip-hop that has not already turned into a contemporary version of rhythm & blues is nearly devoid of familiar melody that is easy to remember, at least in the vocal leads (the backgrounds are another matter). Indeed, rap melodies are more like cadences—modulating phrases, a rising and falling of the voice. Overall, rap is a sharp, clean, lean, linear musical charge. Even when the performance is relaxed, there is an insistence to it. There is boasting, but no vocal basing, no ballads, no floating tenor, no falsetto lead. In contrast, older group harmony in its standard material was melodically familiar; a sweet, soft, full sound—music with a vertical sphere. Even the blues, jump, or gospel-based material has a full sound or dimension to it because of the harmony and the arrangements around those voices. Alongside differences between rap and group harmony however, there are similarities.

On a musical level, both are group sounds and a busy type of music. There are always several things going on at once to keep the listener interested, to fill all of the holes up—polyphonic. What rap and hip-hop lack in melody, they make up in textures and rhythm. In rap, there is no vocal basing, usually, but there is always a backgrounding of some sort, whether it's a repetitive sample or rhythm, riff, or groove. The background grooves, prerecorded or not, derive from 1970s funk, which grew from 1960s black popular music, which was the trap set, bass, and guitar extension of a basic rhythm & blues jump ensemble. The jump ensemble itself was a modified swing feel—and you can feel that in early century stomps, boogies, and New Orleans style.

Old school rap, from New York (e.g., Sugar Hill Gang) had a more melodic component than some later styles, but there were still lots of variations, and the more commercial material in the 1990s moved back to embrace melody a little more. You really cannot stereotype rap any more than you can any other style of music. The L.A. Samoan group, Boo Yaa T.r.i.b.e., was "street," but by their own admission did harmony based on what they heard when they were coming up—"the Delfonics, all the Motown stuff, the Dells" (quoted in Cross 1993: 150).

Both group harmony and rap and hip-hop have an essential dance component, both on stage and in the audience. Also, the strong performative components to both styles define them, much more so than the form of the material. The performance interpretations of pop standards by vocal groups enabled them to cover those standards in the first place. The songs were good to begin with, but the young black male interpretations made them suitable for new and younger audiences (and of course, the white interpretation of black material was supposed to make it suitable for white listeners). Rap and hip-hop artists do not generally cover other artists' material in quite the same way, but they achieve the same results. They do it through referencing, sampling, and through overdubbing tracks.[11] The performances are distinct because the artistry is in the conception and the performance.

Another correlative between rap and group harmony lies in the sexual content of the material. Obviously, the language in some contemporary rap performances is direct and to some, obscene. The references to sex are to the point, sexist, vulgar, vernacular, or intuitive, depending on your point of view. However, white overseers have asked black workers to "sing dirty" for them for centuries. The record industry culled from first female, then male blues artists as entertainment the direct and honest expressions common to the stage and folk blues. The 1980s and 1990s may have been no different and so perhaps on one level raps speak to us in ways that we expect. In the 1940s and 1950s, as we indicated already, rhythm & blues harmony groups maintained a varied repertoire and material like "Feel like Ballin' Some More" was not at all uncommon. The perception among rhythm & blues detractors was, in fact, that all of it was vulgar. Even those sympathetic to black experiences, who tried to understand and explain rhythm & blues and called it a "superior music," referred to it oddly: "Its very vulgarity assured its meaningful emotional connection with people's lives" (Baraka 1963: 174).

Most rhythm & blues vocal groups had at least a few songs with some overt sexual content. In fact, much American popular music of the twentieth century is about sex to one degree or another, even a standard like "Blue Moon." Harold Winley recalled a couple of numbers that the Clovers performed: "We had risqué songs in our repertoire, which we would sing in private parties; sing among ourselves. In fact [Harold] Lucas recorded some of that stuff."

Winley was reminded of a song that Lucas performed in Washington, at the Club Soda, one night in 1989. "Oh, you talking about 'In Derby Town.' We sang that on the corners. We sang that on the corners.

> In Derby Town there are two boys and both of them are rich,
> One's a son of a millionaire and the other's a son of a ——.
> Maybe you think I'm fooling you . . .

"Great, because he [Lucas] didn't sing but two songs. He sang that song and a song called 'Ride Red Ride.' I'm talking about in the Clovers, the original group. There's another song we used to sing, based on the melody of 'Darktown Strutter's Ball.' See, we used to sing 'Darktown Strutter's Ball' and then we would change—sing it down once, and then change into some other lyrics which I don't care to put on tape."

In addition to these musical dissimilarities and similarities—only outlined here— between group harmony and rap and hip-hop, there are reasonable comparisons in the social circumstances of both styles. David Toop realized this in his phrase "doo-wop hip-hop," and in his correct allusion to the "street culture" of both group harmony and rap (Toop 1991: 22). The contiguities between group harmony and rap and hip-hop lie strongly in historical and social relationships. Both styles emerged from local, grassroots urban beginnings. Both styles have used the "street" as a strong frame of reference, both literally and as a term to describe a particular substyle. The *territorality* and *geocentricity* of both group harmony and rap and hiphop is strong. The (initially) male imperative of both styles is strong. The activities of 1940s- and 1950s-era vocal groups inside of neighborhood social clubs and gangs were common. The competitive aspect to both styles is strong. Both group harmony and rap and hip-hop share the tension between groups making a style of music and the music industry trying to commodify and market it, turning it into a genre they too easily categorize and stereotype. At the same time, both styles, for their respective generations, contain much possibility and potential. Aspects of both music styles became dominant commercial styles.

One of the strong elements of group harmony is the performance of pop standards or original songs that convey similar "mainstream" sentiments. The machinations of the music industry, not black musicians, marginalized that music—along with what the performance style, rhythms, or skin color represented. The larger point is that ultimately, if you don't pay attention, the distinctions between these categories of marginal and mainstream blur. The "purely" musical distinctions, really, are meaningless, save that people feel a need to make them to begin with. Now that issue, of course, cuts both ways. We do not wish to make distinctions in some cases between "black" and "white," otherwise we are back to separate water fountains. On the other hand, we have to continue to make those distinctions and some of us want to make those distinctions. The reasons are many, arguable, divisive, very personal, broadly social, historical, and still current. Every conscious citizen, of good or bad intent, black or white, has a different reason. Unfortunately, in our world of constructed realities, we often do not have a choice—at least not yet. If you do not make the distinction yourself, someone will make it for you. People construct and use categories to reinforce inclusiveness as well as enforce exclusivity, and therein again lies the conundrum of black popular music like rhythm & blues and rap—be black, but not too black.

The record industry initially marginalized group harmony when they labeled voices and sounds "rhythm & blues," whether the song was a suggestive "Sixty-Minute Man" or a standard like "Red Sails in the Sunset." Then, group harmony moved back into the mainstream again, because by 1954 rhythm & blues became the dominant sound in popular music and group harmony was a dominant sound in rhythm & blues. Rap began on the outside in the late 1970s and moved into the mainstream later. By the mid-1990s it became the dominant sound in American popular music, just as group harmony did forty years earlier. The two musics are opposites in sound, style, and sentiment, yet there are remarkable contiguities in the social crucible that helped create those styles.

Group harmony and rap and hip-hop are both part of a broad spectrum of interrelated black styles, but both are also of their respective times and places. When Eazy E said, "We're telling the real story of what it's like living in Compton. We're giving the fans reality. We're like reporters. We give them the truth" (quoted in Cross 1993: 37), he meant that rap artists were a reflection of their circumstances. When it was suggested to Andy Magruder that rap was a product (you can take product both ways here) of its time, he replied, "It's adding to it." By that he referred to violence, but there is also something deeper in what he says. He infers that rap—broadly speaking, art—is a constituent determiner of what people do, that it has a real impact on what happens in life, not to mention that artists construct it from experiences to begin with. Clearly, vocalists used group harmony as a way to map their lives just as the lives they led, the values they developed, mapped their music. As with rap and hip-hop, the lines between entertainment and everyday experience blur at times.

For some, in the past, group harmony was a reality, a way of life. To others, in the present, group harmony is nostalgia. The common denominator between the past and present is that group harmony was and is entertainment. The very same can be said for rap and hip-hop. Both styles, after a period, flirted with being formulaic or in some cases, parody. What perhaps ultimately unite group harmony and rap are their narrative elements, the stories they tell, what black music communicates for us and to us. If Andy Mack did not hear the message in rap, then it was because he could not make the adjustments that would have allowed him to hear. Not all of us can. Perhaps some stories are for the young to keep among themselves. At any rate, vocalists in group harmony use the phrase "tell a good story" to describe a song that appealed to them, as in Tin Pan Alley standards. And the singular aspect of rap, as a verbal and music expression, is the story, message, and ideas that it conveys. Good rap tells a good story also.

On another level, however, group harmony and rap narrate the circumstances behind each style's respective development and popularity, as do the participants in those styles when they speak about what they do. Some rap styles clearly have oppositional stories from which we can learn. Group harmony, on the other hand, performed songs that were more inclusive, assimilative in a way. Yet both styles resisted the inclinations of whites—rap through its oppositional messages; group harmony through its inclusive (read "mainstream") attitudes. Is it not ironic that Atlantic Records insisted that the Clovers stop singing standards for a while in favor of written blues-based, dance material, that is, "black" music?

Group harmony and rap began at opposite ends of the black music sphere and ended up twisting together. They are more similar than you might expect. The similarity between group harmony and rap is further evidence of the tension between blacks having the power to define themselves and their experiences, and whites doing it for them. It seems as if it is again a variation of the riddle, be black, but not too black. Put another way, it means be black, but on white terms. Black voices in white society have been consistent, albeit in seemingly contradictory ways. Herman Denby at the opening of this chapter says, "The only thing that has changed now — there are no chains around my ankles, as a people, but they're around my brain now." Andrew Magruder, in his shorthand manner of speaking, says, "everything changed" — even though, he says, he has not. Those contrary sentiments are also part of the riddle.

The point is not to try to solve the riddle, but to try to understand why there is a riddle in the first place. For African Americans, by necessity a fundamental goal always has been self-direction, self-determination, and self-definition in white America.

Epilogue

Black Voices in White America

Of stories, the Nigerian author Chinua Achebe writes, "It's one of the things humans do. Not just have a story, but tell a story."[1] The voices in this book also have their stories. They are for us the ties that bind the experiences of those both before and after, past and present. Stories tell us something.

One problem historically for African Americans, especially around music, is that whites do a lot of the telling, the analyzing, capitalizing, constructing, deconstructing, framing, interpreting, theorizing—whatever. It's that imponderable white milieu. Black scholars such as Houston Baker, Derrick Bell, Henry Louis Gates, bell hooks, Cornel West, and many others have done much to establish a black critical voice. It's a voice that attempts to reference both the black intellectual and the black vernacular; a voice that tries to trasverse popular and academic; unfortunately, it often remains fairly inaccessible to the audience that most needs that voice. There is no question that blacks over the centuries have not had access to the commercial means that whites have had to tell their stories and histories. They initially created alternatives—slave narratives, folk tales, songs, music—and succeeded in rewarding if not always remunerative ways in the face of exclusion. Today, even with a greater variety of media available for blacks to write, speak, or otherwise depict and comment on their own behalf, in their own voice, we still find that myth and stereotype rudely persist. It leaves us to wonder what role perspective has in all the things we are.

Deborah Chessler, for one, has retold for us the Orioles' story from *their* perspective. Hers is a noteworthy example because she stresses the participation and not passivity of the Orioles. I do not want to diminish her own role in the group's work, because it was both significant and remarkable, especially given the time, but the Orioles clearly had a collective, decisive role in their own success. Success is an end and in modern America it is paramount. However, attempting to understand the importance of process for black group singers, whether they succeeded by capitalist standards or not, offers an alternative view to a landscape so often painted by whites. The Orioles' story as told through Deborah Chessler is a good one to use as an example because it constitutes a kind of oppositional voice, a form of "counterstorytelling" (Delgado 1995: 65), even though the original voices are absent. It contradicts the prevailing popular notion that the Orioles and black artists in general had somewhat less to do with their own success than white sponsors, and Chessler was a witness, reliable because she was on the inside. Herman Denby inserted the issue into this project very early when he shook his head slowly one day and commented on veracity. "The only things I have problems with are there are some books that are out. And they have false information in them. I don't know where they got the information from."

To some observers from the outside, the Orioles' story was not theirs alone, but for others to own. When compared to what Deborah Chessler tells—and we take a leap of faith that she spoke for them—other accounts of the Orioles' beginnings seem at best disingenuous toward the group in assigning responsibility for their success. These narratives reassign responsibility for the "discovery" of the Orioles. They in effect reassign control of group harmony as a resource and take it out of the hands of seemingly passive singers, save for their luck, good looks, or "innate" talent. Compare Deborah Chessler's words with this version spun by writer Arnold Shaw, who did not cite his source. The facts are one matter; the questionable tone another.

> The Orioles came from Baltimore, where they sang on street corners after Earlington Tilghman (later known as Sonny Til) came out of the service. They were singing on the corner of the Pitcher Street station of the Pennsylvania Railroad when a friendly bar owner invited them into his place to perform. There they were discovered by Deborah Chessler, an enterprising and aggressive songwriter. Changing the name of the group to that of the Baltimore bird, she packed them into her second-hand Ford, drove them to New York City, and parked directly in front of the Apollo Theatre. Not without some difficulty, she managed to persuade Frank Schiffman to audition the group even before they changed their clothes. (Shaw 1978: 135)

Here Shaw places the control of what took place firmly in the hands of the "aggressive" white manager. In contrast to Chessler, Shaw, who had worked in the music industry as a publicist, fails to consider the singers and their voices, their interpretive skills, their energy, and their will to succeed. According to Shaw, the manager did the discovering. The manager was aggressive and enterprising. The manager managed and persuaded. The manager changed the name of the group. The manager did the driving.

Deborah Chessler, on the other hand, attributed the success of the Orioles to the group's own abilities: "They were very anxious to succeed." Chessler says, in fact, that the Orioles "heard" of Abe, their first manager, and "got to him," meaning they took some kind of initiative and sought management out themselves. The way Chessler describes Abe, he in no way sounds like someone on the prowl for black talent; nor, for that matter, was Deborah Chessler. The group mostly chose its own material and "had long rehearsals" to develop its sound. When Shaw credits the Orioles at all, he does so in a questionable manner, evoking pernicious stereotypes. Their first recording was "unfinished," the vocalists unsure of their parts. The lead vocals of Sonny Til "affected the girls like an aphrodisiac. Sonny's voice was full of heartbreak and a palpably horny sound" (Shaw 1978: 135–36).

To press this point just a bit further, compare Shaw's version with the writer Phil Groia's.

> The birth of the Orioles can be traced to the often reported, and now famous, Deborah Chessler story. Upon returning home to Baltimore from military service in 1946, Earlington (Sonny Til) Tilghman's girlfriend persuaded him to enter an amateur talent show at a local club. Much to his surprise, Sonny won first prize on two successive Wednesday nights and began harmonizing with subsequent winners who were personal friends and members of the band.
>
> Tommy Gaither (guitarist), George Nelson (baritone), Alexander Sharp (first tenor), Johnny Reed (bass and bassist), and Sonny, nicknaming themselves the Vibranaires, continued to sing on local street corners. One night, while harmonizing on the corners of Pennsylvania and Pitcher Streets in Baltimore, The Vibranaires (not to be confused with The Vibranaires from Asbury Park, New Jersey—After Hours and Chariot labels) were invited to sing inside the bar located on that Baltimore street corner. Inside they were discovered by Deborah Chessler who had written a song called "It's Too Soon to Know." She coached and rehearsed the group at her house while they continued to do local gigs in Baltimore. In 1948, she managed to get them a spot on The Arthur Godfrey Show. The penniless Vibranaires traveled to New York City and in circumstances that were to haunt other R&B groups on The Godfrey Show for years to come, finished second to young George Shearing. Broke and defeated, The Vibranaires returned to Baltimore. (Groia 1983: 15–16)

Groia's telling of the story is far more level than was Shaw's version. It reads more like Groia did research, which he did, using the group's original name and naming the members beyond just Til. He still retells the Chessler-in-the-bar myth. We have to assume the group had to audition for the spot on the Godfrey show, just like everybody else, because there simply is no evidence that Chessler "managed" to get them on Godfrey's show any other way. To Groia's credit, he gets the race issue right.

There are other published stories about the Orioles, but two more examples are sufficient to illustrate differing perspectives, ones that reposition power. There is no question that in 1948 the Orioles made important changes to American popular music, just as the *Afro-American* predicted. Thus, the question becomes—who made the Orioles?

Jack Schiffman was the son of Apollo Theater owner Frank Schiffman. In his book about the history of the famous New York venue, he wrote about the Orioles. His subtext is that the Orioles were talented, but lucky, as other benevolent forces (like Frank Schiffman) created if not the actual sound, then at least the group's success. In Shiffman's story, the Orioles were only a footnote (or preface) to larger forces already at work. They were practically anonymous and easily replaceable.

> Their name was the Orioles, and their leader was a handsome, talented young man named Sonny Til. And the Apollo remembers them very well, for it was there that their act was launched.
>
> Conditions in the pop music world were such at the time that if the Orioles hadn't come along when they did, another group would have arrived at the same place around the same time. Indeed, the Orioles almost didn't make it themselves, for they'd spent their last penny getting to New York from Baltimore and their 1934 Ford literally gave up the ghost after depositing them at the Apollo's front door.
>
> They hadn't been booked and didn't even have an appointment, but Sonny Til and the boys' manager, Deborah Chessler, somehow got to see Dad and persuaded him to give them an audition.
>
> Partly out of compassion (how were they all going to get back to Baltimore?) and partly out of his showman's instinct, Dad gave them a hearing. He liked them and hired them. (Schiffman 1971: 86–87)

This story reads like the paternalistic vision of the mythic, benevolent white man. Schiffman, though, worsens matters in a description of Sonny Til's performance.

> And when Sonny himself canted his lean body and caressed the air around the mike as if it were a ripe female—pure lust! Girls started hug-

ging, kissing, and clawing their dates or whatever other males happened to be handy. And that cry of "Ride my alley, Sonny! Ride my a-l-l-e-y!" Wow! (Schiffman 1971: 88)

Ralph Cooper, who for many years hosted Apollo shows, wrote the Orioles' story yet another way:

A vocal group I brought up from Baltimore to play the Apollo—Sonny Til and the Orioles—helped start the doo-wop craze. I was in Baltimore with a tour I had packaged that was playing the Royal Theatre, which was part of the Around the World circuit, along with the Lafayette in New York, the Lincoln in Philadelphia, and the Howard in Washington. I was walking around one night and this group caught me right there in the street. They said they were a quartet and all they wanted was a chance to get started. They knew who I was and they wanted a spot in my Amateur Night show at the Apollo. I said, "Well, can you sing?" They put on a show right on the spot. As soon as I heard them, I knew they'd win a week at the Apollo if they could handle the Amateur Night audience.

They handled it, all right. Sonny Til was the lead singer, and he would get down on his knees and cry and beg the girls for their lovin'. And love them he did. As soon as the Orioles finished, the audience started hollering: "Give 'em a week, Coop! Hell give 'em two weeks!" (Cooper 1990: 183–84)

All these narratives on the origins of the Orioles fail in crucial ways and reveal subtle prejudices. Arnold Shaw undermines his own effort to understand the Orioles in particular and rhythm & blues as a whole. To begin with, he first praises "R&B" (as a category, a creation of the music industry) and then assigns it to the ranks of the "artless," "a product of fumbling amateurs," "body music rather than head or heart music" (Shaw 1978: xx). Phil Groia wrote a seminal and important first work on vocal groups—it's still a great read. Unfortunately, and by his own admission, he "partially fictionalized [the book] to add excitement and color" (Groia 1983: 5) and thus weakens his otherwise good work. Schiffman clearly reassigns responsibility for the Orioles' success to luck, paternalism, and his father. Cooper's version of the story also reassigns responsibility for the group, manages to contradict all the other versions, and even misses the fifth member of the group, for the Orioles were a quintet, not a quartet, as Cooper writes.

The reason to scrutinize published accounts like these is not just to determine what "really" happened—memories could be faulty, myths in the music industry are plentiful, objective truths elude us (although, as Chessler put it, "There's only one story that's true"). Truth and reality from the vocalist's point of view is one important basis for this study, but even here absolute truth is not absolute—nor is it the point. Narratives like the ones above articulate more than just perspectives; they also de-emphasize process, work that the singers themselves did and the circumstances in which they lived and worked. They also reveal socially constructed truths—that the dominant culture dominates the music industry and the success that lies just beyond actual performing. Shaw, Schiffman, and Cooper—whether intentionally or not—strongly articulate the dominant perspectives (even though Cooper is African American).

These narratives create and perpetuate stories that shift the control of group harmony away from vocalists and reassign it to others—mostly whites. On the other hand, Chessler, as a manager and to her credit, articulates the Orioles' perspectives quite well, in their absence, as do the other singer-storytellers above. They provide for us "counter-accounts of social reality" (Crenshaw et al. 1995: xiii), accounts that tell us what the dominant

The Four Bars, "to Mama," 1955. Courtesy of Al Feemster..

culture does not. Black vernacular expressions in literature, music, dance, drama, poetry, and folk tales have always done that; ethnographic research and scholarly writing should as well.

Al Feemster once saw Sonny Til perform, but it was late in Til's career. Feemster's story is about loyalty to his friends and to his vocal group, the Four Bars.

"Ah, well, on a couple of occasions—not being boastful myself, though, but they wanted me, not them. And me—said the same as I said to Clyde, 'I want to stick with my guys.' "

Feemster is talking about record people who wanted his lead voice, but not the rest of the group. He conveys precisely the same sentiment as Ernest and Herman—it's important to stay together.

"Because they would say [to the group], 'We can't use you, but we can use that skinny kid over there.' They would say it. Right in front them. And of course the guys would always say, 'Yeah, go ahead man, this is your break,'—when I'm saying, 'No, we're gonna do this together.' "

The Four Bars did make some records for Josie (a subsidiary of Jubilee, the company the Orioles were with). They recorded, according to Feemster, eight songs in 1954. Josie released six of the sides.

After a period in the music business Feemster returned to D.C., to a day job. "Yeah, went in to it full-time; just concentrated on going to work every day." He left music "completely," he said, and ended up working for the Navy Department and then the Commerce Department, in the printing office. After twenty years, he retired.

"I don't regret nothing I did. I wouldn't give nothing for the experience that I had out there, though. I mean, even though I didn't make a big splash, it was good enough, you know, just to have been there.

"Like Sonny Til. I saw him down to a, a little old rinky-dink theater down in the shopping center down here at Capitol Plaza. And they had just begun, they had closed the movie session of it and they had just start opening up for live entertainment, and he was up on the stage singing. One his legs already been amputated, because he had diabetes so bad. And I remember him getting out of the car going in on crutches, and he sit, he sit down and sang everything he sang—me and my wife went down there. I told her I got to go down and see Sonny. And he start talking about old days and he started crying, I mean about how the arenas used to be full. I know what it was, you know. And he saying, you know, that he's still trying to pray and get better. He sang a lot of his old records."

Although Sonny Til's career lasted from 1948 until he died in 1981 (at age seventy-three), the original Orioles remained together only two years, until the auto wreck that killed Tommy Gaither and injured George Nelson and Johnny Reed. The second group remained together until 1954, when Til put yet a third version together.

The original Clovers remained together for a decade (Buddy Bailey was replaced only for the time he spent in the service). They were the most successful and longest lasting of the vocal groups from Washington and still remain one of the more recognizable nationwide. Many of the rhythm & blues era vocal groups, for one reason or another, simply could not, would not, sustain. The men changed, the times changed, the industry changed, and the musical tastes of the listening and purchasing public changed. Sometimes the singers just drifted apart from one another, as Buddy Slaughter says about the Buddies and the Cap-Tans.

"It just drifted, you know. Les [Fountain] went in the army. This is in the fifties on up. Les went in the service, we tried somebody; it wouldn't work. We dropped off a little while. We picked up Raymond Reeder from Southeast (who used to sing with the Armstrong group). Guitar player. Took him to New York and recorded these other records, with Coral records, but that didn't do anything, so Reeder had to go back to work."

Slaughter tried to continue singing in Washington, but moved away after a period. He returned to manage a club in Maryland for a while, and to sing again.

"Moved back to D.C. in '65. I worked right around the project where I was living and we were rehearsing every night—the Master Tones."

You have to have done it, really, to understand it, to understand what it is like to drag yourself to a day job and then come home and go to work rehearsing or to a music job. With playing out at clubs, or even rehearsal, comes the joy of making music—the anguish of learning material and working it out notwithstanding. With music, especially in rehearsal, there is always the optimism. Putting a music group together and going into rehearsal is the ultimate act of hope and faith. You always have within you the expectancy of making it. You have a few—or maybe a lot of—playing or singing jobs along the way to keep the flame burning. At a certain point, though, even those with unfathomable energy and faith grow tired and just have to wash away that kind of life. Without the imponderables that youth provides, it is difficult to sustain yourself with just the hope of making it. An awful lot have done it, and still do it, weekenders, but for some it is just not enough. Eventually Buddy Slaughter drifted away from music and settled permanently into a day job as a security guard.

After 1955 the Hi Fis also "just sort of drifted," as Howard Davis put it. The group had remained "adamant" about not doing rhythm & blues. It was just something they could not do, he said. By the mid-1950s the members had families, day jobs, or college obligations. Looking back on what he did as a vocalist, Howard says a familiar line.

"But it was an experience that I would not, you know, change for anything."

Davis went on to become Dr. Howard Davis, a dentist. Mel Lipscomb had a career at the National Institutes of Health. You could not spend any time at all with Howard Davis and Melvin Lipscomb and not understand how their singing past, their singing experiences, still so deeply resonated within—and would continue to do so.

James McPhail sang in the Armstrong Four, the "rival" vocal group to the Dunbar Four who became the Hi Fis. The Dunbar singers remained together as a group for a while, but the Armstrong singers quickly went their own separate ways.

McPhail says that after his time in the vocal group he performed as a solo singer and had good success at it.

"We [Armstrong Four] never got to make a record together. And I wanted us to stay together, even when I went to college, you know, but Raymond [Reeder] went to the navy. Earl [Brent] went to the navy and Julian [Ward] went to the army. Well, I was too young at the time. That gave me a chance to go to school and that's why I didn't go to the service."

Jimmy McPhail graduated from Shaw College in 1950 and returned to Washington, D.C. He got a job in Howard County, Maryland, teaching school. He took a leave in order to fulfill an obligation with the Duke Ellington Orchestra, which he won through the thirteen-week talent show run-offs on radio station WWDC. McPhail had jobs on his own through the Gale Agency of New York around 1951, 1952. Afterward he returned to Washington to substitute teach and play local clubs such as the Caverns, the Seventh and T Cocktail Lounge, and the Oddfellows Hall. He would perform at what he called a "cabaret," when private social clubs got together to give an affair of some sort. McPhail built a reputation in Washington. He was a good vocalist, a classy singer, and a hard worker. McPhail clearly used his singing career to his advantage, like an entrepreneur.

"I would be at the Seventh and T Cocktail Lounge working, and then in-between I would have to go over here and do a show or cabaret, you know, not too far from the club, on my break. Then, I'd come back to my regular job; it was something. I look back on it now, it was exciting. That was how I managed to save money for a down payment on a house, man."

He also used to work at a place called the Melody Inn, which is now Jimmy McPhail's Gold Room. He bought the place. He also worked at the Cotton Club on Benning Road, which booked a lot of black groups in the 1950s and other acts in the 1960s.

"A white fellow used to own it, and we would make five dollars a night apiece. That was years ago. That's when we were in high school, five dollars a night."

He said that occasionally he did a "spot" there at the Blue Mirror, downtown. At the mention of Buddy Slaughter's name (Slaughter also sang at the Blue Mirror) McPhail exclaims "Buddy!" He knew Slaughter, but hadn't seen him in years.

"It's amazing how you could be in this town and not see people for years.

"I've been lucky. I really been lucky."

He worked hard, too. "I tried to. You know, that's one thing my mother and father sort of tried to instill in us. In order to get something you had to work and you had to work for it."

George "Icky" Tillman performed with the Melodaires when he was younger and then sang solo as an adult, like McPhail. As good as he was, like the Hi Fi's and Armstrong Four, he never made a commercial record.

"No, we never recorded. And then, while I was in the army, during the time I was an instructor at Camp Gordon, I got involved with some gentlemen. About five of us, and we were called Four Hearts. We performed on the local TV stations down in Augusta. It was segregated at that time and what happened, they had a black TV program and then they had a white TV program, a variety. First they had the white program and then the black program came on. We would sing on that program, you know it was a local show, and this quartet, the Four Hearts, we'd sing Oriole-type stuff and we, during my stay in the army, sort of kept that quartet together until the guys started shipping out and getting discharged."

Tillman maintained his interest in music, even though married and working at a naval gun factory. There, he "came through the ranks" as messenger, clerk, supervisor, then management and analyst. When he worked days at the Navy Yard, Tillman attended the Modern School of Music in the evening, where he studied composition and piano. He also formed a little combo. Tillman worked hard his whole life.

"But anyway, I came up through the ranks, and my government—I worked very hard in the government. I worked very hard, coming from a laborer. I always kept myself neat. I believed in wearing a tie at all times, even as a laborer, I'd be sweeping the floor with a tie on. And they used to kid me about that. I said, well my mama always told me hygiene is like being holy."

When Herman Denby left Baltimore, he left music completely, at least for a while. When he got out of the Marines, he did not return to Baltimore, the Swallows, or to singing, but to Detroit and a day job. He had stopped thinking about singing until, he says, the opportunities he had to return to music were gone. By the 1980s, he moved once more back to Baltimore. His thoughts returned to music. He wrote songs and began to play saxophone.

"It was a struggle man. It was. It was. And for one, the strangest thing, I used to have parties with Berry Gordy's private secretary. We used to party together, you know, when Motown was beginning to move up. And I never had it in mind about the music thing, because she was aware of what I had done, you know. And she used to talk to me about it sometime but I, I really had no desire to do it until the opportunity left. And then I said, 'Wait a minute. I still can sing.' You know what I mean? And by that time, the opportunities that I had there was gone. And it was hard to get in touch with people to get somebody to listen to something, you know."

Herman may have left music for a while, but your past always has a way of hanging around, even if you don't carry it around as baggage. When Herman moved back to Baltimore and began to work again, someone at his job recognized his name on a name tag and asked if he was *the* Herman Denby. That person was Alan Lee, who had an oldies radio program in the Baltimore area and was a record collector and record store owner. He was a big fan of the music. Alan reconnected Herman's present and past for him.

Ernest Warren in 1990 lived up near Pimlico Racetrack in Baltimore. He worked, he had a family, and he seemed to place an intellectual distance between what he did as a singer, and who he was in the present. Ernest was a hard worker, and that comes out in all of his stories. He had a matter-of-fact attitude about his life. "We had a job to come back to, yeah. We could have went anywhere and worked. We were that type of group, you know. But Jack [Donald Johnson], like I said, Jack had about eleven, eleven babies at that particular time. And we were doing, we were doing alright for being young guys. You know. Nobody never got in trouble. They took care of their obligations. Everybody did what they were supposed to do in this group."

Ernest Warren reached a point in the early 1960s when he had a day job and turned his attention away from music to his family. For some musicians there comes a point when you have to, or simply want to, give it up. For some, it came down to family. "Things got slow for us and—families. It was mostly it, everybody had families and the families was increasing. And if we come in off a tour today, we had to wait and see when the next one was coming up. We didn't work continuously throughout the year. And it got bad, it got bad enough for us to go work, and stay that way, you know, because you had to have a weekly income every week."

A musician will use the term "work" to refer to playing jobs, music jobs, but in this case, Ernest means his day job, "real" work to non-musicians. "By that time I was working at a detective agency, and they sent me on different jobs, and on this one particular job—they make airplane propellers and piston rings. And they had an orderly there and he used stop and talk to me all the time and he was a seaman. Every time he get ready to change jobs he go sail ships. And I just talk to him and ask him could he get me a job sailing on a ship. And he told me, 'yeah.' And we kicked that thing around until he carried me down to customs house and got me some seaman's papers.

"Sailed ships out of Baltimore. National Maritime Union. That's the Merchant Marines. My son was born in '65 and I started sailing after that. I sailed up to about '66 and I quit that and went to work as a longshoreman. I got hurt on that job ten years ago. I got both legs broken on that job—bad."

Ernest retired after his accident, in 1980. "It's not been a bad life for me, I had a good life. Very good life. It won't be back, but it's not over, you know, but those times are. The older you get you got to start acting your age."

Andrew Magruder says otherwise, at least for himself. He asks, "Excuse the scratches, allright?"

He's playing a recording he made with James "Pookie" Hudson and the Spaniels, on the Vee Jay label, around 1960. "Hey, I'm a tell you something, I'm the same guy I was when I was twelve years old."

Maybe. By the time he was twelve he was playing the guitar his mom gave him and singing in his Washington neighborhood of Georgetown, around school, around town. "I was about eleven, ten, eleven years old. Because every time I went to the studio, I used to have an old wooden guitar and I'd lay it across—I'm left handed. I used to lay it across my lap and chord, you know, just chord, up at George Washington Circle. So, we save our money and, you know, I go up there and we pay a dollar and we get two sides. Seventy-eights. I used to go up there every Saturday. Every Saturday we'd go up there, and if we had three dollars, we did six sides, which is three records. It was Circle Music. I can't remember his name, but he used to look for me every Saturday. Yeah, he was a white guy. And we go up in the studio, he be sitting down there in his little room, and the records were made of tin."

The place was Circle Recording Studio, at 2138 Pennsylvania Avenue Northwest. At that time they used a record cutting machine that Tex Gathings called a "Recordo." Anyone could come in and cut a disc.

"They grooved; I could see them taking the thing and doing it, you know."

The owner of the store took note of young Magruder.

"And then he came out one day and told me, he says, 'Man, you so sincere. You so sincere about what you doing.' "

He is slight, handsome, light-skinned with wavy hair that kids would give Andy a hard time about when he was young. On October 17 1989, one day after his 53rd birthday, he looked a decade younger than that and still carried that map around in his head.

"Rose Park, Twenty-seventh and P, where Jerusalem Baptist Church is right near. That's where it all started at, and we were a city within a city, in that little area. It was mostly white, above on Wisconsin Avenue going toward Bethesda and whatnot. But from Twenty-first and P, when you cross P Street Bridge, and you went up to Wisconsin Avenue. But, you know, make a long story short, man, like the kids are going through now. We didn't go through that. We didn't have anything."

By "we didn't go through that," Andy is referring, to the prevailing violence in Washington, in the late 1980s. He voices the sentiments of many from his generation. Though very poor, kids didn't shoot one another. "I had three sisters; no brothers. But we had pinball machines. We had popcorn machines. And paper route was the thing then. And then, all of a sudden Sonny Til and the Orioles. That group generated every group."

Andy did not sing in church. "I was a Catholic. My father was Catholic, too. The only thing I did as far as the Catholic religion was, I became an altar boy and learned Latin."

He sang with the Five Blue Jays, and then they changed the name to the Five Blue Notes. He made a number of records over the years, from the 1954 Sabre recordings with the Blue Notes, through the 1960s. He joined the Marines. In 1989, Andy worked as a mechanic for Washington Metro Bus, at the North Station. He had worked for Metro for years, but his co-workers didn't know a thing about his earlier singing career.

He puts a Flamingos record on. It's a late 1950s version of the group. You can hardly hear the song for the scratches. "But here's Tommy Hunt."

He likes old pop standards. For him, he says, it was "music." He says the very same thing about those tunes that Buddy Bailey said about them. "Anything that tells a story."

He loved, he said, "that body contact," of the slow dance love songs that back in his day helped a guy get over with the girls. Like most of the men his age, he doesn't like rap. It's as if, when he hears some, he can not pull the story from the poetry. He does not hear the message in the music. "But it's no message. It's just the beat."

Perhaps rap and hip-hop simply reflected the decade, but Andy must have been thinking again about the street violence in Washington at the time, in the late 1980s. You could not have been in Washington, especially if you had children, as Andy did, and not be aware and just a little bit frightened by it all. Newspapers used to publish the murder rate in the nation's capital—called it the "Murder Capital."[2] Most of the violent crime centered in overwhelmingly poor black districts, like Ward 8 in Anacostia.[3] Nonetheless, the entire city, outside of the federal enclaves, suffered from political, financial, and social problems that bottomed out by the mid 1990s. Was rap music a reflection of or an agent in urban problems?

"It's adding to it," he says of rap, not referring to anything specific, just the tenor of the time.

When Andy was young, he worried about crossing over into a white neighborhood and getting beat up or having someone call the police. In 1989, he worried about his kids crossing a street in Washington, D.C., and getting caught in a shooting. The terrible violence in Washington at the time was mostly black-on-black violence. Maybe this is why he doesn't hear the message in rap music.

"But I'm just saying—street corners underneath of the lamplight, church things, I know what has happened. I know what has happened. Everything changed, when the Korean War broke out, they took a lot of kids out of the neighborhoods. Some of my friends died there. Then they developed the, people that, what do you call it? Construction people want to run you out. And that's what they did in Georgetown."

He's talking about developers and the gentrification of Washington neighborhoods which forced folks out of their own neighborhoods into smaller and smaller enclaves in less desirable areas. When you talk to Andrew Maguder, though, his past and a group's past, the music's past and the city's past, all run together as one.

"Yeah, they came in and destroyed everything there. Now they still having problems. You resolve one problem, but you got another problem. But I tell you one thing, man we are still the same people. In other words, I say to myself, I'm history."

Andy says this without irony, but then the double meaning of being "history" occurs to him and he corrects himself—he is talking about the past, not *being* past.

"I can take you through Georgetown tomorrow if you want me to. I can ride you past every house on P Street. I can go down Wisconsin Avenue, and come back down M Street, and show where everybody lived and tell you where MacArthur's wife lived, Admiral Nimitz's wife lived. I know that I'm a part of this community, but I have never been recognized."

Again he says this without irony, probably referring to the musical notoriety that eluded him. In another sense though, he might be reflecting more broadly on the lost black presence in Georgetown, like Ellison's invisible man.

Andy remembers the Heartbreakers, an early vocal group from Washington that recorded for RCA in 1951 and 1952. He knew Robert Evans, the lead singer. "Robert was a short, bald-headed guy. I'll never forget him, because we used to go to the quarter hops together. And they were one of the first groups other than the Clovers to come out of D.C. that had a hit record."

Andy mentions Seventeenth and Swann, Northwest, and Seventeenth and R. He said those were the Heartbreakers' neighborhoods. Then he takes me back to the Flamingos recording, "Everybody's got a Home."

"That was Tommy Hunt's number, with the Flamingos, I got it right there. I'll always love that song, about a guy that says:

As I rode by a house, with the windows lighted up
Looking pretty as a Christmas tree
And I said to myself, as I rode by myself
Everybody's got a home but me."

Appendix

PRIMARY CONSULTANTS / AUDIO TAPE RECORDED INTERVIEWS

John Buddy Bailey (Clovers) — September 8, 1989, Washington

Lawrence E. Berry — October 7, 1989, Suitland, Maryland

Alan J. Bloom (Super Music) — April 16, 1990, Vienna, Virginia

Clarence F. Jap Curry (York Records) — October 20, Hampton, Virginia

Howard C. Davis and Melvin F. Lipscomb (Dunbar Four, Rhythmneers, Hi-Fis) — February 24, 1990, Washington.

Herman Denby (Swallows) — August 27, 1989, Catonsville, Maryland

Herman Denby and Lee (Ernest) Warren — October 15, 1989 Catonsville, Maryland

Jack Lowe Endler — March 14, 1990, Rockville, Maryland

Alphonso Feemster (Four Bars) — February 10, 1990, New Carrolton, Maryland

Tex Gathings — November 20, 1989, Washington

Felix Grant — January 20, 1990, Washington

Maurice Hulbert — January 24, 1990, Baltimore

George Jackson (Plants) and Melvin Coles — January 6, 1990, Baltimore

Albert Nathaniel Jefferson — January 25, 1990, Washington

William Andrew Magruder (Five Blue Notes) — October 17, 1989, Hyattsville, Maryland

James McPhail (Armstrong Four) — January 10, 1990, Washington

Miss June Norton (Pam-Nor Records) — November 27, 1989, Washington

Johnny Page, Sr. (Marylanders) — September 16, 1989, Baltimore

Deborah Chessler Reingold (Orioles' manager) — April 1, 1990, telephone interview

Albert Russell (Orioles III) — August 28, 1989, Washington

Alfred H. Buddy Slaughter (Buddies, Cap-Tans) — October 30, 1989, Washington

Jesse Stone (Atlantic Records) — May 29, 1990, telephone interview

George Tillman — February 1, 1990, Washington

Ernest Lee Warren (Cardinals) — September 6, 1989, Baltimore

Carroll Williamson (Howfum Records) — March 10, 1990, Baltimore

Harold Jerome Winley, Sr. (Clovers) — November 9, 1989, Washington

OTHER CONSULTANTS

Mrs. C. C. Coley (Northwest Amusements)

Don Covay (Satisfiers, Rainbows)

Clarence Dillard (Three of Us Trio)

Theodore Gaffney (Flayr Records)
Billy Gordon (Teen-Age Records)
Eugene Hawkins (Magic Tones)
Kimo and Quatro McVay (York Records)
Henry Mont (Harlequines)
Les Moss (Roadhouse Records)
Chevist Parham (Pam-Nor Records, manager for Clarence Dillard)
Robert Stroud (Five Blue Jays, Five Blue Notes)
Ray Tolson, Jr. (University Records)
Rudy West (Five Keys)
Ralph Whittington (collector)

INSTITUTIONAL SOURCES

Secondary source material included books, maps, monographs, newspapers, periodicals, photographs, sound recordings, in the following special collections and files.

Afro-American Newspapers Archives and Research Center
Baltimore City Archives
Baltimore Enoch Pratt Library
Howard University Moorland-Spingarn Research Center
Library of Congress
  General Collections, Recorded Sound Reference Center, Performing Arts Reading
  Room, Sound Lab, Newspaper and Periodical Reading Room, the library's film,
  photo, map records, and telephone directory collection
National Archives, District of Columbia Records
National Museum of American History
  DeVincent Collection on popular music, Programs in Black Culture
Washington D.C. Martin Luther King Library

GROUPS IN BALTIMORE AND WASHINGTON

This is a partial list of vocal groups from the Washington and Baltimore areas between 1945 and about 1960. It includes record labels, dates, and the names of the singers if known. Sources include primary and secondary consultants, Les Moss, and the fan magazine (no longer in print), *Yesterday's Memories*. This list is incomplete and in no way definitive, nor is it guaranteed free of errors, but serves as a general guide.

Baltimore

1. **Baltineers.** Teen-Age. 1956. Percy Cosby
2. **Blendtones.**

3. **Cardinals.** Atlantic. 1951. James Adyelotte, Meredith Brothers, Leon Hardy, Donald (Jack) Johnson, Ernest Warren.

4. **Cubits.**

5. **Encores.** Checker. 1953.

6. **Four Buddies.** Savoy. 1950. Gregory Carroll.

7. **Goldtones.** YRS. 1960s.

8. **Honey Boys.** Modern. 1955. John Billy, Roland Jackson, Calvin Rollette, Dixon Stokes.

9. **Jolly Jacks.** Teen-Age. 1956.

10. **Kings.** Jalo. Adolphus (Pop Diddy) Holcomb (Bobby Hall).

11. **Cool Gents.** (see Twilighters).

12. **Magic Tones.** King 1953, Howfum 1957. Gene Hawkins, et al.

13. **Marlettes.** Howfum. 1957.

14. **Marylanders.** Jubilee. 1952. Johnny Page.

15. **Orioles** (Vibra-Naires). National, Jubilee. 1948. Lloyd (Tommy) Gaither, George Nelson, Alexander Sharp, Earlington (Sonny) Tilghman, Richard Williams (replaced by Johnny Reed).

16. **Plants.** J&S. George Jackson.

17. **Quintones.** Jordan. 1958.

18. **Sonnets.**

19. **Sonny Womack and The Montereys.**

20. **Swallows.** King. 1951. Herman Denby, Earl Hurley, Fred Johnson, Norris Mack, Eddie Rich.

21. **Wayward Sons.** Hope. 1965. Syng McGowan.

22. **Twilighters.** Marshall. Deroy Green.

Washington, D.C.

1. **Armstrong Four.** 1940s. Earl Brent, Jimmy McPhail, Raymond Reeder, Jullian Ward.

2. **Bachelors.** (All or some recorded as the Jets on Rainbow, Links on Teenage, and Knickerbockers). Circa 1950. Charles Booker, John Bowie, Herbert Fisher, Waverly Buck Mason (later replaced by Robert Russell), Walter Taylor, James Toy Walton. Also, Don Covay sang in the group briefly, maybe around 1953, but did not record.

3. **Capitols.** Triodex (see Ontarios).

4. **Cap-Tans.** Dot, D.C. 1950s. Harmon Bethea, Floyd Slum Bennett, Sherman Buckner, Lester Fountain, Alfred Buddy Slaughter. The group was the Buddies when they hired Bethea, who came up with the new name. They were managed by Lillian Claiborne. Bethea came out of a spiritual group called the Progressive Four (Progressiveaires) and later had groups called the Octaves and the Agents.

5. **Carusos.**

6. **Cavaliers.** A Northeast group that did not record. Sonny Mobly.

7. **Chessmen.** Pac. Willie Hardman, who told Les Moss he sang in the Dippers Quintet. Also, according to Ferlingere (1976), a group named the Chessmen recorded a song called "Du-Whop" on the Mirasonic label (#1868). He gives no year.

8. **Chords.** Gem. 1953. Mark Hill, who wrote the song "In the Woods," published by J & J Music. Jesse R. Barnett, of Washington, D.C., owned the publishing company.

9. **Clefs.** Chess, Peacock. 1952. Scotty Mansfield.

10. **Clovers.** Rainbow, Atlantic, United Artists. 1950s. John Buddy Bailey, Bill Harris (guitar), Harold Lucas, Mathew McQuater, Harold Winley. Also Billy Mitchell, Charlie White. Original members were Billy Shelton, Tommy Woods.

11. **Coolbreezers.** Bale, ABC. 1957. Alonzo Armstead, William Primrose. Bea Tibbets was the manager.

12. **Cruisers.** V-Tone. 1960. Paul Long (also with the Strollers).

13. **Dippers Quintet**. Flayr. The Washington photographer Ted Gaffney owned the small label and recorded the group in the early 1950s.

14. **Earls.** Gem. 1954.

15. **Five Blue Notes.** Sabre. 1954. (Originally the Five Blue Jays.) Fleming Briscoe, Melvin Lee, Andy Magruder, Robert Stroud.

16. **Four Bars of Rhythm.** Josie. 1954. Melvin Butler, Eddie Daye, Alphonso Feemster, Frances Henry. Mostly from southeast Washington and Barry's Farm.

17. **Four Bel-Aires.** X-Tra. 1956. Vernon Ricks, Warren Ricks, Alfred Reed (Nooky) Robinson, Robert (Slick) Russell. Managed by Al Jefferson.

18. **Four Dots.** Dot.

19. **Four Men.** Pam-Nor.

20. **Gales.** Winn.

21. **Griffins.** Mercury.

22. **Harlequins.** Juanita.

23. **Heartbreakers.** RCA, D.C. 1951. George (Junior) Davis, Robert Evans, Lawrence Green, James Ross, Lawrence Tate.

24. **Hot Tamales.**

25. **Jewells.** 1963. Margie Clark.

26. **Joe Lyons and the Arrows.** Hollywood, Hitmaker.

27. **Jones Boys.** Johnny Stewart.

28. **Five Kingbees.** KRC.

29. **Knickerbockers.**

30. **Marvells.** Winn. 1960s. James Ison.

31. **Meadowlarks.**

32. **Melodaires.** 1950s. George (Icky) Tillman. Anacostia neighborhood.

33. **Five Nobles.**

34. **Ontarios.** Big Time. 1954. Also recorded as the Capitols.

35. **Parakeets.** John Burt. From Georgia Avenue and Lamont area of northwest.
36. **Paramounts.** Dot. 1968.
37. **Playboys.** From Phelps Vocational School, non-recording.
38. **Satisfiers.** 1950s. Don Covay, John Bowie
39. **Senators.**
40. **Serenadors.** Jake Hardy, Quay Martin, Henry Mont, Robert Neil, Shorty Womble, et al. Some members from the Kelly Miller Junior High School.
41. **Skylarks.**
42. **Syncopators Quintet.**
43. **Three of Us Trio.** York. 1950s–1960s. Clarence Dillard, Lawrence Farrell, Charles Kelly.
44. **Truetones.** Josie, LSP, Monument. Ron Henderson.
45. **Velps.**
46. **Velveteers.** Fred Coates, Alphonso Feemster, Charles Wright, Ernest Williams. From Barry's Farm.
47. **Versatiles.**
48. **Warblers.**

RESEARCH DISCOGRAPHY

The following are representative recordings from the Baltimore and Washington areas, circa late 1940s to about 1960. Commercial releases are noted with the label name. (I want to thank Les Moss and Roadhouse Records for help chronicling these sides.)

Dunbar/Rhythmneers acetates and wire recording courtesy of Howard Davis and Mel Lipscomb. Satisfiers rehearsal/demo tape and 1450 Club air-check acetate courtesy of Jack Lowe. All acetates and wire recordings were transferred to audio/cassette tape by Bob Carneal, at the Library of Congress. All other recordings courtesy of Les Moss and Howard Begle (Begle indicated by asterisk).

Arrows (unreleased) "How Late," "No End to True Love" (released Hollywood label, 1956)
Bachelors (Aladdin) "Can't Help Lovin' You" (December 1953)
Baltineers (Teenage) "Tears in My Eyes" (ca. 1957)
Berry Rhythm Boys "Too Young," "Mule Train"
Billee Jones "Every Night," "Satellite Love"
Bobby Hall and the Kings "You Make Me Cry"
Capitols (D.C.) "Honey, Honey"
Cap-Tans (unreleased D.C.) "Goodnight Mother" (ca. 1950)
Cap-Tans (Dot) I'm So Crazy "For Love," "With All My Love" (1950)
Cap-Tans (w/ Frank Motley) "Feel Like Balling Some More" (unreleased boot from D.C. records)

Cardinals (acetate) "I'll Always Love You," "Would I Love You" (Orioles cover)

Cardinals (Atlantic) "Wheel of Fortune" (February 1952), "Shouldn't I Know" (May 1951)*

Carusos Confessions of Love," "Haunting Memories" (ca 1955)

Chords (Gem) "In the Woods," "Daddy Loves Mommy" (1953)

Clefs Sorry (ca. 1952–1955, with Scotty Mansfield)

Clovers (Atlantic) "Don't You Know I Love You" (April 1951), "One Mint Julep" (March 1952)*

Clovers (Rainbow) "Yes Sir, That's My Baby," "When You Come Back to Me" (1950)

Coolbreezers "You Know I Love You," "Just Room for Two"

Demens (NY group on Teenage) "Take Me as I Am" (1956)

Dippers Quintet (Flayr) "It's Almost Christmas," "Look What I Got" (ca. 1954)

Dunbar Four / Rhythmneers / Hi-Fis (acetate transcriptions from Jack Lowe's WWDC amateur show) "Confessions," "That's the Way It Is" (June 10, 1945), "Sunny Side of the Street," Interview with Howard Davis (April 3, 1949), Interview with Norwood Williams, "Without a Song" (1949). The following sides were acetate demos from U.S. Recording Studio: "Pennies from Heaven," "Again," "Moonlight in Vermont," "I Can't Give You Anything But Love," "Lover Come Back to Me," "Danny Boy" (mid-1950s). "Symphony of Love," vocal duet with piano accompaniment, Howard Davis and Mel Lipscomb, from a wire recording likely around 1950, perhaps earlier. Recorded in Mel Lipscomb's stepparents' home, Washington, D.C.

Earls (Gem) "Love Tears"

Five Blue Notes (Sabre) "The Beat of Our Hearts," "You Gotta Go" (1954)

Five Bluejays (Circle Music acetate) "Could I Adore You," "Pauline" (ca. 1951)

Five Nobles (Circle Music acetate) "Beatrice My Darling," "Love Me When I'm Old"

Four Bars (Josie) "If I Give My Heart to You" (1954)

Four Dots (Dot) "My Dear"

Four Men (Pam-Nor) "Drink Everywhere They Go"

George Torrence and the Dippers "Juanita"

Harmon Bethea and the Octaves (with Chuck Conners and his Rhythm Steps) (unreleased from D.C. Records) "The Fox and the Grapes"

Heartbreakers (Live from Howard Theater) "Heartbreaker," "Embraceable You" (October 19, 1951)

Heartbreakers (RCA) "Why Don't I" (1951), "There Is Time" (1952), "It's O.K. with Me" (1952), "Heartbreaker" (1951), "Wanda" (1951)

Heartbreakers, "Goodbye Baby," "We're Gonna Have Some Fun" (unreleased from D.C. Records)

Heartbreakers w/Frank Motley and His Crew (unreleased boot from D.C. Records), "Don't Stop Baby," "I Swear by the Stars Above (w/TNT Tribble Orchestra), "Cry Wind Cry" (w/TNT Tribble)

Jets (Rainbow) "The Lovers" (1/53)

Joe Lyons and the Arrows "What's New with You"

Jones Boys "Alone in the Night"

King Bees "Look My Way"

L' Cap-Tans "Give Me My Love," "Chicken"

Magic Tones (Howfum) "Spanish Love Song," "Tears in My Eyes" (ca. 1957)

Marylanders (Jubilee) "I'm a Sentimental Fool" (April 1952)

Ontarios "I Really Had a Ball" (ca. 1954)

Orioles (Jubilee) "I Love You Mostly" (January/55)

Parakeets "My Love Is True"

Paul Crawford "I'm Your Man"

Quintones (Jordan) "Lonely Telephone," "Just a Little Lovin' "

Rainbows (Pilgrim) "Stay, Shirley" (1956)

Satisfiers (demo tape) "Shake That Thing," "Telephone," "You Broke My Heart (ca. 1954)

Serenaders "Lonesome," "Korea" (1953)

Swallows (King) "It Ain't the Meat (It's the Motion)," "Eternally" (1951)*

Swallows "Good Time Girls," "My Baby"

Three of Us Trio (Pam) "Lonely House Blues"

Twilighters (Marshall) "Please Tell Me You're Mine," "Wondering

(Unknown group audition for RCA) "I Really Don't Care"

"You Won't Let Me Go" (1951)

Velps "The Korea Song (Naka Naka Nooka Nooka)," "Little Girl" (late 1950s)

Warblers "Scheming"

Warblers "She's Too Tall for Me"

WWDC *1450 Club* (May 10, 1949, 9–9:30 p.m.), 78) This 30-minute radio program segment was taped from Jack Lowe's 16" transcription disc (which he's been keeping in his cellar since 1949). It contains various artists that were played over the air and may well be the only example of radio programming in Washington from this period.

Notes

1. All the dialogues in this book, unless otherwise noted, occurred with the author in 1989 and 1990. See Appendix.

CHAPTER 1. ANTECEDENTS

1. From an unpublished manuscript by Mihaly Csikzentmihalyi, "Play and Intrinsic Rewards," cited in Turner (1982: 55–56).

2. Listed by Document Records, "Earliest Negro Vocal Quartets Vol. 2 1893– 1922" DOCD-5288. The title of the song is indicative of the novelty role black artists had to confront, as well as other issues.

3. Funk (1991) annotates a compilation, "The Earliest Negro Vocal Quartets: 1894–1928. "The groups include, in addition to the Standard Quartette, the Dinwiddie Colored Quartet (1902), the Male Quartet (1910), the Apollo Male Quartet (1912), and Polk Miller and His Old South Quartette (1909, 1928). The style of these groups sounds remarkably contemporary. A reviewer of an earlier draft of this manuscript wrote that the Unique Quartet recorded in 1893, according to a Document Records release available on a Document Records Website.

4. There were of course white male and female harmony groups, especially those that emerged from vaudeville and theater after 1900; they do not appear to have been as numerous as African American pop and gospel groups, but they did receive a lot of play on radio, recordings, and in film. Probably the two most famous and influential of the female groups were the Boswell Sisters from New Orleans, in the 1930s, and the Andrews Sisters in the 1940s. Both groups were trios and lacked the harmonic depth and complexity of quartets and quintets; they borrowed heavily from swing music. The Modernaires were a harmony group (four males and a female) that recorded swing style from around 1935 through the 1950s, and the Pied Pipers were another male/female group which recorded in the 1940s, giving way to a style in the 1950s called "modern harmony," which the harmony style of the Beach Boys in the 1960s references. There were also important and popular country harmony groups, such as the Sons of the Pioneers (formed in the 1930s). No one claims that there were not influences across and between all of these types of groups—quite the opposite is probably the case—but the subject of this study, the street and neighborhood tradition of vocal groups, prevailed specifically among blacks initially. See also note 7, below.

5. Billy Eckstine (from Washington) had "12 top 30 hits on MGM" between 1949 and 1952 (Clarke 1989: 373). This was right at the start of group harmony's dominance as a rhythm & blues sub-style and Eckstine was very popular with

young vocalists. Many of his hits were standard ballads, such as "My Foolish Heart."

6. There were few, if any, white male vocal groups in the 1930s and 1940s quite like the Ink Spots, Mills Brothers, Cats and the Fiddle, Four Clefs, Deep River Boys, Delta Rhythm Boys, Red Caps, or any of the other pre-rhythm & blues secular groups. One exception was the Rhythm Boys—three singers that included Bing Crosby. They sang for Paul Whiteman beginning in 1926. Neither were there any white, male gospel quartets. Despite the Inks Spots' conventional material, their rhythmic phrasing, vocal shading, tonal emphasis, and subtle stylistic innuendos marked clearly that they were a "black" group, given the period. On the other hand, youngsters today listening to the group and not knowing who they were would more than likely not consider their sound as "black."

7. Jump bands were scaled-down big bands, popular by the mid-1940s. The sound was focused and very danceable. Louis Jordan and his Tympany Five is a prime example. Jordan was enormously popular and influential, especially from 1939 to 1949. He recorded on the Decca label.

8. When Ivory "Deek" Watson left the Ink Spots he formed the Brown Dots.

9. "Mainstream" in general usage refers to the taste of the middle of a general, dominant culture, e.g. white. Its precise meaning, however, remains a matter of perspective; cf. Amiri Baraka's (1963) use of the same term to refer to a particular "core" segment of black culture and society below the middle class.

10. According to Stearns (1968: 1–7), there was something of a lull in popular dance music from about 1945 until 1954, at least among whites. In the early 1950s, white teenagers especially discovered older African American dances, which became popular again under new names and simplified rhythms. They called it rock 'n' roll.

11. Female Classic Blues singers and big band swing probably did the most to move blues into the mainstream in the 1920s through the 1940s.

12. This quotation and the preceding biographical paragraph are from a typed, unedited article from the morgue of the *Baltimore Afro-American*, dated June 21, 1948.

13. Tin Pan Alley refers generally to sentimental, popular songs rooted in music publishing and professional composers (Irving Berlin, George Gershwin, Jerome Kern, and Cole Porter, among many others), Broadway shows, and later Hollywood movies. These "standards" were aimed at more or less mainstream tastes from before the 1920s through the 1950s, although this cultural assertion is arguable, as is any cultural identification with Tin Pan Alley. I will not argue the case. However, African American involvement in Tin Pan Alley was considerable—from composers to performers to jazz use of the material—and this would include consumers and listeners.

14. The 1950s honking tradition included players such as Frank "Floorshow" Culley, Willis "Gatortail" Jackson, Big Jay McNeely, Red Prysock, Hal "Cornbread" Singer, Sam "The Man" Taylor, and later, King Curtis. There were many others over the years.

15. When whites made black music "their own," they often did so by *copying* style or co-opting publishing rights, but when Magruder talks about making

music his own, he is talking about something more fundamental and cultural—taking any kind of music and performing it in a manner consistent with black musical sensibilities. All of this is a comment on the different dynamics established by the politics of race and the struggle to control cultural resources.

16. We can only speculate as to the reason why most of the vocal harmony groups before the mid- to late 1950s were all male. It may have had to do with limited mobility, social and geographic, of young girls. What Amiri Baraka wrote of life in the nineteenth century was still true in the twentieth: "In those times, unless she traveled with her family it was impossible for a woman to move about like a man" (Baraka 1963: 91). Although females sang in every place that males did—school, church, home, social club—you would not find them on the street corners. Their sense of place was more limited than males in that regard, even though it was less likely that white folks felt as threatened by African American girls. The proclivity of male groups has much to do with the notion of "grouping," and doing so within a particular territory. It is more than possible that young males had a territorial imperative and a grouping impulse that young girls simply did not need to articulate—or they simply channeled it in other ways.

Nevertheless, a more pronounced territorial imperative among males perhaps was the result of segregation—certainly segregation was a factor in how black males mapped their territory in any given neighborhood.

CHAPTER 2. TIME AND PLACE

1. Scherer (1972) describes men as like trees, needing roots, with groups of men creating a social attachment to a particular locality. Ley (1974) makes a similar argument about the black "inner city" and "sense of place."

2. This kind of model is not problem-free, however. Dennis (1968: 168) refers to the "elusiveness of neighborhood" where there is little or no correspondence between territory and human behavior; social relationships that fail to synchronize with geography.

3. Baltimore City Archives, "Negroes/Music" file RG 29 S1.

4. "Forgotten Anacostia," *New York Times*, July 26, 1996, front page.

5. I found both letters in a Metropolitan Police Department, Government of the District of Columbia folder in the National Archives. The incidents described were from "The Biggest Rock 'n' Roll Show of '56," featuring Bill Haley, the Platters, Clyde McPhatter, Lavern Baker, Big Joe Turner, the Teenagers, the Teenqueens, Bo Diddley, the Drifters, Flamingos, Colts, and Red Prysock and his Rock & Roll Orchestra.

6. For instance: "The Athletic Department, which conducts all tournaments and athletic events for colored schools, is seriously handicapped in its program because there is only one Negro worker available for educating the community, promoting the activities and carrying out the program. In addition, this one colored worker is supposed to supervise athletic events throughout the state" (Reid 1935: 28). In 1930 there were approximately 150,000 Blacks living in Baltimore alone (Reid 1935: 6).

7. There remain under-explored gender relationships here. The patriarchy

(power relationships) of the city meant that while young males could be out on the streets running together and harmonizing, young females generally could not. The issue of female harmonizing moves beyond the scope of this study, but it did not take place out on the block in the same way that male harmonizing did. To be sure, females did not have the same public mobility that males did, and their "awareness of space" may have been different from males (McDowell 1982). Their public music patterns no doubt developed differently, as has been the case historically. Baraka (1963) observed that after the Emancipation African American women did not have the mobility that men did. They did not travel alone, but in minstrel and vaudeville shows and thus participated in blues development differently. Popular rhythm & blues female harmony groups emerged as early as 1954 (the Queens) and later (the Bobbettes, Chantels, Shirelles, et al.), and then based their style only partly on male models. You will note, however, that several of the male singers in this study indicate that girls were around them, often on the periphery at playgrounds, or at rehearsals or performances at social clubs or schools. Indeed, some singers have said that they participated in singing a little more readily because the girls liked singers.

8. Knox 1957 provides precise figures and Strayer 1949 alludes to inequities.

9. Green, while writing about the prestige of Washington's black schools of the 1930s and 1940s, alludes to a "fortified" class structure (Green 1962, 2: 341), and the "class consciousness" of Black Washington—especially the schoolteachers (Green 1962, 2: 361). See also Battle (1982), Fitzpatrick and Goodwin (1990).

10. "Capital's Loss is One County's Gain," *New York Times*, July 27, 1997.

11. The insistence of or for a unified black America for political and economic purposes is another matter.

CHAPTER 3. ENTREPRENEURSHIP

1. For both sides of the issue see, just for example, Austin (1995) Billingsley 1992, Butler (1991), Green (1990), Walker (1998), and vis-à-vis music see George (1988), Sanjek (1997).

2. See *Washington Post*, Thursday, May 12, 1988, D1. *Newsweek* also ran a story, on November 7, 1988. The specific issue had to do, according to the Post article, with "payments the company had reduced by making foreign royalty payments at a disputed lower rate and by charging artists for production and packaging costs not called for in the original contracts" (D1).

3. Record people used to call Atlantic "the house that Ruth built," because her success was also the success of her label. It was as a play on the famous relationship between Yankee Stadium and Babe Ruth.

4. Louis Armstrong once said something about always having a good "white man" behind you (Kenny 1991: 54–55). This, perhaps, was an old habit and one of expediency as well—an extension of the old slave notion of a white "sponsor" to freedom? In the twentieth century, some white performers could say the same thing about having a good black musician behind you.

5. From Ralph Ellison, *Invisible Man*. In the opening chapter the narrator falls into a dream and hears the sermon in a cave, "Blackness of Blackness" (Ellison 1952: 9).

6. Ellison (1952: 213–14).

7. A group of theater professionals organized the Theater Owners Booking Association in 1920 to help facilitate a nationwide black theater circuit. See Southern (1997: 298).

8. "Shindig Presents Soul," Rhino Home Video, 1991.

9. Franklin recorded "Rock-A-Bye" for CBS/Columbia in 1961, and it was the *only* recording she did for CBS (she was with them until 1966) that charted in the Top 40 (Clarke 1989: 434). In 1967 she went with Atlantic Records and stopped, according to one writer, "watering herself down" (434).

10. The separation of black artists from the music they created—or perhaps it is more like white folks lifting the music from their back pockets—is a phenomenon that continues into the twenty-first century. Who would want their picture on a beer can anyway, but that's not really the point: "Miller Brewing is celebrating the "50th anniversary of rock 'n' roll" with eight beer cans that feature Rolling Stone cover shots of Elvis Presley, Blondie and others.What is missing, some say, is a black artist." Robert Thompson, a professor of popular culture at Syracuse University, called the absence "beyond conspicuous," because black artists are often credited with inventing rock music. "It would be like doing a set of cans of six great Impressionist painters and not including any French people on it," he said (*New York Times*, August 16, 2004).

11. Neil Leonard's (1987) discussion of white (and assimilated black) reaction to ragtime and jazz is applicable also to rhythm & blues rock 'n' roll.

12. By the 1960s, after the specific time and place of group harmony came and went, many other individuals and groups (record collectors, "oldies" devotees, writers, and scholars) seized what remained of that original entrepreneurial moment and spun off a new one.

13. The Cardinals covered a version of "Wheel of Fortune" in 1952 with lead singer Ernest Warren sounding remarkably similar to Kay Starr (the entire arrangement was similar). Sometimes it was a case where the vocalists knew and liked the song, but the record companies were right with them in trying to get a cover out, whether it fell into a "black" mold or not. The Kay Starr version came out on Capitol Records in early 1952; the Cardinals recorded it about a month later for Atlantic, Ernest Warren recalled. "That was Kay Starr. Well, Sonny Gale did it too, didn't she? Yeah, well see, Atlantic was like this. You take even 'Off Shore.' 'Off Shore' was done by Ethel Innis, she's from here. And anything that they hear good and they thought I could do, they'd try to get a rush release on it. Like if this song only been out for a couple days and they hear it, they try to get a rush release on it, and the earliest rush release would be something like ten days, and release it then, you know. And that's the way they did 'Wheel of Fortune' and 'Off Shore.' Even a song called 'Come Back My Love' was done by the Wrens, and it didn't take off so they hurry up and got us in the studio to do it and we did better than they did with it. Lou Karpouzie's a Greek, and he just bugged Atlantic about 'Misirlou' and he bugged them so much until they did it. And they had the oboe and everything in there, but we was just ahead of our time for doing things."

14. Les Moss, personal communication.

15. Although this harmonic progression has deep roots in twentieth-century

popular song and much earlier antecedents, today the term generally refers back to George Gershwin's "I Got Rhythm" (1930), an AABA 32-bar song form. These changes show up in countless jazz and pop variations, with the most typical as I vi ii V^7 I in the "head" (A sections), with a distinctive III^7 VI^7 II^7 V^7 bridge (B). It became a paradigm for a good number of jump and rhythm & blues songs.

16. Levine (1977: 31) describes six African Americans rowing a boat in Georgia in 1845: "Occasionally they struck up a hymn, taught them by the Methodists, in which most sacred subjects were handled with strange familiarity, and which, though nothing irreverent was meant, sounded oddly to our ears, and, when following a love ditty, almost profane."

17. The nuances of city life shaped the development of group harmony. Whether each place (Baltimore and Washington) did or did not have a precisely quantifiable and identifiably unique sound is not a question this book can resolve. Vocalists never spoke of any specific regional or neighborhood sound that they imagined or cultivated. As we have seen, though, they did compete against one another from sides of town, or schools. They continually indicated throughout these pages their strong connection to "place." They enacted, when younger, and spoke, when older, more of geographic affiliation than they did of actually *sounding* it. It is the emotional and cognitive connection that performers had to place that is the point, not necessarily whether an outsider can hear it.

18. Claiborne died sometime in the early 1980s. I spoke briefly with her attorney in early 1990 and learned only his last name, Mr. Goodsen.

19. According to Gribin and Schiff (1992), the Antwinetts' two sides — "Johnny" b/w "Kill It" — came out on the RCA label in 1958. It was not possible to determine whether RCA, Howfum, or perhaps both issued the recordings. Given that Howfum left the masters with RCA, though, it is likely that RCA issued them. Ferlingere (1976) also lists RCA as the label.

20. Personal communication.

21. Les Moss, personal communication, 1989.

22. Phil Chaney pieced together a short biography of the Magic Tones for a record collector's trade journal, *Yesterday's Memories* 4 (1976): 18–19.

CHAPTER 4. MEDIATORS

1. The period from the late 1940s through the mid-1950s also saw the beginning of the freestanding record store (up until this time, you would purchase records in department stores, pharmacies, or appliance stores).

2. Washington reported that 79.5 percent of Armstrong High School graduates in 1941owned radios (Washington 1951: 65).

3. Jan Peerce was an American tenor who sang for the Metropolitan Opera in the 1940s and 1950s and who maintained popular appeal as well.

4. Felix Grant began his all-night jazz program on WWDC in 1950, before moving to WMAL in 1953 with an "across the board," five nights per week jazz program.

5. According to author Gilbert Williams, "The first African-American disc jockey with a commercially sustained radio show was Jack L. Cooper, a former vaudeville and ventriloquist who got started in broadcasting on WCAP in Washington, D.C., in 1924." Cooper, like the other few black DJs of the 1920s, 1930s, and 1940s, "reflected a middle-American dialect and enunciation pattern" (1998: 12).

6. This is ironic in light of how, in so many instances, whites insisted that blacks "sound" and thus embody blackness stereotypically in song, on stage, on radio, television, and film. The case of the black DJs is, you could say, an instance of the disembodiment of blackness. Whites wanted to have it both ways.

7. Bob McKuhn hosted Capital Caravan on channel 5, WTTG. Lawrence Berry said that at the time, in the early 1950s, it was "the only all-black" talent variety show. Berry also said that Milton Grant's television dance program in the 1950s had blacks on the show once a week.

8. Vernon Ricks, Warren Ricks, Alfred Reed "Nooky" Robinson, Robert "Slick" Russell.

9. Jackson Lowe worked with at least one other group in the mid-1950s — or at least tried to help them out — a group called the Satisfiers. Along with a transcription disc of his 1450 Club show, Lowe kept in a plain manila envelope an undated demo tape from the 1950s, when he worked on station WOL. He recalled that he must have let the group use one of his studios there to rehearse and record. The tape label had "Satisfiers" written on it. In addition to the tape, a handwritten page — on WOL letterhead — had the titles of 21 songs and the three the group eventually recorded, plus the names of either the song composers or lead singers. The three songs on the tape were obvious demos because of the stops and starts. The names listed as writers or singers were John Berry (who sang and recorded with another Washington group, the Rainbows), David Scott, John Woody, and Don Covay. Don Covay, born in 1938 in South Carolina, grew up in Washington, D.C. He recorded for Atlantic Records, first in 1957. Covay was a prolific performer and composer, who wrote a number of hits from around 1961 ("Pony Time") through that decade ("Chain of Fools," a hit for Aretha Franklin). Covay attended Shaw Junior High School and first sang with the Bachelors, a D.C. group. "They painted a mustache on me to make me look older." He also sang with the Rainbows, and duets with singer Billy Stewart, who was originally from Washington. Covay worked places like the Hayloft and the Casino Royale, where he did an imitation of Little Richard as a single act. Richard nicknamed Covay "Pretty Boy."

Of the Satisfiers, Covay recalled very little, other than the original name for them was the Cherokees and that "a lot of guys were in and out of the group." He said Jack Lowe used to tell them that they could be a basketball team (referring either to their individual size or the sheer number of them at any one time).

10. Circle's 1955 telephone directory announced this.

11. "Papa Lou Looks Back on a Golden Era When the Clovers Hit Top in Early 50's," *Baltimore Evening Sun*, March 29, 1972.

12. *Baltimore Afro-American*, April 20, 1957, n.p.

CHAPTER 5. PATTERNS

1. Personal communication.

2. Charles Keil (1966: 45–46) wrote of the crosscurrents between African, African American, and (white) American popular music and included falsetto as a vocal characteristic.

3. Falsetto among twentieth-century white males singing pop probably came to modern fruition with Frankie Valli and the Four Seasons, around 1962, when they had the first of many hits. The association between falsetto and black was so strong that the group "passed" for black on radio (at least with white listeners) because of Valli's voice, until they had an appearance on *American Bandstand* (Clarke 1989: 430). Valli was a good singer, but few other white singers could sing falsetto very well. One notable exception was the Beach Boys' use of falsetto. Many others tried, like John Lennon, but the likes of the Bee Gees and Michael Bolton never helped matters.

4. *Dictionary of Philosophy*, ed. Dagobert D. Runes, s.v. "utopia."

5. Carroll sang with the Four Buddies and Four Buds from 1950 through about 1953.

6. See Andrews (1986: 5), and his discussion of white sponsors for very early black autobiographies. Related is Louis Armstrong's strategy of a white sponsor as a manager, in Kenny (1991: 54–55). As Armstrong wrote, "always have a good white man behind you."

7. The Orioles were with Jubilee from 1948 to 1956. They returned to record six sides for the label in 1959, according to Ferlingere (1976).

8. "Crying in the Chapel" was written and originally recorded by Darrell Glenn as a country song, although at the time *Billboard* would use terms like "pop" and "hillbilly" versions to describe the different covers. Sonny Til and the Orioles recorded it in 1953, 1959, and again in 1964.

9. Of categories, Duke Ellington wrote: "The category is a Grand Canyon of echoes. Somebody utters an obscenity and you hear it bouncing back a million times" (Ellington 1973: 38).

10. See the *New York Times*, May 28, 1889, B1.

11. A good example was Puff Daddy's 1997 cover of Sting's "I'll Be Missing You." It wasn't street or hard, but commercial and well done nonetheless.

EPILOGUE

1. *New York Times*, "A Storyteller far from Home," January 10, 2000, B6..

2. *New York Times*, "Trying to Fix the Nation's Capital," July 25, 1996, A8.

3. *New York Times*, "Toll is Even Greater in Forgotten Anacostia," July 26, 1996, front page.

Bibliography

Abbott, Lynn. 1992. "Play That Barber Shop Chord: A Case for the African-American Origin of Barbershop Harmony." *American Music* 10 (3): 289–324.

Alexander, Lois K., ed. 1948. *Dee Cee Directory: A Business, Professional and Social Directory of Negro Washington*. Washington, D.C.: James Terry.

Alston, John C. 1940. "An Ecological Study of the Negro Population in the District of Columbia." Master's thesis, Howard University.

Anderson, Jervis. 1978. "Our Far-Flung Correspondents." *New Yorker*, March 20, 94–121.

Andrews, William L. 1986. *To Tell a Free Story: The First Century of Afro-American Autobiography*. Urbana: University of Illinois Press.

Armstrong, Louis. 1954. *Satchmo: My Life in New Orleans*. New York: Prentice-Hall.

Austin, Regina. 1995. "A Nation of Thieves: Consumption, Commerce, and the Black Public Sphere." In *The Black Public Sphere: A Public Culture Book*, ed. Black Public Sphere Collective. Chicago: University of Chicago Press.

Babchuck, Nicholas and Ralph V. Thompson. 1962. "The Voluntary Associations of Negroes." *American Sociological Review* 27 (5): 647–55.

Baker Associates. 1947. *Baker Handbook of Negro-Owned Businesses, Professional Persons, Churches, and Organizations*. Washington, D.C.: Baker Associates.

Baker, Houston A., Jr. 1984. *Blues, Ideology, and Afro-American Literature: A Vernacular Theory*. Chicago: University of Chicago Press.

Banton, Michael. 1987. *Racial Theories*. Cambridge: Cambridge University Press.

Baraka, Amiri Imamu (LeRoi Jones). 1963. *Blues People: The Negro Experience in White America and the Music That Developed from It*. New York: William Morrow.

———. 1976. *Black Music: Negro Music in White America*. New York: William Morrow.

Battle, Thomas Cornell. 1982. "Published Sources for the Study of Blacks in the District of Columbia: An Annotated Bibliography." Ph.D. dissertation, George Washington University.

Bauman, Richard, ed. 1992. *Folklore, Cultural Performances and Popular Entertainments: A Communication-Centered Handbook*. New York: Oxford University Press.

Berman, Paul. 1994. "The Other and the Almost Same." *New Yorker*, February 28, 61–71.

Billingsley, Andrew. 1992. *Climbing Jacob's Ladder: The Enduring Legacy of African-American Families*. New York: Simon and Schuster.

"Black Disc Jockeys." 1949. *Afro Magazine Section*, March 5.

Black Public Sphere Collective, ed. 1995. *The Black Public Sphere: A Public Culture Book*. Chicago: University of Chicago Press.

Borchert, James. 1982. *Alley Life in Washington: Family, Community, Religion, and Folklife in the City, 1850–1970*. Urbana: University of Illinois Press.

Bourdieu, Pierre. 1991. *Language and Symbolic Power*. Ed. John B. Thompson. Cambridge, Mass.: Harvard University Press.

Buffalo, Audree. 1993. "Sweet Honey in the Rock: A Cappella Activists." *Ms.* 3 (5): 24–29.

Butler, John Sibley. 1991. *Entrepreneurship and Self-Help Among Black Americans: A Reconsideration of Race and Economics*. Albany: State University of New York Press.

Caldwell, Paulette M. 1995. "A Hair Piece: Perspectives on the Intersection of Race and Gender." In *Critical Race Theory: The Cutting Edge*, ed. Richard Delgado. Philadelphia: Temple University Press.

Carby, Hazel V. 1998. *Race Men*. Cambridge, Mass.: Harvard University Press.

Cater, John and Trevor Jones. 1989. *Social Geography: An Introduction to Contemporary Issues*. London: Edward Arnold.

Chambers, Ross. 1991. *Room for Maneuver: Reading (the) Oppositional (in) Narrative*. Chicago: University of Chicago Press.

Clarke, Donald, ed. 1989. *The Penguin Encyclopedia of Popular Music*. London: Penguin.

Cohen, Abner. 1974. *Two-Dimensional Man: An Essay in the Anthropology of Power and Symbolism in Complex Society*. Berkeley: University of California Press.

Cooper, Ralph. 1990. *Amateur Night at the Apollo: Ralph Cooper Presents Five Decades of Great Entertainment*. New York: HarperCollins.

Cortez W. Peters Business School. 1946. *Bulletin and First Directory*. Baltimore: Cortez W. Peters Business School.

Crenshaw, Kimberlé, Neil Gotanda, Gary Peller, and Kendall Thomas, eds. 1995. *Critical Race Theory: The Key Writings That Formed the Movement*. New York: New Press.

Cross, Brian. 1993. *It's Not About a Salary: Rap, Race, and Resistance in Los Angeles*. London: Verso.

de Certeau, Michel. 1984. *The Practice of Everyday Life*. Berkeley: University of California Press.

Delgado, Richard, ed. 1995. *Critical Race Theory: The Cutting Edge*. Philadelphia: Temple University Press.

Dennis, Norman. 1968. "The Popularity of the Neighborhood Community Idea." In *Readings in Urban Scoiology*, ed. R. E. Pahl. London: Pergamon.

Doo Wop Songbook. 1989. New York: Goodman Group; Milwaukee: Hal Leonard.

Doty, Francis A. 1938. "Junior High School Music in Six Large Cities." Master's thesis, George Washington University.

Du Bois, W. E. B. 1903. *The Souls of Black Folk*. Reprint New York: Bantam, 1989.

Durst, Lavada. 1953. *The Jives of Dr. Hepcat*. Austin: Lavada Durst.

Ellington, Duke. 1973. *Music Is My Mistress*. New York: Doubleday.

Ellison, Ralph. 1952. *Invisible Man*. New York: Random House.

——. 1964. *Shadow and Act*. New York: Random House.

Entrikin, J. Nicholas. 1991. *The Betweenness of Place: Towards a Geography of Modernity*. Baltimore: John Hopkins University Press.

Federal Writers' Project. 1937. *Washington: City and Capital*. Washington, D.C.: U.S. Government Printing Office.

Ferlingere, Robert D. 1976. *A Discography of Rhythm and Blues and Rock 'n' Roll Vocal Groups, 1945–1965*. Hayward, Calif.: Robert D. Ferlingere.

Fitzpatrick, Sandra and Maria R. Goodwin. 1990. *The Guide to Black Washington: Places and Events of Historical and Cultural Significance in the Nation's Capital*. New York: Hippocrene Books.

Flack, Horace E. 1912. "Segregation Ordinances." *National Municipal Review*, April.

Floyd, Samuel A., Jr. 1980. "Black American Music and Aesthetic Communication." *Black Music Research Journal* 1 (1): 1–17.

Fox, Ted. 1983. *Showtime at the Apollo*. New York: Holt, Rinehart and Winston.

Frazier, E. Franklin. 1940. *Negro Youth at the Crossways: Their Personality Development in the Middle States*. Washington, D.C.: American Council on Education.

Funk, Ray. 1991. Liner notes for *The Earliest Negro Vocal Quartettes: 1894–1928*. Document Records DOCD-5061.

Gale, Dennis E. 1987. *Washington, D.C.: Inner-City Revitalization and Minority Suburbanization*. Philadelphia: Temple University Press.

Garofalo, Rebee. 1995. "Culture Versus Commerce: The Marketing of Black Popular Music." In *The Black Public Sphere: A Public Culture Book*, ed. Black Public Sphere Collective. Chicago: University of Chicago Press.

Gart, Galen, ed. 1986. *First Pressings: Rock History as Chronicled in Billboard Magazine*. Vol. 2, *1951–1952*. Milford, N.H.: Big Nickel Publications.

Gates, Henry Louis, Jr. 1979. "Dis and Dat: Dialect and the Descent." In *Afro-American Literature: The Reconstruction of Instruction*, ed. Dexter Fisher and Robert B. Stepto. New York: Modern Language Association of America.

——. *The Signifying Monkey: A Theory of African-American Literary Criticism*. New York: Oxford University Press.

——. 1994. *Colored People: A Memoir*. New York: Knopf.

Genovese, Eugene D. 1974. *Roll, Jordan, Roll: The World the Slaves Made*. New York: Pantheon.

George, Nelson. 1988. *The Death of Rhythm & Blues*. New York: Pantheon.

Giles, Peter. 1994. *History and Technique of the Counter-Tenor: A Study of the Male High Voice Family*. Hants, England: Scolar Press.

Gillett, Charlie. 1983. *The Sound of the City: The Rise of Rock and Roll*. Rev. ed. New York: Pantheon.

Gilroy, Paul. 1993. *The Black Atlantic: Modernity and Double Consciousness*. Cambridge, Mass.: Harvard University Press.

Goldberg, Marv and Mike Redmond. 1973. "The Clovers." *Record Exchanger* 3 (4): 5–6.

Goldberg, Marv, Mike Redmond, and Marcia Vance, eds. 1975. *Yesterday's Memories* 1 (4), issue 4.

———, eds. 1976. *Yesterday's Memories* 2 (4), issue 8.

Goosman, Stuart L. 1992. "The Social and Cultural Organization of Black Group Harmony in Washington, D.C. and Baltimore, Maryland, 1945–1960." Ph.D. dissertation, University of Washington.

Granda, Megan. 1992. "Aunt Jemima in Black and White: America Advertises in Color." Master's thesis, University of Texas at Austin.

Green, Constance McLaughlin. 1962. *Washington*. 2 vols. Princeton, N.J.: Princeton University Press.

———. 1967. *The Secret City: A History of Race Relations in the Nation's Capital*. Princeton, N.J.: Princeton University Press.

Green, Shelly and Paul Pryde. 1990. *Black Entrepreneurship*. New Brunswick, N.J.: Transaction Publishers.

Gribin, Anthony J. and Matthew M. Schiff. 1992. *Doo-Wop: The Forgotten Third of Rock 'n' Roll*. Iola, Wis.: Krause.

Groia, Philip. 1973. *They All Sang on the Corner: New York City's Rhythm and Blues Vocal Groups of the 1950s*. New York: Edmonds.

———. 1983. *They All Sang on the Corner: A Second Look at New York City's Rhythm and Blues Vocal Groups*. Port Jefferson, N.Y.: Phillie Dee Enterprises.

Guralnick, Peter. 1986. *Sweet Soul Music: Rhythm and Blues and the Southern Dream of Freedom*. New York: Harper and Row.

Habermas, Jürgen. 1989 (1962). *The Structural Transformation of the Public Sphere*. Cambridge, Mass.: MIT Press.

Hall, Edward T. 1959. *The Silent Language*. Greenwich, Conn.: Fawcett.

Hall, Stuart. 1992. "What Is This 'Black' in Black Popular Culture?" In *Black Popular Culture*, ed. Gina Dent. Dia Center for the Arts Discussions in Contemporary Culture 8. Seattle: Bay Press.

Hansen, Barret. 1967. "Negro Popular Music, 1945–1953." Master's thesis, University of California, Los Angeles.

Hannerz, Ulf. 1969. *Soulside: Inquiries into Ghetto Culture and Community*. New York: Columbia University Press.

Haralambos, Michael. 1974. *Right On: From Blues to Soul in Black America*. London: Edison Press.

Hayden, Dolores. 1995. *The Power of Place: Urban Landscapes as Public History.* Cambridge, Mass.: MIT Press.

Heilbut, Anthony. 1971. *The Gospel Sound: Good News and Bad Times.* Rev. ed. New York: Limelight Editions, 1985.

Herbert, David. 1972. *Urban Geography: A Social Perspective.* Newton Abbot, Great Britain: David and Charles.

Hinckley, Dave. 1976. "The Cap-Tans." *Yesterday's Memories* 2 (4), issue 8, 8–10.

hooks, bell. 1994. *Outlaw Culture: Resisting Representation.* New York: Routledge.

———. 1995. *Art on My Mind: Visual Politics.* New York: New Press.

Jameson, Fredric. 1984. "Postmodernism, or the Cultural Logic of Late Capitalism." *New Left Review* 146: 53–92.

Jaynes, Gerald D. and Robin M. Williams, eds. 1989. *A Common Destiny: Blacks and American Society.* Committee on the Status of Black Americans, Commission on Behavioral and Social Sciences and Education, National Research Council. Washington, D.C.: National Academy Press.

Johnson, Gwendolyn Z. 1949. "The Transformation of Juvenile Gangs into Accommodated Groups: A Study of Eight Boys' Gangs in Washington, D.C." Master's thesis, Howard University.

Johnson, James Weldon and Rosamond J. Johnson. 1925. *The Books of American Negro Spirituals.* Reprint New York: Viking, 1951.

Jones, William H. 1927. *Recreation and Amusement Among Negroes in Washington, D.C.* Reprint Westport, Conn.: Negro Universities Press, 1970.

Keil, Charles. 1966. *Urban Blues.* Chicago: University of Chicago Press.

Keller, Suzanne I. 1968. *The Urban Neighborhood: A Sociological Perspective.* New York: Random House.

Kenney, William. 1991. "Negotiating the Color Line: Louis Armstrong's Autobiography. In *Jazz in Mind: Essays on the History and Meanings of Jazz,* ed. Reginald T. Buckner and Steven Weiland. Detroit: Wayne State University Press.

———. 1993. *Chicago Jazz: A Cultural History, 1904–1930.* New York: Oxford University Press.

Knox, Ellis O. 1957. *Democracy and the District of Columbia Public Schools: A Study of Recently Integrated Public Schools.* Washington, D.C.: Judd and Detweiler.

Landis, Kenesaw M. 1948. *Segregation in Washington: A Report of the National Committee on Segregation in the Nation's Capital, November 1948.* Chicago: The Committee.

Lee, Antoinette. 1986. *School Building Survey, District of Columbia. Historical Summary.* Sumner Archives, Washington, D.C.

Lefebvre, Henri. 1991. *The Production of Space.* Oxford: Blackwell. French original 1974.

Leonard, Neil. 1987. *Jazz: Myth and Religion.* New York: Oxford University Press.

Levine, Lawrence W. 1977. *Black Culture and Black Consciousness.* Oxford: Oxford University Press.

Ley, David. 1974. *The Black Inner City as Frontier Outpost: Images and Behavior of a Philadelphia Neighborhood.* Monograph Series 7. Washington, D.C.: Association of American Geographers.

Lornell, Kip. 1988. *Happy in the Service of the Lord: African-American Sacred Vocal Harmony Quartets in Memphis.* Urbana: University of Illinois Press.

Lott, Eric. 1996. "Blackface and Blackness: The Minstrel Show in American Culture." In *Inside the Minstrel Mask: Readings in Nineteenth-Century Blackface Minstrelsy,* ed. Annemarie Bean, James Vernon Hatch, and Brooks McNamara. Hanover, N.H.: Wesleyan University Press.

Lovell, John, Jr. 1972. *Black Song: The Forge and the Flame.* Reprint, New York: Paragon House, 1986.

Lynch, Kevin. 1960. *The Image of the City.* Cambridge, Mass.: MIT Press.

Marable, Manning. 1983. *How Capitalism Underdeveloped Black America: Problems in Race, Political Economy, and Society.* Boston: South End Press.

——. 1992. "Race, Identity, and Popular Culture." In *Black Popular Culture,* ed. Gina Dent. Dia Center for the Arts Discussions in Contemporary Culture 8. Seattle: Bay Press.

Maryland Commission on Interracial Problems and Relations. 1955. *An American City in Transition: The Baltimore Community Self-Survey of Inter-Group Relations.* Baltimore: Baltimore Commission on Human Relations.

Maultsby, Portia. 1986. "Rhythm & Blues (1945–1955): A Survey of Styles." In *Black American Popular Music: Rhythm and Blues, 1945–1955, a Symposium.* Program notes edited by Niani Kilkenny and Robert Selim. Smithsonian Institution, National Museum of American History, Program in Black American Culture.

McDowell, Linda. 1983. "Towards an Understanding of the Gender Division of Urban Space." *Environment and Planning D: Society and Space* 1: 59–72.

McGarvey, Seamus. 1988. "It's Those 'Lovey Dovey' Clovers: An Interview with Harold Winley, Part 1." *Juke Blues* 13: 25–27.

Mintz, Sidney and Richard Price. 1976. *An Anthropological Approach to the Afro-American Past: A Caribbean Perspective.* Philadelphia: Institute for the Study of Human Issues.

Moskowitz, Les. 1976. "The Twilighters." *Yesterday's Memories* 2 (4), issue 8, 16.

Murray, Albert. 1970. *The Omni-Americans: New Perspectives of Black Experience and America.* New York: Outerbridge and Dienstfrey.

Murry, Catherine M. 1938. "The Development of Music Appreciation." Master's thesis, Catholic University of America.

Myrdal, Gunnar. 1944. *An American Dilemma: The Negro Problem and Modern Democracy.* New York: Harper and Brothers.

Nast, Lenora Helig, Laurence N. Krause, and R. C. Monk, eds. 1982. *Baltimore: A Living Renaissance.* Baltimore: Baltimore Historical Society.

Nisbet, Robert A. 1966. *The Sociological Tradition.* New York: Basic Books.

Oliver, Paul, Max Harrison, and William Bolcom. 1986. *The New Grove Gospel, Blues, and Jazz.* New York: W.W. Norton.

Olson, Sherry H. 1976. *Baltimore.* Cambridge, Mass.: Ballinger.

———. 1980. *Baltimore: The Building of an American City.* Baltimore: Johns Hopkins University Press.

Pack, Louise Howard. 1945. "The Status of Music in Secondary Schools of Washington, D.C." Master's thesis, Howard University.

Palmer, Robert. 1981. *Deep Blues.* New York: Viking.

Pruter, Robert. 1996. *Doowop: The Chicago Scene.* Urbana: University of Illinois Press.

Rampersad, Arnold. 1983. "Biography, Autobiography, and Afro-American Culture." *Yale Review* 73 (1): 1–16.

Reagon, Bernice Johnson. 1975. "Song of the Civil Rights Movement, 1955–1965: A Study in Culture History." Ph.D. dissertation, Howard University.

Redd, Lawrence N. 1985. "Rock! It's Still Rhythm and Blues." *Black Perspective in Music* 13 (1): 31–47.

Reid, Ira De A. 1935. *The Negro Community of Baltimore: A Summary Report of a Social Study Conducted for the Baltimore Urban League.* Baltimore: Department of Research, National Urban League.

Riis, Thomas L. 1989. *Just Before Jazz: Black Musical Theater in New York, 1890–1915.* Washington, D.C.: Smithsonian Institution Press.

Robinson, Elaine M. 1959. "The Characteristics of the Membership of Baker's Dozen Youth Center from 1952–1957 in Relation to Program Planning." Master's thesis, Howard University.

Rose, Arnold M. 1954. *Theory and Method in the Social Sciences.* Minneapolis: University of Minnesota Press.

Runes, Dagobert D., ed. *Dictionary of Philosophy.* New York: Philosophical Library.

Sanjek, David. 1997. "One Size Does Not Fit All: The Precarious Position of the African American Entrepeneur in Post-WWII American Popular Music." *American Music* 15 (4): 535–62.

Sbarbori, Jack. 1985. "The Ravens." Annotation for Savoy Jazz SJL 1156. New York.

Scherer, Jacqueline. 1972. *Contemporary Community: Sociological Illusion or Reality?* London: Tavistock.

Schiffman, Jack. 1971. *Uptown: The Story of Harlem's Apollo Theatre.* New York: Cowles Book Company.

Shaw, Arnold. 1978. *Honkers and Shouters: The Golden Years of Rhythm and Blues.* New York: Macmillan.

Shepp, Archie. 1981. Foreword to Ben Sidran, *Black Talk.* New York: Da Capo Press.

Silverman, Albert J., ed. 1953. *Baltimore: City of Promise.* Baltimore: Department of Education.

Southern, Eileen. 1997. *The Music of Black Americans: A History.* 3rd ed. New York: W.W. Norton.

Stacey, Margaret. 1979. "The Myth of Community Studies." *British Journal of Sociology* 20 (2): 37–47.

Stearns, Marshall and Jean Stearns. 1968. *Jazz Dance: The Story of American Vernacular Dance.* New York: Macmillan.

Strayer, George D. 1949. *The Report of a Survey of the Public Schools of the District of Columbia.* Washington, D.C.: U.S. Government Printing Office.

Toop, David. 1991. *Rap Attack 2: African Rap to Global Hip Hop.* London: Serpent's Tail.

Tosches, Nick. 1984. *Unsung Heroes of Rock 'n' Roll.* New York: Scribner's.

Trow, George W. S. 1978. *Within the Context of No Context.* Boston: Little, Brown.

Turner, Victor. 1982. *From Ritual to Theatre: The Human Seriousness of Play.* New York: PAJ Publications.

Walker, Juliet E. K. 1998. *The History of Black Business in America: Capitalism, Race, Entrepreneurship.* New York: Simon and Schuster.

Washington, Bennetta Bullock. 1951. *Background Factors and Adjustment: A Study of the Socio-Economic and Personal Factors in the School and Subsequent Adjustment of a Select Group of High School Students.* Washington, D.C.: Catholic University of America Press.

Wexler, Jerry and David Ritz. 1993. *Rhythm and Blues: A Life in American Music.* New York: Knopf.

Williams, Gilbert, L. 1998. *Legendary Pioneers of Black Radio.* Westport, Conn.: Praeger.

Wilson, Olly. 1983. "Black Music as an Art Form." *Black Music Research Journal* 3: 1–22.

Wirth, Louis. 1938. "Urbanism as a Way of Life." *American Journal of Sociology* 44 (1): 1–25.

X, Malcolm and Alex Haley. 1964. *The Autobiography of Malcolm X.* New York: Ballantine.

Index

Acknowledgments

The project that led to this book never lost its initial impetus, which was to build a narrative from the ground up, that is, to have the material I was able to collect be the basis for what I wrote. The momentum behind it all was what people told me in their oral histories, and to them I am deeply grateful: John (Buddy) Bailey, Lawrence E. Berry, Alan J. Bloom, Melvin Coles, Clarence F. Curry, Howard C. Davis, Herman Denby, Jack Lowe Endler, Alphonso Feemster, Tex Gathings, Felix Grant, Maurice Hulbert, George Jackson, Albert Nathaniel Jefferson, Melvin F. Lipscomb, William Andrew Magruder, James McPhail, Miss June Norton, Johnny Page, Sr., Deborah Chessler Reingold, Albert Russell, Alfred H. Slaughter, Jesse Stone, George Tillman, Junius (Ernest) Lee Warren, Carroll Williamson, and Harold Jerome Winley, Sr.

I am also grateful to Mrs. C. C. Coley, Don Covay, Clarence Dillard, Billy Gordon, Eugene Hawkins, Kimo and Quatro McVay, Henry Mont, Chevist Parham, Robert Stroud, Ray Tolson, Jr., and Rudy West.

I would also like to thank other individuals for their help during the research phase of the project, beginning with Dr. Bernice Johnson Reagon; also Gloria Beck, Howard Begle, Spencer Crew, Cary Beth Cryor, Theodore Gaffney, Marvin Goldberg, Phil Groia, Alan Lee, Les Moss, Bill Nolan, and Ralph Whittington.

In addition, I want to acknowledge the following organizations: The Smithsonian Institution, for a one-year Pre-Doctoral Research Fellowship in 1989–1990, The Afro-American Newspapers Archives and Records Center, The Library of Congress Recorded Sound Reference Center, Roadhouse Records, The Rhythm & Blues Foundation, Spirit in the Dark Productions, Antique Blues, The Rhythm & Blues Rock'n Roll Society, Inc., and *Yesterday's Memories*.

Finally, I would like to thank Samuel A. Floyd, Jr., James Borchert, and Charles McGovern, who, at separate times and in different ways, helped me with this book project.